Anatomy of a Medieval Islamic Town: Al-Basra, Morocco

Edited by

Nancy L. Benco

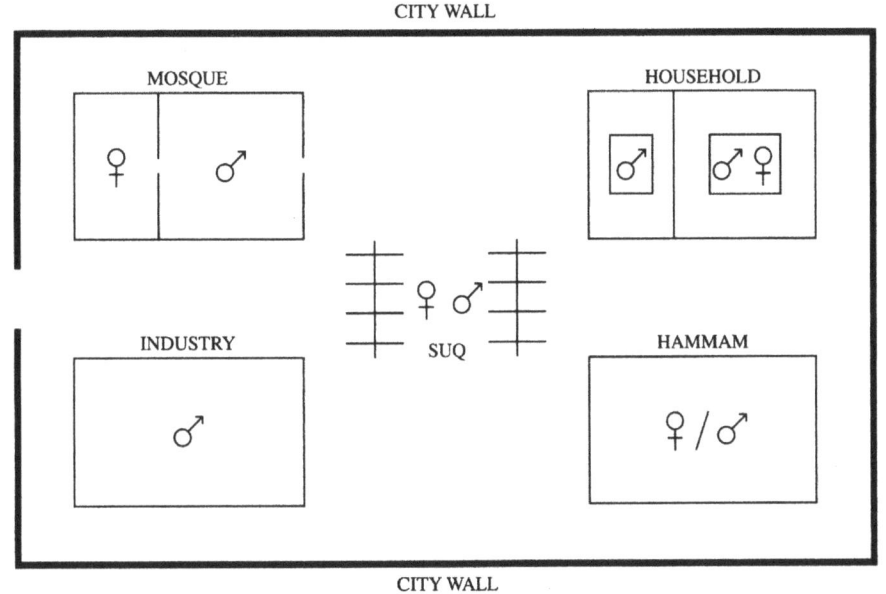

BAR International Series 1234
2004

Published in 2016 by
BAR Publishing, Oxford

BAR International Series 1234

Anatomy of a Medieval Islamic Town: Al-Basra, Morocco

ISBN 978 1 84171 593 3

© The editors and contributors severally and the Publisher 2004

The authors' moral rights under the 1988 UK Copyright,
Designs and Patents Act are hereby expressly asserted.

All rights reserved. No part of this work may be copied, reproduced, stored,
sold, distributed, scanned, saved in any form of digital format or transmitted
in any form digitally, without the written permission of the Publisher.

BAR Publishing is the trading name of British Archaeological Reports (Oxford) Ltd.
British Archaeological Reports was first incorporated in 1974 to publish the BAR
Series, International and British. In 1992 Hadrian Books Ltd became part of the BAR
group. This volume was originally published by Archaeopress in conjunction with
British Archaeological Reports (Oxford) Ltd / Hadrian Books Ltd, the Series principal
publisher, in 2004. This present volume is published by BAR Publishing, 2016.

Printed in England

PUBLISHING

BAR titles are available from:

          BAR Publishing
          122 Banbury Rd, Oxford, OX2 7BP, UK
EMAIL   info@barpublishing.com
PHONE +44 (0)1865 310431
  FAX   +44 (0)1865 316916
          www.barpublishing.com

To the generous people of Jaouna-Basra

CONTENTS

LIST OF ILLUSTRATIONS iv
LIST OF TABLES vi
LIST OF CONTRIBUTORS vii
ACKNOWLEDGMENTS viii

THE SITE OF AL-BASRA

Chapter 1
Al-Basra in Historical and Archaeological Perspective
Nancy L. Benco 3

Chapter 2
Al-Basra's Fortification Walls and Towers
Nancy L. Benco, James E. Franklin, and Azzedine Karra 9

SUBSISTENCE ECONOMY AND THE ENVIRONMENT

Chapter 3
Food, Fuel, and Raw Material: Faunal Remains from Al-Basra
Michelle Loyet 21

Chapter 4
Agriculture, Industry, and the Environment: Archaeobotanical Evidence from Al-Basra
Nancy Mahoney 31

CRAFT PRODUCTION

Chapter 5
Pottery and Ethnic Change at Al-Basra
Jennifer F. Hembree 45

Chapter 6
View from the Rooftops: Clay Tiles and Roof Construction at Al-Basra
Lance Lundquist, and Nancy L. Benco 51

IDEOLOGICAL PERSPECTIVES

Chapter 7
Speaking Stones: Islamic Burial Practices at Al-Basra
Rachel Kluender 61

Chapter 8
Urban Women in Early Islamic Morocco
Hannah Dodd 69

BEYOND THE CITY

Chapter 9
Beyond Al-Basra: Settlement Systems of Medieval Northern Morocco in Archaeological and Historical Perspective
Said Ennahid 79

SCIENTIFIC APPLICATIONS

Chapter 10
An Archaeomagnetic Study of Two Kilns at Al-Basra
AbdelKrim Rimi, Donald H. Tarling, and Sidi Otman el-Alami 95

ILLUSTRATIONS

1.1	Map of Northern Morocco, showing location of al-Basra.	4
1.2	Topographic map of al-Basra, showing location of excavation units. Map prepared by James E. Franklin.	5
1.3	Map of valley floor, showing industrial (F) and residential (G) excavation units. Map prepared by James. E. Franklin.	6
2.1	View of city wall and towers (Towers 2, 3, and 4), looking toward the east.	10
2.2	Map of al-Basra, showing extant city wall in northwest quadrant and projected city wall elsewhere. On east side, A is projected wall circuit based on aerial photo interpretation; B is projected wall circuit based on topography. Map was prepared by James E. Franklin.	11
2.3	Plan of existing city wall, showing 10 semicircular towers (T) with distance between towers in meters. Drawn by James E. Franklin.	12
2.4	Method used to measure wall segments and tower radii. Drawn by James E. Franklin.	14
2.5	Cross-section of city wall near Tower 10, showing core of coursed stone rubble and mortar.	15
2.6	View of Tower 3, showing alternating courses of blocky and flat stones and interlocking stones at the juncture of the tower and wall.	15
3.1	Sheep/goat (*Ovicaprine*) mortality profile. N = 736.	22
3.2	Cattle (*Bos*) survivorship curve. N = 258.	23
3.3	Cattle (*Bos*) body part distribution in the residential area (G).	25
3.4	Sheep/goat (*Ovicaprine*) body part distribution in the residential area (G).	25
3.5	Cattle (*Bos*) body part distribution in the industrial enclave of the residential area (G-enclave).	26
3.6	Sheep/goat (*Ovicaprine*) body part distribution in the industrial enclave of the residential area (G-enclave).	27
3.7	Cattle (*Bos*) body part distribution in the metal-working sector of the industrial area (F-metal).	27
3.8	Sheep/goat (*Ovicaprine*) body part distribution in metal-working sector of the industrial area (F-metal).	28
4.1	Density of seeds (number per liter) and charcoal (volume per liter), by area.	40
4.2	Density of seeds (number per liter) and charcoal (volume per liter), by occupation phase.	40
5.1	Fragments of al-Basra cream ware pottery with painted motifs.	46
5.2	Al-Basra pitcher styles. (a) and (c): cream ware pitchers with rounded shoulders; (b) and (d): buff ware pitchers with sharply carinated shoulders.	46
5.3	Relative frequencies of al-Basra pitchers, by ware and occupation phase.	48
6.1	Generalized shape and dimensions of a typical roof tile at al-Basra.	51
6.2	Three nearly complete roof tiles found in the F3 kiln at al-Basra. They belong to Type A.	52
6.3	Schematic drawing of a tiled roof, illustrating five typical al-Basra tile types (A, B, C, D, and E). Cutaway (on right) shows the probable method of layering top and bottom tiles. Dashed lines represent 1 m^2 area. Drawing is based on data collected from excavation unit G4S10E0 roof collapse.	53
6.4	Roof slopes (in degrees) and tile requirements, derived from excavation unit G4S10E0 roof collapse.	57
7.1	View of a rectangular grave (foreground) in the western cemetery, looking eastward toward al-Basra's city walls.	62
7.2	Map showing the location of the western cemetery outside al-Basra's city walls. Map prepared by James E. Franklin.	63
7.3	Map showing location and orientation of 108 graves and structures in al-Basra's western cemetery. Map prepared by Rachel Kluender.	64
7.4	Distribution of graves, by shape of construction stone.	64
7.5	Distribution of graves, by general shape.	65
7.6	Distribution of graves, by their compass orientation.	66
7.7	Orientation of a typical al-Basra grave (facing 160° azimuth) compared with actual *qibla* direction in northern Morocco (97° azimuth).	67
8.1	Schematic drawing of male and female spaces within a mosque, industry, suq, household, and hammam within an idealized Islamic city.	71

8.2	Map of al-Basra, showing residential and industrial areas. (Adapted from Benco 1987: Figure 4.1)	73
8.3	Photo of copper applicator, probably used for kohl.	73
8.4	Photo of glass vessel rim.	74
8.5	Photo of polished stone beads.	74
9.1	Number of toponyms cited in textual evidence, by name of chronicler. (Based on Massignon 1906:46-47)	80
9.2	Schematic classification of settlement data found in textual evidence.	81
9.3	Number of archaeologically identified and unidentified settlements that are historically documented in northern Morocco, by time period.	82
9.4	Schematic drawing of the main premises of the conceptual model used in this research. (Based on Boone et al. 1990)	82
9.5	Map showing survey area in region of al-Basra and the location of identified archaeological sites (LLM, ARB, and MBS). Potsherds collected from the surface of these sites were analyzed using instrumental neutron activation analysis (INAA).	83
9.6	Hierarchy of urban settlements in early medieval Morocco. (Based on al-Muqaddasî 1950)	85
9.7	Distribution of settlement size classes, by dynastic period.	86
9.8	Correlation between city tax payments and settlement size classes during the Marinid period. (Based on Godinho 1947:134-135; Massignon 1906:148; al-'Umarî 1927:171)	88
9.9	Distribution of settlements, by length of occupation. (All periods are combined)	88
9.10	Percentage of occupied settlements, by dynastic period.	89
10.1	Sketch plans of the sampled floor areas: (top) Kiln F3, (bottom) Kiln F1. Shading indicates the areas that were sampled for archaeomagnetic analysis.	96
10.2	Stereographic projections of the sample directions for Kiln F3: (a) most stable directions for each sample, (b) most linear vector directions. The projection is an equal area, lower hemisphere projection in which upward directions are shown as circles. The present geomagnetic field direction is marked by a cross.	99
10.3	Stereographic projections of the sample directions for the northwestern, southwestern, and southeastern edges of Kiln F1: (a) most stable directions for each sample, (b) most linear vector directions. The projection is an equal area, lower hemisphere projection in which upward directions are shown as circles. The present geomagnetic field direction is marked by a cross.	102
10.4	Stereographic projections of the sample directions for the northeastern edge of Kiln F1: (a) most stable directions for each sample, (b) most linear vector directions. The projection is an equal area, lower hemisphere projection in which upward directions are shown as circles. The present geomagnetic field direction is marked by a cross.	102
10.5	Mean declination and inclination values for relevant sites (200 B.C. to A.D. 600). The mean values are shown with the standard deviation of the age estimate. The errors on inclination are α_{95} and twice α_{95} for declination (to approximate the solid angle error).	105

TABLES

1.1	Al-Basra Phases, Dates, and Dynasties.	7
2.1	Dimensions of al-Basra's 10 Extant City Wall Towers	13
3.1	Counts and Percentages of Identifiable and Unidentifiable Fauna, by Functionally Distinct Spatial Areas.	21
3.2	Counts and Percentages of Identifiable Faunal Taxa, by Functionally Distinct Spatial Areas.	
3.3	Distribution of Cattle (*Bos*) and Sheep/Goat (*Ovcap*) Body Parts, by Functionally Distinct Spatial Areas. (Shaded areas indicate butchery waste elements).	24
4.1	Counts of Seeds in Samples from Metal-Working Contexts at al-Basra, by Genus.	33
4.2	Counts of Seeds in Samples from Ceramic Kilns and Other Contexts at al-Basra, by Genus.	35
4.3	Counts of Seeds in Samples from Residential Contexts at al-Basra, by Genus.	36
4.4	Identification and Weights of Hand-Collected Charcoal, by Excavation Unit.	38
5.1	Counts and Percentages of al-Basra Pottery, by Ware Type.	45
5.2	Counts and Percentages of al-Basra Wares, by Occupation Phase.	47
5.3	Counts and Percentages of Pitchers, by Occupation Phase.	48
6.1	Counts and Weights of Roof Tiles and Pottery from Ten Roof Collapses at al Basra.	55
7.1	Relationship between Grave Shape and Type of Construction Stone.	65
8.1	Counts and Percentages of Female Artifacts in Residential and Industrial Areas.	74
9.1	Tax Payments of Marinid Cities.	87
9.2	Settlement Size Estimates for Selected Medieval Moroccan Cities, Based on Documentary Data.	87
10.1	F3 Kiln Intensity, Coercivity, and Consistency Characteristics.	97
10.2	F3 Kiln Principal Component Analyses.	98
10.3	F3 Kiln Mean Sample Directions from Different Edges and the Combined Mean Direction.	99
10.4	F1 Kiln Intensity, Coercivity, and Consistency Characteristics.	100
10.5	F1 Kiln Principal Component Analyses.	101
10.6	Mean Directions for F3 Kiln Southwestern, Northeastern, and Northwestern Edges.	103
10.7	Relevant Archaeomagnetic Observations from Morocco (300 B.C.-A.D. 500) and Spain.	104

CONTRIBUTORS

Sidi Otman el-Alami
Institut Scientifique
Service de Physique du Globe
Rabat, Morocco

Nancy L. Benco
Department of Anthropology
George Washington University
Washington, D.C.

Hannah Dodd
Department of Anthropology
University of New Mexico
Albuquerque, New Mexico

Said Ennahid
School of Humanities and Social Sciences
Al Akhawayn University
Ifrane, Morocco

James E. Franklin
Licensed Land Surveyor
Candia, New Hampshire

Jennifer Hembree
American Studies Program
University of Maryland
College Park, Maryland

Azzedine Karra
Monuments Historiques et des Sites Adjoint
Safi, Morocco

Rachel Kluender
Department of Anthropology
University of New Mexico
Albuquerque, New Mexico

Michelle Loyet
Department of Anthropology
University of Illinois
Champaign-Urbana, Illinois

Lance Lundquist
Department of Anthropology
University of New Mexico
Albuquerque, New Mexico

Nancy Mahoney
Department of Anthropology
Arizona State University
Tempe, Arizona

Abdelkrim Rimi
Institut Scientifique
Service de Physique du Globe
Rabat, Morocco

Donald H. Tarling
Department of Geological Sciences
University of Plymouth
Plymouth, United Kingdom

ACKNOWLEDGMENTS

This volume is based on findings from five seasons of archaeological fieldwork at the Islamic site of al-Basra in Morocco. This research could not have been accomplished without the dedication of dozens of archaeological students, both Moroccan and American, and scores of men and women from the small village of Jaouna-Basra whose labor allowed us to uncover the remains of one of Morocco's earliest Islamic cities. The research was inspired by the earlier Moroccan excavations of Charles Redman. It was enabled by permissions from the Institut National des Sciences de l'Archéologie et du Patrimoine (INSAP), Ministry of Culture, in Rabat, and by the assistance of many of their personnel, in particular Joudia-Hassar Benslimane and Ahmed Ettahiri. The fieldwork and analyses were funded by the National Science Foundation (NSF-SBR-9618369); the U.S. Fulbright Senior Scholars program; the National Geographic Society; the American Institute for Maghrib Studies; and the Cotlow Foundation at George Washington University. Logistical and other support was also provided by INSAP through the years.

The Site of Al-Basra

Chapter 1

AL-BASRA IN HISTORICAL AND ARCHAEOLOGICAL PERSPECTIVE

Nancy L. Benco

This volume grew out of a symposium held at the 23rd Annual Meeting of the Society for American Archaeology in Philadelphia in 2000. Entitled "Anatomy of a Medieval Islamic City," the symposium highlighted a series of papers presented by graduate students and specialists who had worked at the archaeological site of al-Basra in Morocco. These papers focused on specific aspects of the medieval city that, when presented altogether at the symposium, offered a rich mosaic of urban Islamic life during the first millennium A.D. in the western Mediterranean. The analyses presented in these papers were based on archaeological research conducted at al-Basra during the course of five summer field seasons in the 1990s.[1]

Of the 10 chapters in this volume, five (Benco, Loyet, Hembree, Kluender, Dodd, and Ennahid) were presented as papers at the symposium. Two other papers that were given at the symposium (Morgan and Waters) are not included in this volume. Of the other five chapters, two (Benco, Franklin, and Karra; Lundquist and Benco) are drawn from ongoing analyses of excavation data; one (Mahoney) is based on an ethnobotanical study written as a master's thesis in the mid-1990s; and one presents the results of archaeomagnetic work conducted at al-Basra in the early 1990s (Rimi, Tarling, and al-Alami).

The chapters focus on the economic and social aspects of the early Islamic city. Several of them examine the underlying economic structure—food production (animals and plants), the manufacture of craft goods (pottery, roof tiles), and the environment. Others explore the less tangible social aspects of medieval urban life, such as ethnic identity, the status of women, and the treatment of the dead. One chapter looks beyond the city to reconstruct its economic ties with settlements in the region.

In this introduction, I provide the historical and archaeological context for the studies that follow. This chapter traces the main highlights of the city's history, briefly describes the archaeological work that has been conducted there, and outlines the chronological framework for the ancient site.

Highlights of Al-Basra's History

The Islamic city of al-Basra was located in the foothills of the Rif Mountains, about 40 kilometers from the Atlantic coast, midway between Fez and Tangier (Figure 1.1). Enclosed by stone fortifications, the 35-hectare city extended across two ridges and the valley between them. Its strategic location gave it a commanding view of the broad Mda River valley to the north, the Rif foothills to the east and south, and the Atlantic coastal plains to the west.

According to Arab historians, the city of al-Basra was established during the fragmentation of the Islamic empire in North Africa and Spain. Following the overthrow of the long-standing Ummayid Caliphate by the Abbasids in the Middle East in ca. A.D. 750, dozens of refugees fled to safety in the Maghreb (the Far West). Many of them established independent dynasties in North Africa and southern Spain, severing their political ties to the Islamic heartland. One of these refugees founded the Idrisid dynasty in northern Morocco in A.D. 789. Idris I built the city of Fez as his royal capital, and his successors founded al-Basra and other cities in about A.D. 800. The Idrisids named al-Basra after the port city in southern Iraq from where they had fled.

While the city of Fez has been continuously occupied during the past 1,200 years, al-Basra met an entirely different fate. The city was abandoned about 300 years after it was built and its walls and buildings eventually disappeared from sight. According to Arab chroniclers, al-Basra served as an important Idrisid administrative and commercial center in the ninth and tenth centuries. Its population of about 10,000 consisted of both Arabs and indigenous Berbers (see Hembree this volume). In about A.D. 979 century, al-Basra was destroyed during a regional conflict between the Ummayids in Spain and the Fatimids in Tunisia; around the same time, the Idrisid dynasty came to an end. The chronicles confirm that al-Basra was subsequently rebuilt and continued to flourish as a small urban center. Although it is not clear when the city was finally abandoned, reports from the thirteenth and fourteenth centuries indicate that the town was in ruins.

Today, the city of al-Basra has disappeared almost entirely from sight. The only visible remains include a small segment of the thick fortification walls and towers that once encircled the town (see Benco and Franklin this

---

[1] The excavations at al-Basra in Morocco were conducted during summer field seasons in 1990, 1994, 1995, 1998, and 1999. The fieldwork was funded by the National Science Foundation (NSF-SBR-9618369), U.S. Fulbright Senior Scholars program, National Geographic Society, American Institute for Maghrib Studies, and the Cotlow Foundation at George Washington University. The Institut National des Sciences de l'Archéologie et du Patrimoine (INSAP), Ministry of Culture in Rabat provided permissions and logistical support. Ahmed Ettahiri of INSAP, who helped direct the 1998 and 1999 field seasons, was invited to give a paper at the symposium but was unable to attend at the last minute.

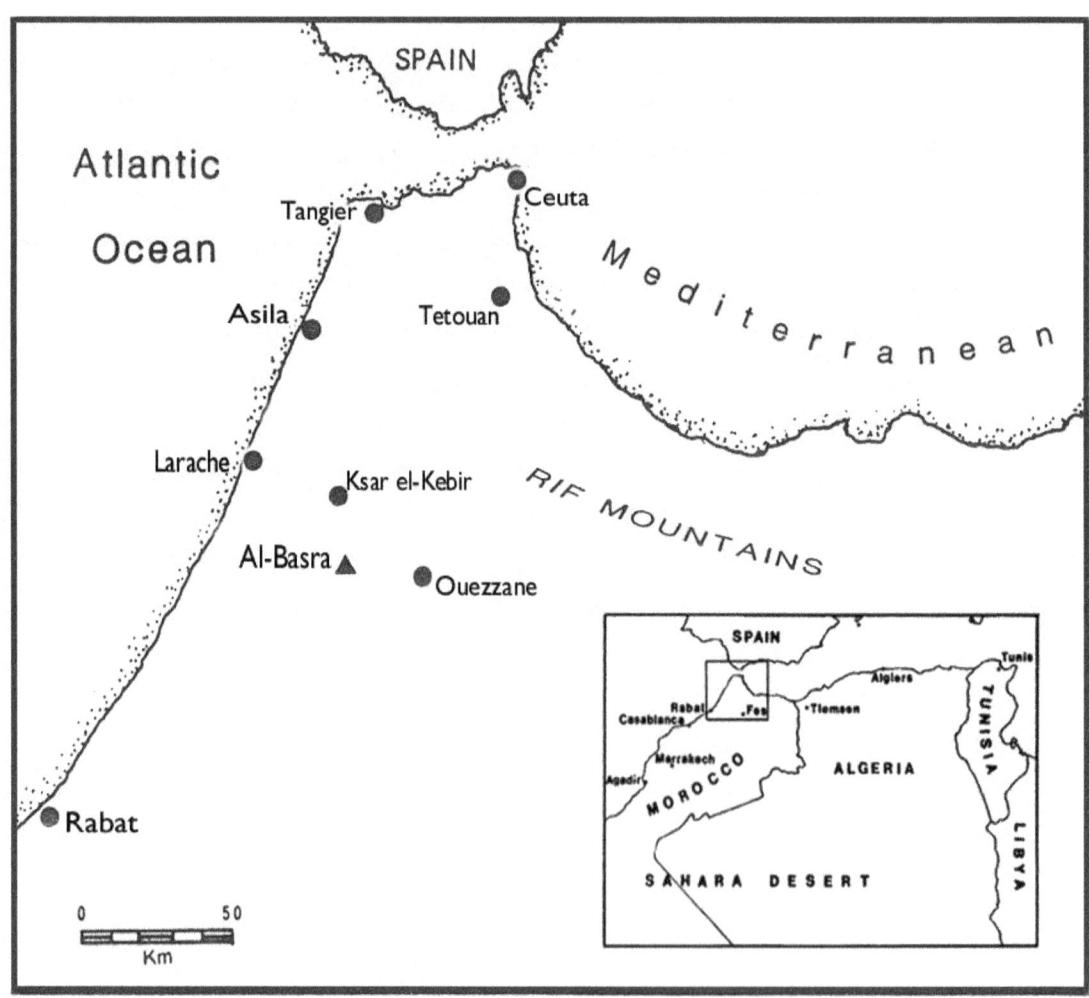

Figure 1.1 Map of Northern Morocco, showing location of al-Basra.

volume). The rest lie buried below ground. A small Moroccan village (Jaouna-Basra) and the villagers' gardens and fields extend across much of the ancient site today.

Archaeological Research at Al-Basra

The earliest documented archaeological work at the site of al-Basra was conducted in the 1950s by French archaeologists who mapped the city walls and dug soundings along them (Eustache 1955). Some 25 years later, in 1980 and 1981, American archaeologists under the direction of Charles L. Redman remapped the site. They also excavated several test units, selected by probability sampling techniques, inside the city walls to determine what kind of architectural and artifactual remains lay below ground (Redman 1983-84; Benco 1987). The test units revealed two updraft kilns near the western city wall and residential structures closer to the center of the site. They also indicated that deposits were deep (up to 3 meters) and well-stratified in the lowest part of the site—the valley floor—and shallow and disturbed along the hill slopes leading to the ridge tops (Figure 1.2).

Starting in 1990, I conducted five additional field seasons to expand the work that Redman had initiated (Benco 1994, 1995, 2001, 2002; Benco and Ettahiri 1998, 1999; Benco, Ettahiri, and Loyet 2002).[2] The main thrust of this research was to investigate the spatial layout of the Islamic town and reconstruct its medieval economy, including the organization of food and craft production in the urban center. To accomplish this, we focused our work on two functionally distinct areas: an industrial sector in the western zone and a residential sector in the center of the site. These two sectors are shown in Figure 1.3. In addition, we continued to examine other parts of the site with small test units, topographic mapping, and remote sensing techniques, including proton magnetometry and ground-penetrating radar, to determine the extent of the city and circuit of its fortification walls.

---

[2] I directed the 1990, 1994, and 1995 field seasons. In 1998 and 1999, I codirected the project with Ahmed Ettahiri of INSAP. Archaeology students from the United States and Morocco participated in the project each year. In addition, several dozen residents of the village of Jaouna-Basra, which is located on part of the site, worked with us to unearth the remains of the early Islamic city.

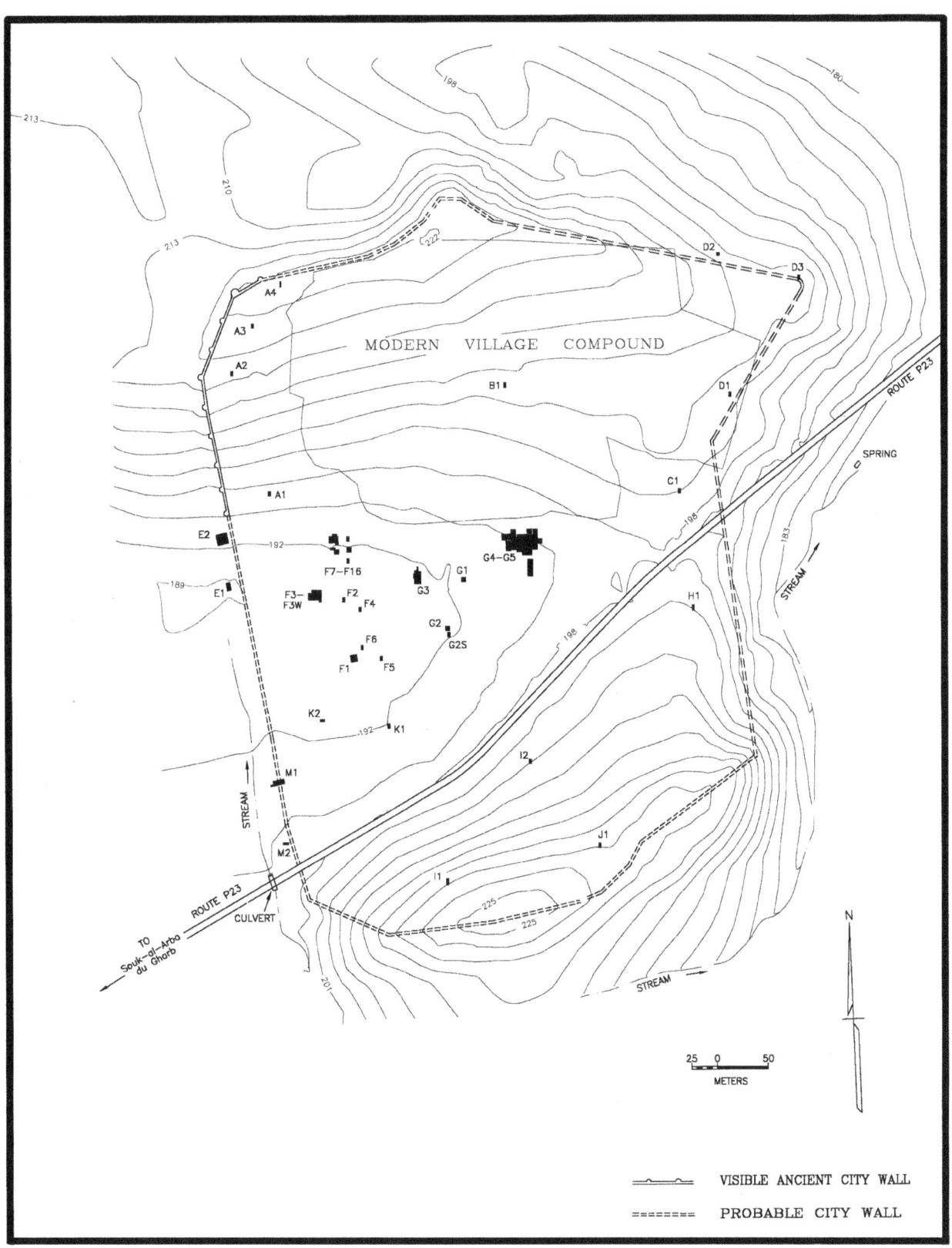

Figure 1.2 Topographic map of al-Basra, showing location of excavation units. Map prepared by James E. Franklin.

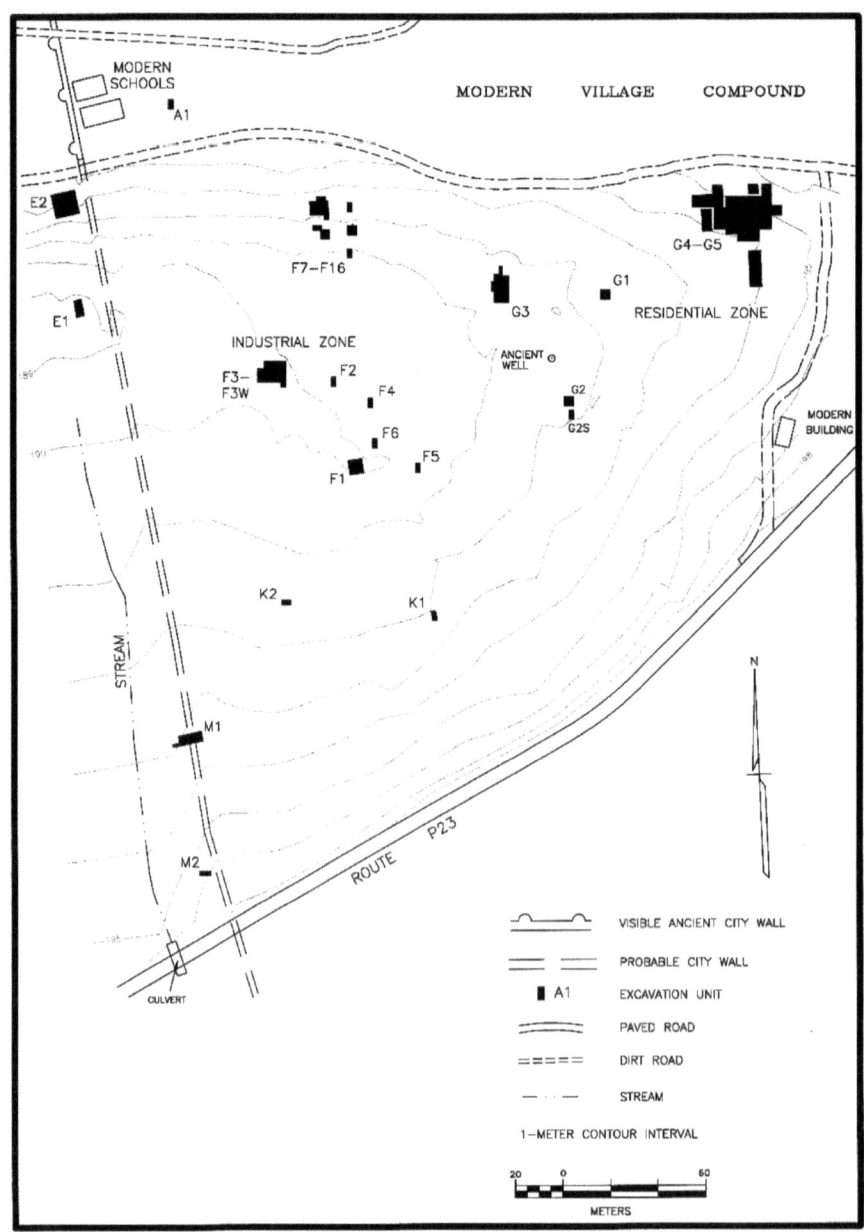

Figure 1.3 Map of valley floor, showing industrial (F) and residential (G) excavation units. Map prepared by James. E. Franklin.

Industrial Sector

Archaeological work in the western zone revealed that this area shifted from an industrial sector to a residential neighborhood during the city's history. During the early and middle occupation phases (pre-Idrisid and Idrisid periods), industrial activities took place in this part of the site (Table 1.1).[3] Excavations have revealed the remains of two rectangular-shaped updraft kilns. Potters used the earliest kiln (unit F3) to fire both pottery and rooftiles and the later kiln (unit F1) to fire only pottery (see Lundquist and Benco this volume; also Rimi, Tarling, and el-Alami this volume). About 50 m north of the kilns along a hill slope was a metal-working industry (units F7-F16) that

---

[3] The site chronology has been developed using several pieces of evidence. The medieval Arab histories and geographies provide the basic historical framework, with the succession of early Islamic dynasties (Idrisid, Spanish Ummayid, Almoravid, and Almohad) clearly identified and sometimes dated. A body of numismatic evidence provides further details on the reigns of various rulers and the minting of coins at al-Basra. Coins minted at al-Basra exist in a collection published by Eustache (1970-71), although their provenance is not known. In the course of excavations at al-Basra, additional coins were unearthed. Although most of them were badly worn and illegible, a few have been identified variously as Idrisid, Almoravid, Almohad, and Spanish Ummayid. Finally, radiocarbon dating of charcoal samples from various components at the site offers some additional dates, although these often span more than one historical period.

Table 1.1. Al-Basra Phases, Dates, and Dynasties

Phase	Dates	Dynasty
Abandonment	1150-1250	Almohad
Post-urban	1105-1150	Almoravid
Late (urban)	970-1050	Post-Idrisid/Spanish Ummayid
Middle (urban)	800-970	Idrisid
Early (pre-urban)	600-800	Pre-Idrisid/Late Roman

appears to have spanned the early and middle occupation phases at al-Basra. In this area, metalworkers smelted iron ore and forged large quantities of iron nails and other objects (e.g., door hinges). They used small bowl furnaces, as evidenced by charcoal-filled circular pits dug into the ground, to smelt the ores, and they constructed more elaborate facilities, including plaster-lined basins and stone-walled workshops for smithing activities. They used animal bones as a fuel and flux for metal production, as well as to fashion a variety of bone tools (Benco, Ettahiri, and Loyet 2002; Loyet this volume). During the late occupation phase (post-Idrisid/Ummayid), the western sector took on a more residential character with compounds that contained evidence of domestic activities, such as cooking and food storage.

Residential Sector

Excavations in the central part of the walled city have revealed the remains of several extensive residential compounds with paved courtyards and an elaborate underground water system. These date primarily to the middle phase (Idrisid and post-Idrisid periods). One partly uncovered house compound (G3) featured two rooms with white plaster floors and red-painted walls along with a bent-axis entryway, which is commonly found in Islamic houses in North Africa.

Nearby were two large house compounds located next to each other (G4-G5). Each compound consisted of several small rectangular rooms surrounding a central courtyard. The courtyards featured pebbled or flagstone surfaces and roofed porticos. The houses were well built of stone, mortar, and pisé walls and had pitched tile roofs (see Lundquist and Benco this volume). In addition to the ubiquitous undecorated pottery, rooftiles, and faunal remains, these residential structures yielded unusually large quantities of glass objects (glass weights and vessels), jewelry (glass and stone beads, stone pendants, gold beads, and copper rings), and glazed pottery, attesting to the presence not only of high-status households but also of women (see Dodd this volume). Like many other structures, these residential compounds were rebuilt. The walls of the new structures were not as well consolidated, and they often followed a new spatial layout. At some point, most of the buildings collapsed as a result of a major conflagration. Buildings throughout the city collapsed and roof tiles fell to the floors below (see Lundquist and Benco this volume), leaving a thick layer of bright orange clay (from the pisé walls) and traces of charcoal across most of the urban center. Subsequently, parts of the site were rebuilt and reused, but only scattered building stones remain from this final phase (Almoravid-Almohad periods).

South of the residential sector, the excavations revealed traces of industrial activities, including large quantities of iron slag, charcoal, and animal bones in relatively early deposits (possibly pre-Idrisid). These remains suggest that the function of this area also changed—from industrial to residential—between the earliest, pre-Idrisid settlement and the Idrisid city that flourished as a commercial and administrative center in the ninth and tenth centuries.

References Cited

Benco, N.
1987 *The Early Medieval Pottery Industry at al-Basra, Morocco*. BAR International Series 341. British Archaeological Reports, Oxford.
1994 Preliminary Report on Archaeologial Excavations at Al-Basra, Morocco, June 26-July 17, 1994. Submitted to the Institut National des Sciences de l'Archéologie et du Patrimoine, Rabat.
1995 Preliminary Report on the 1995 Season of Archaeological Excavations at al-Basra, Morocco. Submitted to the Institut National des Sciences de l'Archéologie et du Patrimoine, Rabat.
2001 Five Seasons of Archaeological Research at al-Basra, Morocco. *Actes des Premièrs Journées Nationales d'Archéologie et du Patrimoine. vol. 3: Archéologie Islamique*, pp. 130-142. Société Marocaine d'Archéologie et du Patrimoine, Rabat.
2002 1990 Archaeological Investigations at al-Basra, Morocco. *Bulletin d'Archéologie Marocaine* 19:293-340. Rabat.

Benco, N., and A. Ettahiri
1998 Report on the 1998 Season of Excavations at al-Basra, Morocco. Submitted to Institut National des Sciences de l'Archéologie et du Patrimoine, Rabat.
1999 Report on the 1999 Season of Excavations at al-

Basra, Morocco. Submitted to Institut National des Sciences de l'Archéologie et du Patrimoine, Rabat.

Benco, N., A. Ettahiri, and M. Loyet
  2002 Worked Bone Tools: Linking Metal Artisans and Animal Processors in Medieval Islamic Morocco. *Antiquity* 76:447-457.

Eustache, D.
  1955 El-Basra, Capitale Idrissite, et Son Port. *Hespéris* 42:218-238.
  1970-71 *Corpus des Dirhams Idrisites et Contemporains.* Banque du Maroc, Rabat.

Morgan, M.
  2000 Reconstructing Islamic Metal Production: The View from North Africa. Paper presented at the symposium, Anatomy of a Medieval Islamic Town, at the 23rd Annual Meeting of the Society for American Archaeology, Philadelphia.

Redman, C.
  1983-84 Survey and Test Excavation of Six Medieval Islamic Sites in Northern Morocco. *Bulletin d'Archéologie Marocaine* 15:311-349.

Watters, M.
  2000 Geophysical Survey at al-Basra. Paper presented at the symposium, Anatomy of a Medieval Islamic Town, at the 23rd Annual Meeting of the Society for American Archaeology, Philadelphia.

Chapter 2

AL-BASRA'S FORTIFICATION WALLS AND TOWERS

Nancy L. Benco
James E. Franklin
Azzedine Karra

Medieval Islamic cities in North Africa were nearly always enclosed by a city wall. The enclosure wall served as a fortification to protect the city's inhabitants from the armies of their enemies. After nightfall when the gates were closed, it protected urban residents from wild animals and common thieves who roamed outside the walls. In a symbolic way, the city wall clearly marked the boundary between urban and rural life in medieval Islamic times.

Today, the only visible remains of the once flourishing urban center of al-Basra are its fortifications (Figure 2.1). A segment of its enclosure walls and the remains of 10 semicircular towers can still be seen in the northwest corner of the ancient city while the rest of the urban center lies buried below ground.

In this chapter, we trace the development of al-Basra's city walls through the accounts of medieval geographers and historians, many of whom may have actually visited the city. We also provide a detailed description of the existing walls and towers and its projected circuit around the city and a discussion of the construction technology. Finally, the chapter places al-Basra's city wall into a historical and chronological perspective by a comparative study with other Islamic city walls in the Maghreb.

Historical Views of the City Wall

During the course of several hundred years, scores of Arab and other geographers, historians, and archaeologists have visited the Islamic city of al-Basra. Although brief, their eyewitness accounts provide informative glimpses of the urban center and, in particular, the nature and condition of its enclosure walls and towers.

In one of the earliest accounts, the mid-tenth-century Arab geographer Ibn Hawqal (1842:192) described al-Basra as a city of average size enclosed by a weak wall. During his visit—sometime between A.D. 936 and 951 (Miquel 1971)—Ibn Hawqal noted that the inhabitants got their drinking water from a source outside the city wall, a precarious situation especially during times of conflict.

A few years later, the late-tenth-century Arab geographer al-Muqaddasi (1950:273) noted that the city of al-Basra had fallen into ruins. Very likely, he visited the city sometime between A.D. 979-980, the year it presumably was destroyed—or badly damaged–and A.D. 985, the year his chronicles were published. This destruction took place during a conflict between the Ummayids of Spain and the Fatimids of Ifriqiya (Tunisia) for control of northern Morocco. These two competing dynasties attacked cities throughout northern and central Morocco, including Fez and al-Basra. Al-Muqaddasi's account does not mention the city's fortification walls, but it is likely that they too had fallen into ruins.

The next glimpse of al-Basra comes in the mid-eleventh century. The Andalusian geographer al-Bakri (1965:216-217), who based his account on firsthand reports of travelers returning from North Africa, wrote that al-Basra had been rebuilt next to the earlier Idrisid town. Moreover, it had been enclosed by a stone (and brick) wall pierced by 10 gates. The principal gate, called Bir ibn Delfa, was located on the east side near the city's main water source. Al-Bakri's chronicles, which are considered by historians to be highly reliable (Lévi-Provençal 1960), document the reconstruction of the city and its fortification walls sometime between ca. A.D. 980 and A.D.1060, the eve of the Almoravid invasion of the Maghreb.

In the twelfth century, the geographer al-Idrisi (1969:202) reported that the city of al-Basra was in decline. By the sixteenth century, the Arab historian Leo Africanus (1956:259) noted that only the walls of the formerly prosperous town remained intact. Three centuries later, the late nineteenth-century French diplomat and scholar Charles Tissot (1877:296) found only the northwestern segment of the city wall still standing, with rubble and debris scattered across the rest of the site.

In the 1950s as part of an archaeological reconnaissance along the Atlantic coastal plain, M. A. Luquet, the Moroccan Inspector of Antiquities, visited al-Basra where he conducted some test excavations and mapped the site (Eustache 1955). His map shows the remains of walls and towers in the northwestern corner of the ancient city. This segment still stood in the early 1980s when Charles Redman (1983-1984) began test excavations at the site.

Drawing on these historical accounts, it is possible to suggest that al-Basra had two city walls during its 300-

Anatomy of a Medieval Town

Figure 2.1 View of city wall and towers (Towers 2, 3, and 4), looking toward the east.

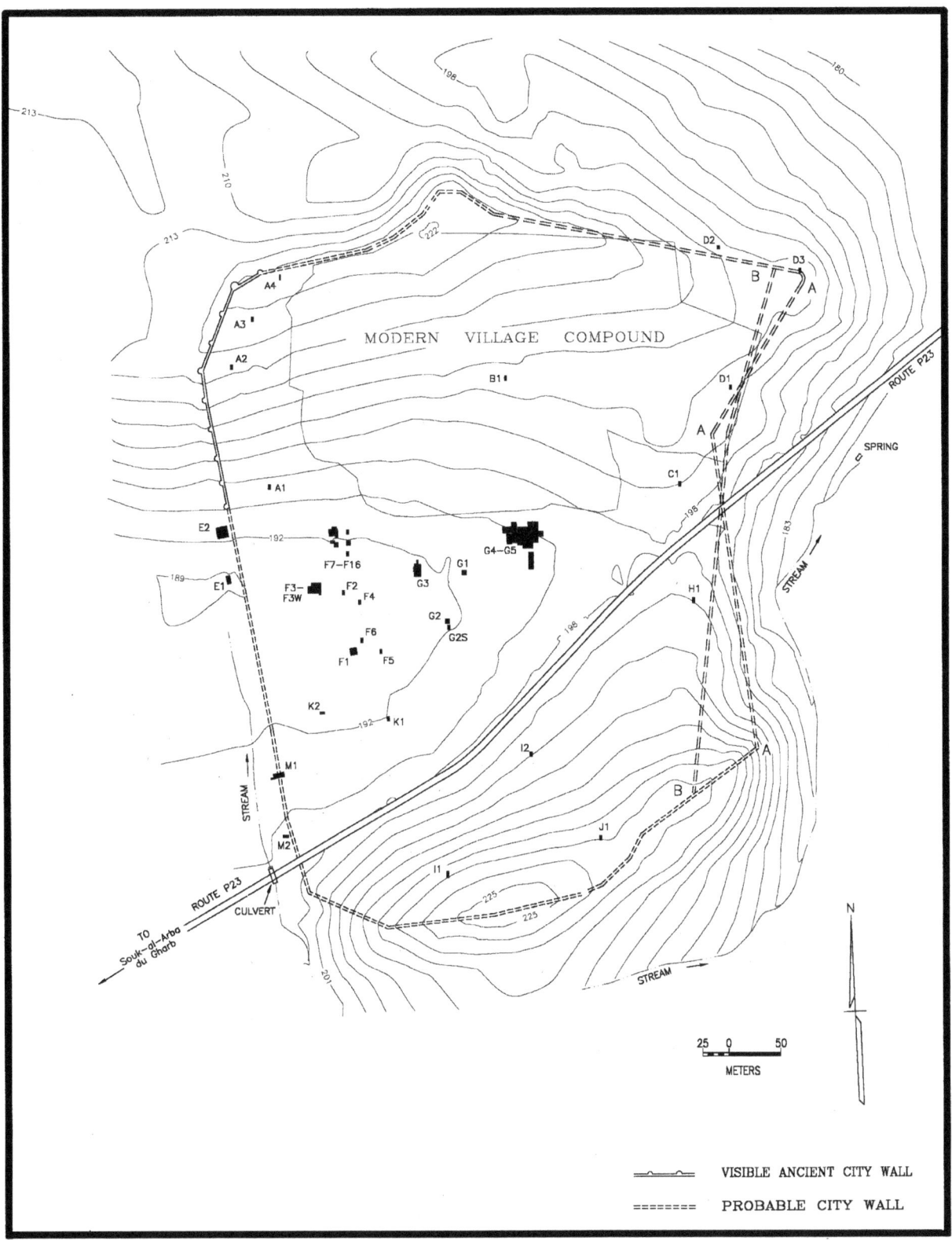

Figure 2.2 Map of al-Basra, showing extant city wall in northwest quadrant and projected city wall elsewhere. On east side, A is projected wall circuit based on aerial photo interpretation; B is projected wall circuit based on topography. Map was prepared by James E. Franklin.

year-history. The earliest one—a poorly fortified wall—may have been constructed sometime around A.D. 800, when the Idrisids first established the city; this wall was likely damaged, or destroyed, in A.D. 979-980. A later wall—part of which may still be extant—seems to have been built sometime between the end of the tenth and the last half of the eleventh century, when the Almoravid dynasty from southern Morocco began its conquest of northern Morocco.

If al-Basra's fortification wall and supporting towers were similar to the portion that exists today, they would have constituted an impressive sight. The wall would have extended more than 2 km around the perimeter of the city (Figure 2.2). It would have been supported by nearly 100 semicircular stone towers, rising to heights of 8 m or more. Of the 10 gates leading into the urban center, the main gate would have been located on the east side, nearest the road that led to Fez, the major administrative and commercial city in northern Morocco at the time.

Description of City Walls and Towers

The existing city walls and towers were mapped during Redman's 1980 field season (Redman 1983-84; Benco 1987:Figure 4.1). They were remapped, measured, photographed, and test excavated during the 1998 and 1999 field seasons (Figures 2.2-2.3; see Benco and Ettahiri 1998, 1999). Their projected circuit around the rest of the city has been estimated on the basis of surface traces of foundation stones, topography, aerial photography, and a remote sensing survey.[1]

Existing Walls and Towers

The segment that still stands today extends for a length of approximately 242 m on the city's northwest periphery (Figures 2.2-2.3). This section represents an estimated 12 percent of the original city wall. Starting on the south end of the section, the existing wall runs uphill in a northwesterly direction (N11°W)[2] from Tower 10 to Tower 6 and then turns a few degrees north (N6°W) to Tower 5; between Towers 5 and 2, it changes from a westerly to an easterly direction (N23°E), and on the top of the ridge it shifts more easterly (N62°E). These directional changes follow the steep topography of the hill slope and keep the long axis of the walls at a right angle to the slope.

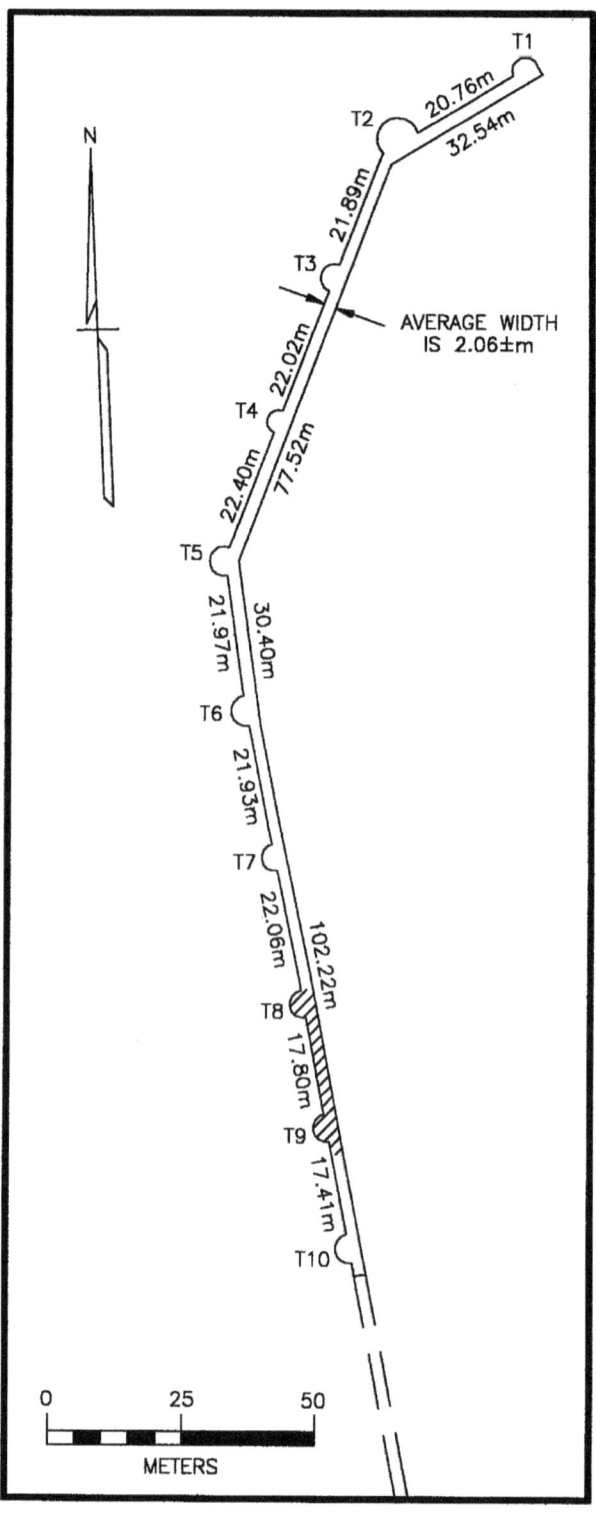

Figure 2.3 Plan of existing city wall, showing 10 semicircular towers (T) with distance between towers in meters. Drawn by James E. Franklin.

The existing walls average 2.06 m in thickness. Although their original heights are unknown because their upper courses have been removed, the highest existing wall

---
[1] James E. Franklin, an independent licensed surveyor from Candia, New Hampshire, measured and mapped the walls in 1998 and conducted a topographic survey in 1998 and 1999. In 1999, Meg Watters of IMAC, Minneapolis, conducted a remote sensing (magnetometer) survey of portions of the projected wall circuit and field staff undertook test excavations. In addition, Arthur Ireland, National Park Service, Southwest Region, Santa Fe, New Mexico, examined several small-scale aerial photos (scale 1:29,000) to identify structural remains at al-Basra. The photos were obtained from the Moroccan Division of Cartography and Topography in Rabat.

[2] The orientations of the existing city wall are based on solar observations taken in July 1999 that showed a magnetic declination of 3°56'20" west of north.

(between Towers 7 and 8) reaches about 3.8 m in height and consists of some 20 courses of stone.

The walls are supported by 10 still-visible semicircular towers. The towers, which are built outside the enclosure walls, are spaced about 22 m apart (Table 2.1 and Figure 2.3). A shorter distance (17 m) exists between Towers 8 and 9 and Towers 9 and 10, possibly indicating the presence of a city gate. The semicircular towers vary in radii from 2.14 m to 2.78 m, with the largest, Tower 2, achieving a radius of 3.8 m. The arc lengths (distance around the curved surfaces) of the towers range from the shortest (6.8 m) at Tower 4 to the longest (8.6 m) at Tower 2 (Table 2.1; Figure 2.4). The unusually large size of Tower 2 may be due to its pivotal position on the summit of the ridge.

Like the walls, none of the existing towers extend to their original heights. Stones from the upper courses have fallen off or have been deliberately removed. Although the highest remaining tower today is 4.3 m in height, it is probable that the towers reached 8 m or more in antiquity (Eustache 1955). Three of the towers (8, 9, and 10) are visible only at ground surface. One of these, Tower 9, may have been destroyed during the construction of an underground canal system in the late 1980s.

A shorter segment of the city wall extends for another 50 m south of the main section. This segment is represented by two semicircular depressions in the ground rather than by standing architecture. This section appears to have been supported by at least two towers, although their size cannot be determined. About 10 m directly west of this segment is a large stone cistern, which had at one time been covered by a vaulted roof (Benco 1987:45, 49-51, Figure 4.13). The cistern's construction, which consists of alternating courses of roughly hewn blocky and flat stones, is similar to that of the fortification walls and towers and suggests they were built about the same time.

Table 2.1. Dimensions of Al-Basra's 10 Extant City Wall Towers

Tower No.	Radius (m)	Arc Length (m)	Tower Height[1] (m)	Distance to Next Tower (m)	Condition in 1999
T1	2.4	7.2	3.0	20.76	standing
T2	3.8	8.6	3.2	21.89	standing
T3	2.5	7.5	3.0	22.02	standing
T4	2.1	6.8	4.3	22.40	standing
T5	2.7	7.9	1.9	21.97	standing
T6	2.8	7.9	n.m.	21.93	standing
T7	2.4	7.4	3.3	22.06	standing
T8	2.5	7.4	n.m.	17.80	trace
T9	n.m.	n.m.	n.m.	17.41	trace
T10	2.7	7.6	n.m.	n.m.	trace

n.m. = not measured
[1] Existing height of tower in 1999.

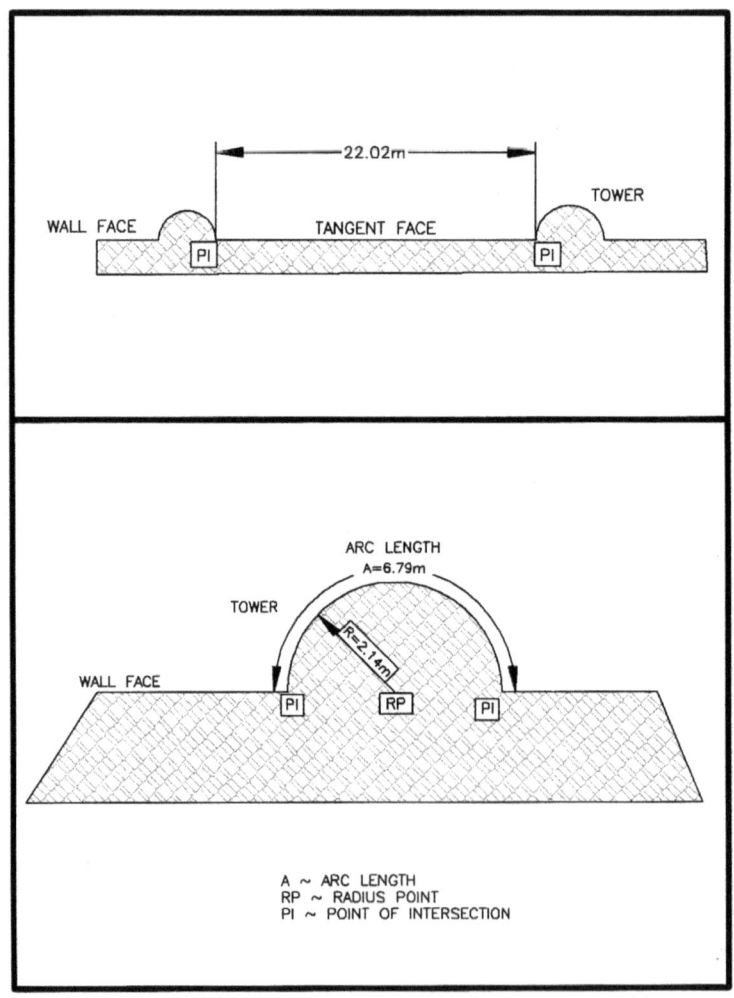

Figure 2.4 Method used to measure wall segments and tower radii. Drawn by James E. Franklin.

Projected Wall Circuit

Although the remaining 1.8 km of the ancient city wall is not visible above ground, its course can be projected on the basis of several lines of evidence, including traces of stones at or just below the surface of the ground, the topography of the hilly site, and possible subsurface features detected on aerial photography. A proton magnetometer survey carried out in 1999 to locate the city wall at various points in its projected circuit proved to be inconclusive perhaps because the stone foundations no longer exist or because the circuit estimates are incorrect.

Starting from Tower 10 (Figure 2.2), the city wall appears to have run southward for about 350 m across the valley floor to the modern-day road (P23). Today, this section is represented by a long narrow depression in the ground and large blocks of stone scattered on the surface. A test unit (M1) dug across the depression revealed the remains of stone architecture that may have belonged to the city wall. Just south of the modern road, the wall turns southeast and climbs a steep hill for about 80 m. At the summit, it turns east and then northeast, running about 390 m to the eastern edge of the south summit. This section also contains a linear depression in the ground and large rocks protruding from the soil.

At this point, traces of the city wall virtually disappear. An examination of aerial photography suggests that it descended the steep hill in a northeasterly direction for a distance of about 60 m and then turned abruptly north/northwest to run along the mid-flank of the hill for about 230 m (Figure 2.2:A). A study of the topography, however, suggests that from the south hill summit the wall may have turned directly north/northeasterly and descended about 280 m along the upper part of the hill (Figure 2.2:B). Just north of the modern road, the wall may have taken one of two paths, either coming to a juncture and turning northeast (Figure 2.2:A) or continuing directly north/northeasterly up the north slope (Figure 2.2:B). At the summit of the north hill, the wall turned northwesterly and then westerly, running for about 550 m to complete the circuit at Tower 1.

Entry Gates

Although the chronicles mention 10 entry gates at al-Basra (al-Bakri 1965:216-217), none of them have been located during archaeological fieldwork. A 1999 magnetometer survey revealed a number of anomalous features southwest of Tower 10, but a large excavation unit (E2) placed over them exposed only a late urban structure, possibly a blacksmith's shop. Additional magnetometer work in other areas along the projected wall circuit yielded little information about either walls or gates.

Construction Technology

The city wall and towers were built of locally available stone, primarily a calcite-cemented quartzose sandstone, a material that is available in outcrops near the site. The roughly hewn building stones were laid in uneven courses on the interior and exterior faces of the enclosure walls and towers. The courses consist of layers of blocky stones and large river cobbles alternating with layers of long flat stones. The stones are bound together with a lime-based mortar. The walls and towers are solid, with the cores filled with coursed stone rubble and mortar (Figure 2.5). The facing stones at the juncture of the walls and towers interlock (Figure 2.6), indicating that they were designed and built as a whole.

The foundations of the walls and towers appear to be relatively shallow. A test pit dug at the foot of the wall

Figure 2.5 Cross-section of city wall near Tower 10, showing core of coursed stone rubble and mortar.

Figure 2.6 View of Tower 3, showing alternating courses of blocky and flat stones and interlocking stones at the juncture of the tower and wall.

near Tower 10 revealed two stone courses below the present-day surface of the ground. Adjacent soils contained ash lenses and highly calcareous concretions, suggesting that construction materials, such as lime mortar, were manufactured directly next to the city wall where they were used.

Comparison with Other Early Islamic Walls

Despite the existence of many cities in medieval Morocco, some of which, like Fez, are still inhabited, and others, like al-Basra, were abandoned centuries ago, no systematic study of their enclosure walls has been conducted to delineate the chronological and geographical variability of their architectural forms and construction technologies. In a recent bibliographical review of Islamic fortifications in Morocco, Cressier (1995) laments the fact that information on Islamic walls, gates, and towers is scattered in a wide variety of sources (art history, history, archaeology); moreover, much of this information was collected during the early part of the twentieth century. Thus, any attempt to situate al-Basra's extant enclosure walls and towers chronological and geographically by a comparative study is limited. In the brief survey that follows, we look primarily at published materials that describe city walls built between the pre-Idrisid and the Almoravid periods in northern Morocco.

Pre-Idrisid Walls

One of the few walls dated relatively securely to the late Roman-early Arab period (ca. A.D. 600-750) is a 660 m long wall that divides the third-century Roman city of Volubilis in half (Akerraz 1985). The wall appears to have been built by late Christian or early Arab inhabitants to enclose the western side of the former Roman city. They used the abandoned east side as a burial ground (see Kluender, this volume). According to Akerraz (1985:420-430), the enclosure wall was faced with recycled Roman building stones, without mortar, and its core was filled with stone rubble and earth. The wall's thickness ranged from 1.5 m to 1.8 m. There is no mention of any supporting towers along the wall.

Idrisid Walls (ca. 800-980)

Although the Idrisids, according to the chronicles, built at least eight cities enclosed by ramparts in northern Morocco (e.g., Ceuta, Tanger, Asila, Aqlâm, Mâsina, Tushummush [Lixus], Hajar al-Nasr, and al-Basra), little is known archaeologically about their fortification walls (Cressier 1983; Cressier et al. 1998:310-314). Most of them were destroyed or rebuilt by later dynastic rulers.

The only enclosure wall that might date to the Idrisid period exists at the recently identified site of Hajar al-Nasr, located about 40 km north/northeast of al-Basra (Cressier et al. 1998). This small, 5-ha mountaintop refuge was established by the Idrisids in the early 900s as a place for the family to retreat to in times of conflict, and it was destroyed in the late 900s. The extant wall runs along the edge of a rocky escarpment. It is built of large, rectangular blocks of cut limestone placed vertically in broad courses. The wall is about 1.5 m thick and has no supporting towers. As Cressier et al. (1998:331) point out, this wall, with its well-cut building stones and absence of towers, differs significantly in construction style from that of al-Basra's.

Spanish Ummayid-Period Walls (tenth to eleventh centuries)

During the tenth-century conflict between the Spanish Ummayids and the Fatimids of Ifriqiya, the Idrisids constantly shifted their allegiance from one side to the other. For a short time, for example, Idrisid al-Basra served as a Fatimid capital before it was destroyed by Ummayid forces. At the same time, the Mediterranean town of Ceuta was controlled by the Spanish Ummayids; in ca. A.D. 931, the Ummayid Caliph, Abd al-Rahman III, built an enclosure wall around the city (Terrasse 1962). The surviving part of this wall is constructed of large rectangular blocks of cut stone, laid horizontally, which alternate with small rounded stones; Terrasse describes this distinctive wall construction technique as an official Ummayid caliphal style, and it differs substantially from that found at al-Basra.

Almoravid Walls (1060-1160)

Following the withdrawal of the Fatimids from the Maghreb in the late 900s, northern Morocco remained under the influence of Spain for nearly half a century until the Almoravids of southern Morocco invaded the north, initiating a period of urban destruction and construction (see Ennahid, this volume). A number of existing fortification walls have been attributed to the Almoravid period, including the fortress of Zagora in southern Morocco (Meunie and Allain 1956) and the fortress of Amargou and the nearby town of Fez-al-Bali (Beni-Taouda), located about 50 km northwest of Fez in northern Morocco (Lévi-Provençal 1918).

At Zagora, the fortification wall encloses an area of about 12 ha. It is constructed of roughly cut stones placed in irregular courses that are interspersed with small flat stones to level them out (Meunie and Allain 1956:311). The stones are mortared with an earth-lime mixture. The walls range from 2.5 m to 3 m thick. The enclosure wall is supported by several square towers, or bastions, which rise up to 9 m high, and one anomalous circular tower. At least two entry gates are visible along the wall. One is located between two projecting bastions and opens directly onto the outside; the other is located inside a large projecting bastion and has a bent-axis entryway.

The fortification walls at Amargou and Fes-al-Bali, which were built by the Almoravids in the late eleventh century, are similar in style. They are about 1.4 m thick, built of roughly cut stone, and bonded with lime mortar (Lévi-Provençal 1918). Fired bricks were used for vaulting in the walls. The wall at Amargou is supported by 12 circular towers, some of which survive up to 5 m high, and at least 6 entry gates.

Dating Al-Basra's City Walls

As Cressier et al. (1998) point out, the early Islamic fortifications in Morocco are both poorly known and highly diverse. Because of this, it is difficult to find exact parallels for the city walls of al-Basra.

The only known Idrisid-period walls are the fortifications at Hajar al-Nasr, which were built in the early tenth century. Their large, vertically placed rectangular block construction and lack of supporting towers, however, differ significantly from al-Basra's.

No enclosure walls are known to date to the few decades between the fall of the Idrisid dynasty and the Almoravid invasion. It is possible that al-Basra's extant walls belong to this period, especially if its walls were rebuilt shortly after the city was destroyed in the late tenth century.

It is equally possible that al-Basra existing walls and towers date to the Almoravid period. The techniques used to construct Almoravid walls, especially their use of roughly hewn facing stone, uneven courses, lime mortar, rubble cores, and supporting towers or bastions, are similar to those found at al-Basra. The main difference appears to be in the shape of towers—the Almoravid fortifications feature circular and square-shaped towers while al-Basra's walls have semicircular towers. It is possible that, while the building technology was highly conservative during this period, architectural style may have been more responsive to change, reflecting regional or cultural variation. Until a systematic study of other early Islamic city walls in Morocco is undertaken, however, the dating of al-Basra's city walls and towers will remain elusive.

References Cited

Akerraz, A.
  1985 Note sur l'enceinte tardive de Volubilis. In *Histoire et archéologie de l'Afrique du Nord: actes du IIe colloque international réuni dans le cadre du 108e Congrès National des Société Savantes, Grenoble, 5-9 Avril 1983*, pp. 429-438. Paris.

al-Bakri, A. (died ca. 1094)
  1965 *Description de l'Afrique septentrionale*. Edited and translated by M. de Slane. 3rd edition. Adrien-Maisonneuve, Paris.

Benco, N.
  1987 *The Early Medieval Pottery Industry at al-Basra, Morocco*. BAR International Series 341. British Archaeological Reports, Oxford.

Benco, N., and A. Ettahiri
  1998 Report on the 1998 Season of Excavations at al-Basra, Morocco. Submitted to Institut National des Sciences de l'Archéologie et du Patrimoine, Rabat.
  1999 Report on the 1999 Season of Excavations at al-Basra, Morocco. Submitted to Institut National des Sciences de l'Archéologie et du Patrimoine, Rabat.

Cressier, P.
  1983 Fortifications du Rif. *Castrum I. Habitat fortifiées et organisation de l'espace en Méditerranée médiévale*, pp. 45-53. Lyon.
  1995 La fortification islamique au Maroc: éléments de bibliographie. *Archéologie islamique* 5:163-196.
  Cressier, P, A. El Boudjay, H. El Figuigui, J. Vignet-Zunz
  1998 Ha↓ar al-Nasr, 'capitale' idrisside du Maroc septentrional: archéologie et histoire (IVe H./Xe ap. J.-C.). In *Genèse de la ville islamique en al-Andalus et au Maghreb occidental*, edited by P. Cressier and M. García-Arenal, pp. 305-334. Casa de Velázquez, Madrid.

Eustache, D.
  1955 El-Basra, capitale idrissite et son port. *Hespéris* 42:218-238.

Ibn Hawqal (died ca. A.D. 988)
  1842 Description de l'Afrique. Translated from Arabic by M. de Slane. *Journal Asiatique*, 3rd series, vol. 13, pp. 153ff.

al-Idrisi (died A.D.1166)
  1969 *Description de l'Afrique et de l'Espagne*. Edited and translated by R. Dozy and M. de Goeje. Oriental Press, Amsterdam.

Leo Africanus (died ca. A.D. 1548)
  1956 *Description de l'Afrique*. Translated by A. Epaulard, T. Monod, H. Lhote, and R. Mauney. 2 vols. Adrien-Maisonneuve, Paris.

Lévi-Provençal, E.
  1918 Les ruins almoravides du pays de l'Ouargha (Maroc septentrional). *Bulletin archéologique*, pp. 194-200.
  1960 Abu Ubayd al-Bakri. *Encyclopaedia of Islam, New Edition*, vol. 1. E. J. Brill, Leiden.
  Meunie, J., and E. Allain
  1956 La forteresse almoravide de Zagora. *Hespéris* 43:305-323.

Miquel, A.
  1971 Ibn Hawqal. *Encyclopaedia of Islam, New Edition*, vol. 3. E. J. Brill, Leiden.

al-Muqaddasi (died ca. A.D. 990)

1950 *Description de l'occident musulman au IVe-Xe siècle*. Edited and translated by C. Pellat. Editions Carbonel, Algiers.

Redman, C.
1983-84 Survey and Test Excavation of Six Medieval Islamic Sites in Northern Morocco. *Bulletin d'archéologie marocaine* 15:311-360.

Terrasse, H.
1962 La forteresse almoravid d'Amergo. *Al-Andalus* 18:389-400.

Tissot, M. C.
1877 *Recherches sur la géographie comparée de la maurétanie tingitane*. Paris.

Subsistence Economy and the Environment

Chapter 3

FOOD, FUEL, AND RAW MATERIAL: FAUNAL REMAINS FROM AL-BASRA

Michelle Loyet

Like other urban centers, the medieval Islamic city of al-Basra required a complex and specialized subsistence economy to feed its inhabitants (Zeder 1988:3). To maintain such an economy, the city supported a variety of specialists who were involved in producing and distributing animal products throughout the city. Among these specialists were herders, who raised domestic animals in the city's hinterland; slaughterhouse personnel, who dismembered the animals; and butchers who sold the meat products to customers in urban markets. It also included a variety of craftspeople who utilized other parts of the animals, such as leather and bones, as raw materials in their manufacturing activities. Despite their diverse interests, these specialists were intimately interconnected with one another within the urban economy.

This chapter investigates the specialized animal economy at medieval al-Basra by (1) describing the types and proportions of animal species exploited by urban residents, (2) reconstructing the herding practices of local pastoralists on the basis of animal mortality profiles, and (3) examining the spatial distribution of animal parts in the city's residential and industrial sectors to interpret the differential usage of animals in the urban center. By tracing the pathways through which animal products passed, this chapter underscores the close linkages that existed in a highly specialized urban economy.

Al-Basra's Faunal Assemblage

Most faunal material used in this analysis was excavated at al-Basra during the 1998 and 1999 field seasons. In addition, remains from the 1990 season, which were studied by Sweeney (1990), were used in the overall counts of various taxa but not in the comparison of body part distribution because of differences in recording technique. The animal remains were primarily recovered from three urban contexts: a residential area (G-residential), a small industrial enclave in the residential area (G-enclave), and the main industrial area, specifically where metal production took place ((F-metal industry).

Recovery Methods

Although two different recovery techniques were used at al-Basra, they do not appear to have affected the numbers or variety of animal species retrieved. Excavation units in the industrial zone (F) were usually sifted with 6-mm screens while in the residential zone (G) archaeological materials were removed by hand. Because of screening, one would expect to find a larger proportion of small, unidentifiable faunal remains in the industrial than in the residential zone but, in fact, the opposite is true. Only 27.5 percent of the fauna from the industrial metal-working area (F-metal) is unidentifiable, while nearly 60 percent of the faunal material retrieved from the residential zone (G) is unidentifiable (Table 3.1). Moreover, one would also expect a screened assemblage to produce a greater proportion of small animals, as these would be more likely to be collected in screening. To the contrary, the industrial units that were screened yielded a lower proportion of small animal remains than did the residential units (Table 3.2). It is possible that the residential area, where domestic activities occurred, would naturally have had a greater variety of species, such as tortoises and birds. Based on these two lines of evidence, however, it appears that the recovery methods that were used at al-Basra had no significant impact on the results of the faunal study.

Table 3.1. Counts and Percentages of Identifiable and Unidentifiable Fauna, by Functionally Distinct Spatial Areas

Type of fauna	G-Residential		G-Enclave		F-Metalworking	
	No.	%	No.	%	No.	%
Identifiable	5,930	40.3	1,974	45.6	6,816	72.5
Unidentifiable	8,795	59.7	2,354	54.4	2,586	27.5
Total	14,725	100.0	4,328	100.0	9,402	100.0

Table 3.2. Counts and Percentages of Identifiable Faunal Taxa, by Functionally Distinct Spatial Areas

Taxon	G-Residential				G-Enclave				F-Metalworking				Total Assemblage			
	NISP	%	MNI	%	NISP	%	MNI	%	NISP	%	MNI	%	NISP	%	MNI	%
Domestic sp.																
Bos	1156	19.5	16	8.9	344	17.4	17	19.4	2911	42.7	73	28.9	4411	30.0	106	0.0
Ovcap	3696	62.3	81	6.0	894	45.3	21	24.0	3310	48.5	130	51.5	7900	54.0	232	5.0
Ovis	145	2.4	18	0.2	404	20.5	12	13.7	267	3.9	13	5.2	816	5.5	43	8.3
Capra	72	1.2	7	3.9	158	8.0	10	11.4	147	2.2	16	6.4	377	2.5	33	6.4
Eq sp.	12	0.2	1	0.7	1	0.1	1	1.2	7	0.1	1	0.4	20	0.1	3	0.6
Eq asinus	44	0.7	2	1.1	14	0.7	1	1.2	31	0.5	3	1.2	89	0.6	6	1.2
Eq caballus	65	1.1	3	1.7	3	0.2	1	1.2	7	0.1	2	0.8	75	0.5	6	1.2
Camel	1	0.0	1	0.7	3	0.2	1	1.2	1	0.0	1	0.4	5	0.1	3	0.6
Canis	33	0.6	4	2.3	15	0.8	2	2.2	11	0.2	2	0.8	59	0.4	8	1.6
Felis	128	2.2	3	1.7	10	0.5	1	1.2	16	0.2	1	0.4	154	1.0	5	1.0
Sus	18	0.3	1	0.7	3	0.2	1	1.2					21	0.1	2	0.5
Aves	297	5.1	26	4.8	77	3.9	12	13.7	44	0.6	3	1.2	418	2.8	41	8.0
Wild sp.																
Fish	24	0.4	2	1.1	6	0.3	1	1.2	4	0.1	1	0.4	34	0.2	4	0.9
Gazelle	4	0.1	2	1.1	3	0.2	1	1.2	17	0.2	2	0.8	24	0.1	5	1.0
Deer					2	0.1	1	1.2	1	0.0	1	0.4	3	0.1	2	0.5
Rodent	3	0.1	1	0.7	2	0.1	1	1.2					5	0.1	2	0.5
Turtle/Tortoise	35	0.6	4	2.3	2	0.1	1	1.2	2	0.0	1	0.4	39	0.2	6	1.2
Gastropod	27	0.5			2	0.1	1	1.2	27	0.4			57	0.3		
Pelycypod	115	1.9			3	0.2			7	0.1			146	1.0		
Cephalopod	43	0.7			24	1.2			2	0.0			46	0.3		
Wild sheep					1	0.1			2	0.0	1	0.4	2	0.1	1	0.2
Wild bovid	7	0.1	1	0.7					2	0.0	1	0.4	9	0.1	2	0.5
Carnivore	1	0.0	1	0.7									1	0.0	1	0.2
Lepus	4	0.1	1	0.7									4	0.1	1	0.2
Wild felis/lynx					4	0.2	1	1.2					4	0.1	1	0.2
Vulpes					1	0.1	1	1.2					1	0.0	1	0.2
Total	**5930**				**1974**				**6816**				**14,720**			

Domestic Species

The al-Basra faunal assemblage consists of 28,455 bone fragments, of which 14,720, or 51.7 percent, can be identified (Table 3.2). The assemblage is dominated by domestic species, which constitute 97.6 percent of all identifiable remains. Of these domestics, 30 percent are cattle (*Bos taurus*), 5.5 percent are sheep (*Ovis aries*), 2.5 percent are goat (*Capra hircus*), and 54 percent are identifiable only as sheep/goat (*Ovricaprines*).[1]

Although these figures suggest that sheep/goat were a more important food resource than cattle, this is probably not the case. A cow yields an average of 226 kg of meat, which is approximately eight times as much as a sheep or a goat, which yield about 27 kg of meat (Clark 1993:162). Based on these calculations, cattle would have actually provided four times as much meat than sheep/goat at the urban center. Cattle would have also provided a greater amount of the milk, although sheep and goat will produce milk in more marginal environments or during times of environmental stress. In terms of the proportion of sheep to goat, if only the numbers of bones identified to species level are used, sheep appear to be about twice as common as goat (5.5 percent vs. 2.5 percent). A similar pattern of high beef and mutton consumption was found in the faunal assemblage from the Islamic levels at the site of Qsar es-Seghir in northern Morocco (Wattenmaker 1978:26). The excavator (Redman 1986:229) interpreted this pattern at Qsar es-Seghir as indicative of a relatively affluent, urban-based production system. The same may be the case at al-Basra.

The environment at al-Basra would have favored raising cattle and sheep. These animals require relatively well watered areas, while goat can survive in more arid and marginal environments. The climate along the Atlantic coastal plain where al-Basra is situated is characterized by rainy winters and dry warm summers. Annual rainfall averages in this area today are about 500 to 700 mm (Mikesell 1961:16, 41). Environmental differences may explain the contrast between faunal assemblages from al-Basra and those from other Islamic sites in North Africa. At the sites of Cherchel and Setif in Algeria and Leptis Magna in Libya, which are located in more arid environments than al-Basra, sheep and goat represent as much as 80 percent of the assemblage (Clark 1993:168;

---

[1] Although sheep and goat bones can usually be distinguished on the basis of metric data or bone morphology, this study has combined the two into a single taxa: *Ovicaprines*. Methods for identifying sheep from goat (Boessneck 1970; Boessneck et al. 1964; Prummel and Frisch 1986) were developed using modern complete skeletons. Because archaeological remains are usually fragmentary, these methods would allow only a small sample to be identified. Most faunal analysts working with medieval or Islamic animal remains combine the two species (Clark 1993:159-160; King 1991:250; Loyet 1999:37; Siracusano 1994:117; Stein 1998:182-183).

King 1991:251-253; van der Veen 1996:252). This may indicate a more conservative production strategy by placing greater importance on the products of drought-resistant species than did the pastoralists at al-Basra. The site of Qsar es-Seghir, on the other hand, which is situated along the well-watered Mediterranean coast, had a cattle to sheep/goat ratio that is similar to that at al-Basra (Redman 1986:229-230).

Another 2.8 percent of domestic species from al-Basra consist of horse (*Equus caballus*), donkey (*Equus asinus*), camel (*Camelus dromedarius*), dog (*Canis familiaris*), cat (*Felis*), and pig (*Sus scrofa*). In each case, these species represent 1 percent or less of the overall faunal assemblage. Birds (*Aves*), which represent 2.8 percent of the assemblage, are also likely domesticated species (possibly chickens), or at least tamed and kept for human consumption.

Although the presence of pigs is surprising in Islamic assemblages because of the Moslem prohibition against eating them, they are not entirely unknown at Islamic sites. For example, pigs have been identified in Islamic contexts at the site of Cherchel in Algeria (Clark 1993:167). It should be noted, however, that the fauna from very few Islamic sites has thus far been published. Whether or not the al-Basra pigs are wild or domesticated species is not possible to determine because of the small number and the types of body parts recovered.

Wild Animal Species

Finally, a very small proportion (2.4 percent) of the al-Basra fauna consists of wild species. These include terrestrial animals, such as wild sheep, gazelle, deer, fox, and hare, and riverine species, such as fish, turtle/tortoise, and freshwater bivalves. Although marine shells also occur (.3 percent), it is unlikely that they were used as a food source. Many of them are cut, drilled, or polished and appear to have been used as decorative objects, such as beads and pendants.

Herding and Culling Practices

During the Islamic period, specialized herders would have maintained large herds of cattle, sheep, and goat and used them for meat and dairy products or, in the case of sheep and goat, for their wool. In addition, they may have used cattle as traction animals to pull plows in the fields.

An understanding of how these domestic animals were utilized can be inferred from mortality patterns and survivorship curves drawn from the al-Basra faunal assemblage. A mortality profile (Figure 3.1) for sheep/goat was constructed using tooth eruption and wear data.[2]

If meat production is the aim for raising a herd of sheep/goat, young male animals are slaughtered when they reach an optimum point in their weight gain, that is, before their weight gain slows in the second year of life and the cost of maintaining their weight increases (Payne 1973:291). Juvenile males that have reached this point are culled from the herd and sent to market, while the females and a few select males are retained as breeding stock (Stein 1998:197-208). If milk production is the goal, once milk production is no longer in danger, surplus lambs are culled. If wool production is the aim, more adult animals are kept and mortality profiles will show a large number of mature animals, both castrate males and females (Payne 1973:291). It is important to note, however, that animals are often kept for more than one product (Payne 1973:291).

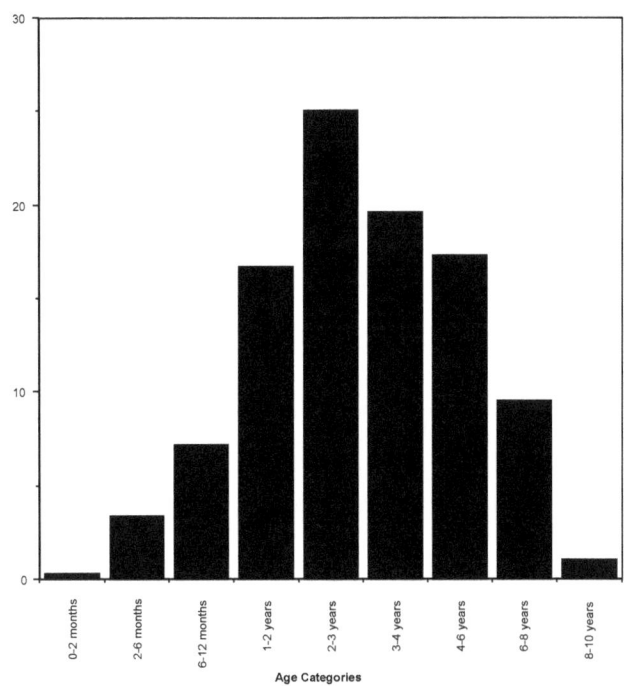

Figure 3.1 Sheep/goat (*Ovicaprine*) mortality profile. N = 736.

As the mortality profile in Figure 3.1 shows, some sheep and goat at al-Basra were slaughtered when they reached one to two years of age, most likely males culled from the herd when their weight gain reached an optimum level. Most of the animals, however, were killed between two and three years of age or older, which is beyond the optimum weight gain and indicates that they were likely kept for their milk and wool byproducts, as well as for their meat (Cribb 1987; Crabtree 1990).

The survivorship information for cattle (Figure 3.2) was drawn from bone fusion rather than tooth eruption data because of the small number of preserved *Bos* mandibles in the al-Basra assemblage. Unlike the mortality curve

---

[2] Ages at death based on tooth eruption and wear were determined by using methods outlined in Deniz and Payne (1982), Grant (1982), and Levitan (1982); also see appendices in Hillson (1986). Ages based on epiphyseal fusion were determined using data from Noddle (1974) and Silver (1969). Mortality curves were constructed using methods described in Zeder (1991:90-91) and Redding (1981:248).

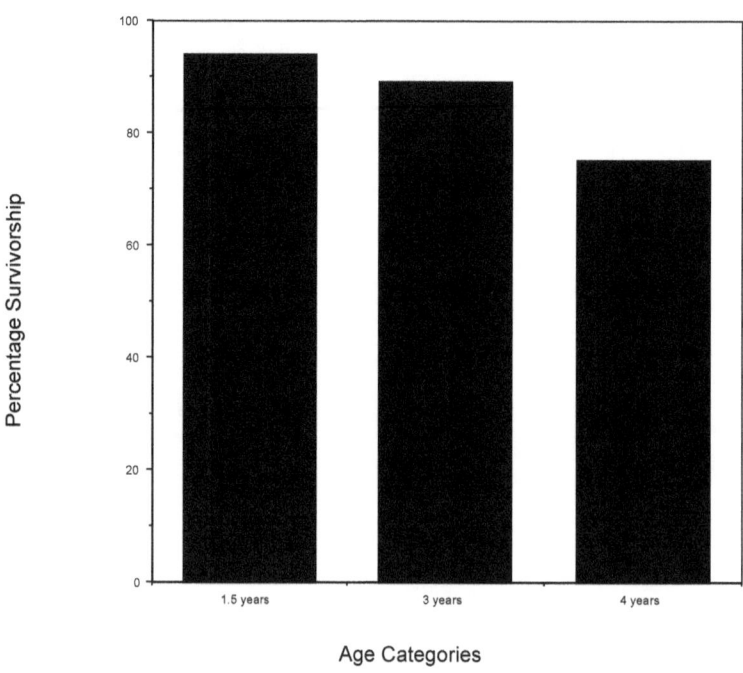

Figure 3.2 Cattle (*Bos*) survivorship curve. N=258

generated for sheep and goat, a survivorship curve, which is based on epiphyseal fusion, provides a different kind of information. A survivorship pattern indicates the age beyond which the animals continue to survive, rather than the age at which they are killed. It is possible to determine only a minimum age from epiphyseal fusion data and not a maximum age, as is the case with tooth wear. The survivorship curve (Figure 3.2) shows that some 75 percent of al-Basra cattle survived beyond four years of age. This suggests that cattle were raised primarily for milk, rather than meat, products. It also indicates that they may have been used as traction animals, a possibility that is further supported by the high incidence of arthritic *Bos* phalanges in the al-Basra assemblage. Cattle that are used for traction develop arthritic growths on their distal limbs (Bartosiewicz et al. 1997). At al-Basra, arthritic growths frequently occur on the first and second phalanges, as well as on the distal metapodials, of cattle.

The mortality data for sheep/goat and cattle point toward an animal economy that maximizes the production potential of the al-Basra herds. While meat is necessary to feed the urban residents of al-Basra, the culling strategies indicate that the production of meat is secondary to the production of milk and other animal products. While older animals do not provide prime meat products, they are far from unpalatable. By slaughtering the animals for food later in their life-cycles, it is possible to extract the maximum number of secondary products from them. This maximization strategy indicates that the animal economy in the urban center relied on all productive aspects of the animal.

Residential Versus Industrial Use of Animal Remains

Species Frequencies

The spatial distribution of animal remains in each of the three excavated areas of the urban center are distinctly different. Based on bone frequencies (NISP), cattle are more common in the metal-working industrial zone (F-metal), while sheep and goat are more common in the residential sector (G), as Table 3.2 illustrates. In the metal-working industrial sector, cattle account for 42.7 percent of the assemblage, while sheep and goat represent 54.6 percent. In the residential sector (G), cattle represent only 19.5 percent of the assemblage, while sheep and goat predominate with 65.9 percent. A similar pattern occurs in a small industrial enclave in the residential zone (G-enclave) where cattle constitute only 17.4 percent while sheep/goat account for 73.8 percent. Wild species and aquatic resources also occur more frequently in the residential area. These contrasts undoubtedly are derived from the different types of activities that took place in each area. Residential area (G) fauna consist mainly of discarded household food remains, while those from the industrial zone (F-metal) represent primarily debris and byproducts from metal-working activities (Benco, Ettahiri, and Loyet 2002).

Body Part Frequencies

The contrasts between the industrial and residential sectors are further underscored by differences in body

Table 3.3. Distribution of Cattle (*Bos*) and Sheep/Goat (*Ovcap*) Body Parts, by Functionally Distinct Spatial Areas. (Shaded areas indicate butchery waste elements.)

Body Part	Bison MGUI	Sheep MGUI	G-Residential Bos %MAU	G-Residential Bos MNI	G-Residential Bos %	G-Residential Ovcap %MAU	G-Residential Ovcap MNI	G-Residential Ovcap %	G-Enclave Bos %MAU	G-Enclave Bos MNI	G-Enclave Bos %	G-Enclave Ovcap %MAU	G-Enclave Ovcap MNI	G-Enclave Ovcap %	F-Metalworking Bos %MAU	F-Metalworking Bos MNI	F-Metalworking Bos %	F-Metalworking Ovcap %MAU	F-Metalworking Ovcap MNI	F-Metalworking Ovcap %
Astragalus	13.6	23.08	72	11.5	5.9	25	26.5	2.9	9	1.5	2.7	3	1.5	1.6	36	26	5	9	14.5	2.2
Vertebrae	60	46.49	20	3	1.5	14	15	1.6	2	0.5	0.8	1	0.5	0.6	7	5	1	3	5	0.7
Calcaneum	13.6	23.08	100	16	7.9	42	44.5	4.8	9	1.5	2.7	4	2	2.2	48	35	6.7	13	20.5	3.1
Carpal	6.6	13.43	8	1	0.5				2	0.5	0.8				6	4.25	0.8			
Cranium	14.2	12.87	10	16	1.9	36	38	4.1	5	1	1.8	4	2	2.2	30	22	4.2	16	25.5	3.8
Proximal Femur	69.4	80.58	12	2	1	25	26.5	2.9	2	0.5	0.8	2	1	1				4	6.5	0.9
Distal Femur	69.4	80.58	32	5	2.5	27	29	3.1	5	1	2.7	3	1.5	1.6	4	3	0.6	7	11	1.6
Horncore	1.03	1.03	92	15	7.5	24	26	2.8	100	17	30.9	100	43	46.5	100	73	14	100	159	23.2
Proximal Humerus	31.6	37.28	12	2	1	8	8.5	0.9				2	1	1	4	3	0.6	2	3	0.4
Distal Humerus	25.1	32.79	60	9.5	4.7	99	105	11.3	2	0.5	0.8	12	5	5.4	28	20.5	4	17	27	3.9
Proximal Metacarpal	3.9	10.11	48	8	4	24	25.5	2.7	2	0.5	0.8	1	0.5	0.6	6	4.5	0.8	26	41.5	6.1
Distal Metacarpal	2.6	8.45	76	12	5.9	48	51	5.5	47	8	14.5	7	3	3.2	16	11.5	2.3	43	68.5	10
Proximal Metatarsal	7.5	15.77	64	10	4.9	28	29.5	3.2	2	0.5	0.8	1	0.5	0.6	41	30	5.8	56	89	12.9
Distal Metatarsal	4.5	12.11	76	12	5.9	38	40	4.3	51	8.5	15.4	9	4	4.3	14	10.5	2.1	33	52.5	7.7
Tarsal	13.6	23.08	12	2	1	2	2	0.2	2	0.5	0.8				21	15.5	3			
Pelvis	54.7	81.5	56	9	4.4	80	85	9.1	7	1.25	2.4	15	6.5	7	17	12.5	2.5	8	13	1.9
First Phalanx	2.4	8.22	56	9	4.4	25	26.5	2.9	7	1.25	2.4	7	3	1	44	32	6.2	13	20.5	3.1
Second Phalanx	2.4	8.22	28	4.5	2.2	3	3	0.3	5	1	1.8	1	0.5	0.6	29	21	4	1	0.5	0.1
Third Phalanx	2.4	8.22	28	4.5	2.2	1	1	0.1	2	0.5	0.8	1	0.5	0.6	26	19	3.7	1	0.5	0.1
Proximal Radius	16.5	24.3	56	9	4.4	39	41	4.4				1	0.5	0.6	41	30	5.8	13	20.5	3.1
Distal Radius	12.1	20.06	24	4	2	56	59	6.4	12	2	3.6	15	6.5	7	41	30	5.8	6	10	1.5
Scapula	31.6	45.06	60	9.5	4.7	64	22	1	5	1	1.8	7	3	3.2	16	11.5	2.3	10	16	2.3
Proximal Tibia	40.8	51.99	24	4	2	21	22	2.4	5	1	1.8	5	2.5	2.7	1	1	0.2	7	11	1.6
Distal Tibia	25.5	37.7	72	11.5	5.9	70	74	8	19	3.5	6.4	10	4.5	4.9	25	18.5	3.7	15	24	3.5
Ulna	20.8		20	3	1.5	42	44.5	4.8	7	1.5	2.7	3	1.5	1.6	6	4.5	0.9	7	11	1.6
Mandible	14.2	11.65	52	8.5	4.2	100	106	11.3							100	73	14	20	32	4.7
% Butchery Waste					37.5			21.8			68.2			57.4			39.7			63.2

part representation, particularly for the two most common taxa, *Bos* and sheep/goat. In general, bone elements that have a considerable amount of meat (i.e., high-meat value) are preferred by consumers. They would be obtained from urban markets, consumed in households, and discarded nearby as food waste. Bone elements with little or no meat on them (low-meat value), on the other hand, would constitute butchery waste. If they were passed along with the meat-bearing parts of the animal, these elements would eventually find their way into domestic or household debris. If, however, some were recycled as raw material for bone manufacture or as a fuel resource, they would ultimately be discarded in an industrial context.

These hypotheses were tested by calculating two indices for cattle and sheep/goat in each of the three areas examined at al-Basra. The first is the modified general utility index (MGUI), a numeric value that represents the amount of meat, fat, and marrow available for each body part. When normalized to a value of 100, it becomes %MGUI[1] (Lyman 1994a:223-234). In essence, this value represents the meat value of the animal bone element. The second is the percentage of minimum animal units (%MAU), which is obtained by normalizing the minimum number of elements (MNE) to 100. This does not affect the relative abundances of the elements but it simplifies graphing (Lyman 1992:253-254, 1994b:40-44).

Table 3.3 illustrates the results of this analysis. The animal debris recovered from the residential zone (G) consists predominantly of high-meat-value bone elements, or food waste (62.5 percent for cattle and 78.2 percent for sheep/goat) and has relatively low proportions of low-meat-value bone elements, or butchery waste (37.5 percent for cattle and 21.8 for sheep/goat). By contrast, the animal remains excavated from a small industrial enclave in the residential zone consists primarily of butchery waste (68.2 percent cattle and 57.4 percent sheep/goat) with smaller proportions of food waste (31.8 percent for cattle and 42.6 percent for sheep and goat).

The faunal debris retrieved from the metal-working sector of the industrial area (F-metal), however, only partially fits the expected pattern. Some 63.2 percent of the sheep/goat remains constitute butchery waste, but only 39.7 percent of the cattle bones belong to this category. It should be noted that the faunal data did not include 169 *Bos* metapodials, which had been modified into bone tools and thus had been recorded as special objects during lab processing. If these worked metapodials are added to the faunal assemblage, the picture changes somewhat. The percentage of butchery waste increases from 39.7 percent to 45.6 percent of the assemblage. While this is closer to the expected values, it is still lower than the percentage of cattle butchery waste found in the small industrial enclave in the residential zone. This unexpected result may be due to a number of reasons, but one of the most compelling is the differential selection of *Bos* metapodials, which are very dense and thus burn well, for fuel in metal-working activities; this selective use of bone as fuel would reduce the number and, thus, the proportion of waste bones left in stockpiles.

Another method to interpret body part distributions consists of utility curves, which are created by plotting the %MAU values against the %MGUI[2] patterns. If an assemblage is dominated by low-value body parts, an L-shaped utility curve will result. The curve will have a high number of low-value bones and a low number of high-value bones. If an assemblage consists primarily of high-value meat-bearing elements, a gourmet or bulk strategy utility curve is created (Lyman 1994a:228-229).

The utility curves (Figures 3.3-3.4) generated by plotting remains from the residential area (G) indicate a predominance of high-value bones for both cattle and sheep/goat, with some low-value elements also present but to a smaller extent. The presence of low-value bones in a domestic context is not surprising, considering the potential variability in waste disposal practices at an urban site.

By contrast, the small industrial enclave in the residential sector shows L-shaped utility curves (Figures 3.5-3.6) for both cattle and sheep/goat remains. This graph indicates the presence of high quantities of butchery waste bones and low amounts of meat-bearing bone elements.

Similar L-shaped utility curves (Figures 3.7-3.8) occur for both cattle and sheep/goat remains in the metal production sector (F-metal). These curves indicate that the faunal assemblage from this industrial sector is clearly butchery waste. The results provide support for the trends found in the MGUI analysis, even without the addition of worked *Bos* metapodials.

Discussion and Conclusions

This study of the al-Basra faunal assemblage clearly indicates that animal remains can provide a wide range of information on the provisioning of an urban center, particularly the pathways through which animal products moved from the rural hinterland into the city.

Although sheep and goat played an important role, the primary animal resource at the center was cattle. The archaeological evidence of herding, especially of cattle, coincides with the historically documented observation by the Andalusian geographer al-Bakri (1965:216) in the

---

[1] This value does not take into account body size or ontogenetic age differences in the initial counting of the element, but the resulting values—MAU—do indicate which carcass portions are more or less abundant than others.

[2] Because a %MGUI value for cattle are unavailable, bison %MGUI values were used. This should not affect the overall pattern since the two species are morphologically similar.

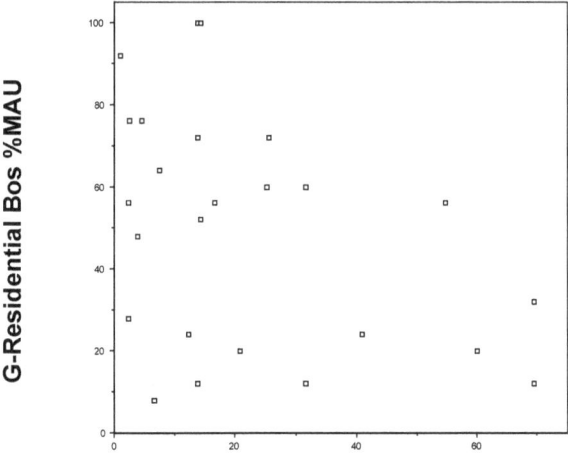

Bison MGUI

Figure 3.3 Cattle (*Bos*) body part distribution in the residential area (G).

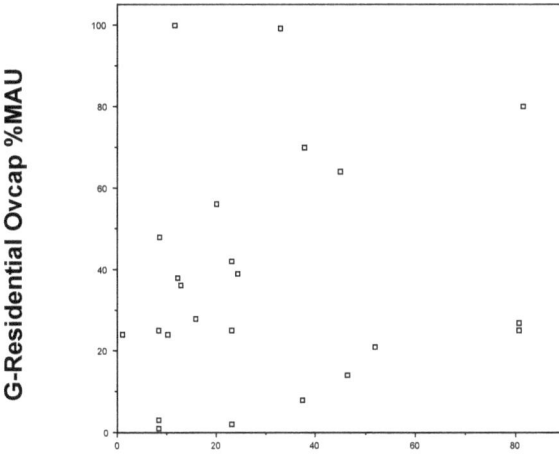

Sheep MGUI

Figure 3.4 Sheep/goat (*Ovicaprine*) body part distribution in the residential area (G).

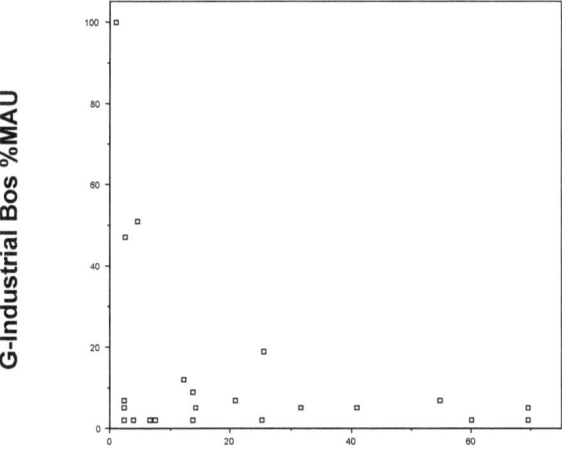

Bison MGUI

Figure 3.5 Cattle (*Bos*) body part distribution in the industrial enclave of the residential area (G-enclave).

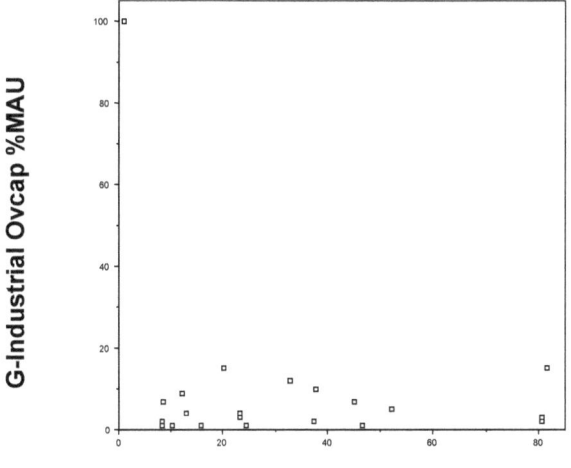

Sheep MGUI

Figure 3.6 Sheep/goat (*Ovicaprine*) body part distribution in the industrial enclave of the residential area (G-enclave).

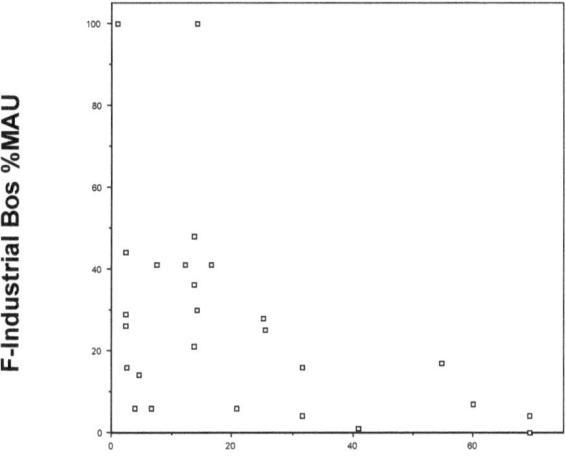

Bison MGUI

Figure 3.7 Cattle (*Bos*) body part distribution in the metal-working sector of the industrial area (F-metal).

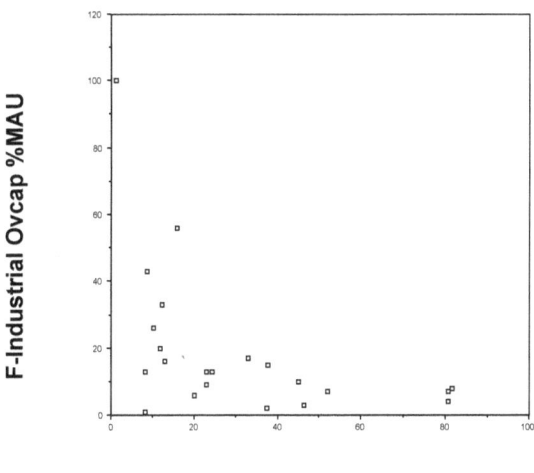

Sheep MGUI

Figure 3.8 Sheep/goat (*Ovicaprine*) body part distribution in metal-working sector of the industrial area (F-metal).

eleventh-century that "the city of al-Basra occupies a large site and surpasses all the neighboring localities in the extent of its pastures and the number of its flocks. There exists such an abundance of milk that the city has been called 'al-Basra-t-ed-Dobban' (al-Basra of the Flies)."

While environmental conditions at al-Basra would have favored a greater reliance on cattle, the raising of sheep and goat, which can survive in more marginal environments, may have been a way of protecting food resources in times of environmental stress. Similar maximization strategies are evident in the population structure of the al-Basra herds. Mortality profiles and survivorship curves show the presence of an older herd composition than would be necessary if the herds were used only to supply meat products to the urban population. By maintaining older animals in the herds, it would be possible to maximize milk and other dairy products and, in the case of sheep, wool production, while still producing meat for the urban butchers.

From the herders, animals intended for use as food would be passed into the hands of other specialists. In my own ethnographic research in the towns of Hasake, Syria (Loyet 1999, 2000), and Fez, Morocco, I found that animals are killed, skinned, gutted, and partially dismembered (the head and feet are removed) at a remote location. From that point, butchers would take the consumable meat portions to their market stalls, complete the butchery, and sell the portions to urban residents. Tanning specialists would take the animal hides to their tanneries, convert them into finished leather, and sell the leather to shoemakers, bookbinders, and others.

As the al-Basra study suggests, animal butchery waste (low-value animal parts, such as metapodials and horns) followed yet another pathway. This waste material appears to have been transported from the slaughterhouses, and perhaps from butchers' stalls, to artisans' workshops in the industrial quarter. At al-Basra, butchery waste was used as raw material for fuel and tools in metal-production activities (Benco, Ettahiri, and Loyet 2002), but in other urban centers animal waste bones may have been utilized by bone-working and horn-working specialists to make consumer products. By tracing the movement of animals and animal products from countryside to urban center, it is possible to begin understanding the complex, interconnected roles of specialists in the urban animal economy.

References Cited

al-Bakri, A. (died ca. A.D. 1094)
 1965 *Description de l'Afrique septentrionale*. Edited and translated by M. de Slane. 3rd edition. Adrien-Maisonneuve, Paris.

Bartosiewicz, L., W. Van Neer, and A. Lentucher
 1997 *Draught Cattle: Their Osteological Identification and History*. Musée Royal de l'Afrique Central, Tervuren.

Benco, N. L., A. Ettahiri, and M. Loyet
 2002 Worked Bone Tools: Linking Metal Artisans and Animal Processors in Medieval Islamic Morocco. *Antiquity* 76(292):447-457.

Boessneck, J.
 1970 Osteological Differences between Sheep (*Ovis aries* Linné) and Goat (*Capra hircus* Linné). In *Science in Archaeology*, edited by D. R. Brothwell and E. S. Higgs, pp 331-358. Praeger, New York.

Boessneck, J., H.-H. Muller, and M. Teichert
 1964 Osteologische Unterscheidungsmerkmale zwischen Schaf (*Ovis aries* Linné) und Ziege (*Capra hircus* Linné). *Kühn-Archiv* 78:5-129.

Clark, G.
 1993 The Faunal Remains. In *Fouilles du forum de Cherchel: 1977-1981*, edited by N. Benseddik and T. W. Potter, pp. 159-195. Agence Nationale d'Archéologie et de Protection des Sites et Monuments Historiques, Algiers.

Crabtree, P. J.
 1990 Zooarchaeology and Complex Societies: Some Uses of Faunal Analysis for the Study of Trade, Social Status, and Ethnicity. In *Archaeological Method and Theory*, vol. 2, edited by M. B. Schiffer, pp. 155-205. University of Arizona, Tucson.

Cribb, R. L. D.
 1987 The Logic of the Herd: A Computer Simulation of Archaeological Herd Structure. *Journal of Anthropological Archaeology* 6:376-415.

Deniz, E., and S. Payne
 1982 Eruption and Wear in the Mandibular Dentition as a Guide to Ageing Turkish Angora Goats. In *Ageing and Sexing Animal Bone Remains for Archaeological Sites*, edited by B. Wilson, C. Grigson, and S. Payne, pp. 155-205. BAR British Series 109. British Archaeological Reports, Oxford.

Grant, A.
 1982 The Use of Tooth Wear as a Guide to the Age of Domestic Ungulates. In *Ageing and Sexing Animal Bone Remains for Archaeological Sites*, edited by B. Wilson, C. Grigson, and S. Payne, pp. 91-108. BAR British Series 109. British Archaeological Reports, Oxford.

Hillson, S.
 1986 *Teeth*. Cambridge University Press, New York.

King, A.
1991 The Animal Bones. In *Fouilles de Sétif (1977-1984)*, edited by A. Mohamedi, A. Benmansour, A.A. Amamra, and E. Fentress, pp. 247-258. Agence Nationale d'Archéologie et de Protection des Sites et Monuments Historiques, Algiers.

Levitan, B.
1982 Errors in Recording Tooth Wear in Ovicaprid Mandibles at Different Speeds. In *Ageing and Sexing Animal Bone Remains for Archaeological Sites*, edited by B. Wilson, C. Grigson, and S. Payne, pp. 207-214. BAR British Series 109. British Archaeological Reports, Oxford.

Loyet, M. A.
1999 Small Ungulate Butchery in the Islamic Period at Tell Tuneinir, Syria. *Journal of Near Eastern Studies* 58:33-45.
2000 The Potential for Within-Site Variation of Faunal Remains: A Case Study from the Islamic Period Urban Center of Tell Tuneinir, Syria. *Bulletin of the American Schools of Oriental Research* 320:23-48.

Lyman, R. L.
1992 Prehistoric Seal and Sea-Lion Butchering on the Southern Northwest Coast. *American Antiquity* 57:246-261.
1994a *Vertebrate Taphonomy*. Cambridge University Press, New York.
1994b Quantitative Units and Terminology in Zooarchaeology. *American Antiquity* 59:36-71.

Mikesell, M. W.
1961 *Northern Morocco: A Cultural Geography*. University of California Press, Berkeley.

Noddle, B.
1974 Ages of Epiphyseal Closure in Feral and Domestic Goats and Ages of Dental Eruption. *Journal of Archaeological Science* 1:195-204.

Payne, S.
1973 Kill-off Patterns in Sheep and Goats: The Mandibles of Asvan Kale. *Anatolian Studies* 23:283-303.

Prummel, W., and H.-J. Frisch
1986 A Guide for the Distinction of Species, Sex, and Body Side in the Bones of Sheep and Goat. *Journal of Archaeological Science* 13:567-577.

Redding, R. W.
1981 The Faunal Remains. In *An Early Town on the Deh Luran Plain: Excavations at Tepe Farukhabad*, edited by H. T. Wright, pp. 233-261. Museum of Anthropology Memoirs 13, University of Michigan, Ann Arbor.

Redman, C. L.
1986 *Qsar es-Seghir: An Archaeological View of Medieval Life*. Academic Press, Orlando.

Silver, I. A.
1969 The Ageing of Domestic Animals. In *Science in Archaeology*, edited by D. R. Brothwell and E. S. Higgs, pp. 283-302. Praeger, New York.

Siracusano, G.
1994 The Fauna of Leptis Magna from the IVth to the Xth Century A.D. *ArchaeoZoologia* 6:111-129.

Stein, G. J.
1998 Medieval Pastoral Production Systems at Gritille. In *The Archaeology of the Frontier in the Medieval Near East: Excavations at Gritille, Turkey*, edited by S. Redford, pp. 181-209. University Museum, University of Philadelphia, Philadelphia.

Sweeney, F. M. G.
1990 Final Descriptive Report on Vertebrate Faunal Remains from al-Basra, 1990 Field Season. Ms. on file, Department of Anthropology, George Washington University, Washington, D.C.

van der Veen, M., A. Grant, and A. Barker
1996 Romano-Libyan Agriculture: Crops and Animals. In *Farming the Desert: The UNESCO Libyan Valleys Archaeological Survey, vol. 1: Synthesis*, edited by G. Barker, D. Gilbertson, B. Jones, D. Mattingly, pp. 227-264. UNESCO, Society for Libyan Studies, Department of Antiquities, Tripoli.

Wattenmaker, P.
1978 An Analysis of the Faunal Remains of the Islamic Occupation of Qsar es-Seghir: Socioeconomic Implications. Ms. on file, Department of Anthropology, University of Michigan, Ann Arbor.

Zeder, M. A.
1988 Understanding Urban Process through the Study of Specialized Economy in the Near East. *Journal of Anthropological Archaeology* 7:1-55.
1991 *Feeding Cities: Specialized Animal Economy in the Ancient Near East*. Smithsonian Institution Press, Washington, D.C.

Anatomy of a Medieval Town

Chapter 4

AGRICULTURE, INDUSTRY, AND THE ENVIRONMENT: ETHNOBOTANICAL EVIDENCE FROM AL-BASRA

Nancy Mahoney

(The following article is abstracted from Nancy Mahoney's 1994 unpublished M.A. thesis, "Economy and Environment at al-Basra: An Archaeobotanical Analysis of a Medieval Islamic Urban Center," Department of Anthropology, George Washington University.)

This chapter utilizes historical and archaeological evidence to shed light on the agricultural economy and on the nature of the environment—and its possible change through time—at the early medieval Islamic town of al-Basra in northern Morocco. It incorporates the observations of various medieval travelers in the region, the record of modern-day flora in the area surrounding the site of al-Basra, and the ethnobotanical evidence, including charred seeds and wood charcoal, to provide a fuller understanding of the medieval landscape and of the agricultural and industrial activities of medieval Moroccan urban dwellers.

Historical Accounts

Several historical accounts briefly describe the types of agricultural products that were found at al-Basra. The tenth-century geographer, Ibn Hawqal (1842:191-192) remarked that during his time the city produced a large quantity of "cotton," as well as wheat, barley, and other cereals. He noted that the city's merchants shipped their products to the Atlantic coast by way of a tributary of the Sagdad River (possibly the Mda River).

In the eleventh century, the Andalusian geographer al-Bakri (1965:216-217) wrote that al-Basra flourished and exceeded all of its neighboring towns in terms of its pastures and its herds. Al-Bakri also mentions that when the city was first inhabited, it was called "al-Basra of the Flax" because flax was used as the main form of currency for commercial transactions. Al-Bakri also notes that agricultural products from al-Basra were transported by river to ports along the Atlantic, from where they were shipped by sea to destinations in North Africa and Spain. Al-Basra's merchants also shipped goods overland to markets in southern Morocco (al-Bakri 1965:294).

While the historical texts provide important information on agricultural production at al-Basra, they do not document the full range of economic activities in which the residents of the city were engaged.

Modern Environment

Northern Morocco has a typical Mediterranean climate, consisting of wet winters and springs, relatively dry summers, mild winters, and a high percentage of sunshine through the year (Mikesell 1961:17). Annual rainfall ranges from 400 mm to more than 1000 mm, depending on the elevation and exposure to prevailing winds. Al-Basra, which lies at approximately 200 m above sea level, receives 500 to 700 mm of annual rainfall; this falls within the range necessary for rainfall, or dry, farming (Mikesell 1961:16, 41).

Most forests in northern Morocco consist of two evergreen oaks; holly oak (*Quercus ilex*) and cork oak (*Quercus suber*), which is used today for its tree bark. There are also cedar forests (*Cedrus atlantica*), a valuable source of timber in the Rif and other mountain ranges (Mikesell 1961:29). In the lower areas of the Rif, the most common fruit and nut trees are the fig, pomegranate, almond, and olive.

The shrub vegetation in the western part of the Rif Mountains consists of the dwarf palm or palmetto (*Chamaerops humilis*), which is exploited for its edible bud and cabbage or harvested for its fiber, which is dried and twisted into loose rope or used for hats, mats, and baskets (Mikesell 1961:23). Another important element of the palmetto shrub vegetation is *Pistacia lintiscus*, a woody plant that grows from 1 to 5 m tall and is prized as a source of charcoal (Mikesell 1961:26). Two other species, which Mikesell does not mention but which were recovered from the site of al-Basra in the form of charcoal, are *Cistus* and *Phillyrea*.

Description of Ethnobotanical Evidence

Methodology

The samples used in this study came from the 1980-1981 (Pollock 1983-1984, n.d.) and 1990 excavations at al-Basra (Benco 1987, 2002). A subsequent study by Perry (1999) is described below.[1] The procedures used to

---

[1] A subsequent study of ethnobotanical remains from the 1994 field season was conducted by ethnobotanist David Perry (1999). The remains came from another excavation unit (F8) in the metal-working area. Of special note, Perry found the remains of olive (*Olea* sp.), both seeds and charred twig fragments, which had not been identified in earlier studies by Mahoney and Pollock. In addition, Perry conducted an SEM (Scanning Electron Microscope) examination to determine if several botanical specimens from F8 were flax (*Linum*). In his report, he

collect and analyze the samples were relatively consistent during each field seasons. Soil samples of 2 liters were collected in 1990, while larger samples were recovered in 1980-1981. Samples were recovered from general fill deposits, pits, kilns, and a burial.

Flotation was conducted manually using a large bucket of water and a 1 mm mesh sieve. Botanical remains were collected with a .2 mm mesh tea strainer as a hand sieve. After flotation, all heavy fractions were collected on newspaper and dried before being bagged. Light fractions were collected in muslim cloth and hung to dry, before being packed in film capsules.

Light fractions were screened through a series of geological sieves. The charred seed and seed fragments from 1990 were identified using a comparative collection of Near Eastern plants at the Museum Applied Science Center for Archaeology (MASCA), University Museum, University of Pennsylvania. Charcoal samples were measured by volume rather than weight because of the presence of a thin film of soil on their surface.

The general state of seed preservation was quite poor, which contributed to the difficulty in species identification. Seed coats were partially or completely missing on many and had a considerable amount of surface pitting (Pollock n.d.:7).

A total of 35 samples were analyzed from 1980-1981 (Pollock 1983-1984, n.d.) and 1990 (see Tables 4.1 to 4.3). The samples came from ten different excavation units: 24 samples from the industrial area (Area F), 8 from the residential/commercial zone (Area G and K); 2 from hill slopes (Area C and I); and 1 from a burial on the valley floor (Area H). Samples numbered 300 to 311 were recovered in 1980-1981 and the rest were collected in 1990.

Cultivated Plants

Cereals

Hordeum. Barley is one of the primary cereals present in the al-Basra assemblage. For most samples, barley grains could not be identified beyond genus because of poor preservation and a clay film on their surface. Five seeds appeared twisted and thus were classified as *Hordeum vulgare*, or six-row barley. In Morocco today, barley is the predominant cereal in terms of land under cultivation. It tolerates saline and alkaline soils and can be grown on calcareous soils. Its primary use is as fodder for livestock, rather than human food. In historical references to al-Basra, barley is recorded as a major crop and thus it was likely consumed in some form by the inhabitants. However, it was probably not brewed for beer, which is prohibited by Islamic tradition.

Triticum. Wheat was slightly more plentiful than barley in terms of overall frequency in flotation samples. It most likely constituted a major crop at al-Basra, as it does today in Morocco. According to the historical chronicles (Ibn Hawqal 1842:192), wheat was an important crop at al-Basra during the tenth century.

Four species of wheat were identified: *T. aestivum* (bread wheat), *T. dicoccum* (emmer), *T. durum* (hard wheat), and *T. monococcum* (einkorn). By far, the most common was *T. aestivum/durum*,[2] which was four and a half times as frequent as einkorn and emmer combined. There is a long tradition of durum wheat use in North Africa. It has a high gluten content and is the semolina wheat from which couscous, a basic staple in northwestern Africa, is made. Durum wheat has the potential for being a temporal marker. Its cultivation seems to have been unknown in the Mediterranean before its introduction by the Arabs (Watson 1983:21-22). Durum wheat is more versatile than bread wheat: it can grow in dry steppe regions where bread wheat cannot (Watson 1983:20) and its low water content permits longer storage over longer periods.

Legumes

Very few legumes were recovered at al-Basra. They consist of: lentils (*Lens culinaris/orientalis*), which occurred in a significant quantity in only one sample (B11)—from an industrial context; one example of field peas (*Pisum* cf. *sativum*); and one of fava bean (*Vicia faba*).

The relatively low frequency of legumes at the site may be due to a number of reasons. In northern Morocco today, legumes are grown only as subsidiary crops (Nuttonson 1961:131). The region around al-Basra may not have had sufficient precipitation or humidity to allow legume cultivation (Pollock n.d.:13). It is possible, too, that legumes were cultivated but, because they are not parched before being eaten, they may be poorly preserved in the archaeological record (Dennell 1978:18).

Other Possible Cultivars

Cannabis sativa. Hemp is cultivated for its fiber and its narcotic properties. Only two seeds were recovered from one sample (C1) recovered from near the surface of the north hill slope at al-Basra. Hemp was cultivated in the

---

concluded that the specimens likely belonged to this taxon: "The anatomy of *Linum* includes a small stem on the outer periphery of which lie the bundles of bast fibers which form the basis of linen cloth. The fibers themselves were present on the three fragments examined (from F8/5-1), and were of the required size and length. That no seeds are present may only indicate that the production of flax was not occurring at the sampled areas of the site. Rather, the byproducts of processing may have been used as fuel, while the storage of seeds for future flax crops was conducted elsewhere."

[2] A distinction between *T. aestivum* and *T. durum* could not be made because of the poor preservation of the samples.

medieval period in the Sous region of southwestern Morocco (Brignon et al. 1967:77), but it may have been widely grown in the north as well (Pollock n.d.:18). Mikesell (1961:53) suggests that hemp was unknown inNorth Africa until it was introduced by the Arabs sometime after the eighth century A.D. Its fibers are commonly used for cordage and its leaves as a hallucinatory drug (hashish).

Ficus cf. *carica*. After wheat and barley, fig seeds constitute the third most abundant cultivar at al-Basra. The large number of seeds, however, may be misleading. Renfrew (1973:135) notes that a single fig may contain as many as 1,600 seeds. Figs are a staple food in modern-day Morocco; they can be eaten fresh or dried for storage (Mikesell 1961:4). They are also reported to have been grown widely in medieval Morocco (Brignon et al. 1967:77). Fig trees are relatively easy to cultivate because they are drought resistant and require little tending (Nuttonson 1961:52). It is possible that they represent a cultivated crop at al-Basra.

Vitis vinifera. Seven grape pips were found in four al-Basra samples. Historical references indicate that dried grapes were exported from Morocco to West Africa in the Middle Ages (Lewicki 1974:76). Thus, it is likely that grapes constituted a significant crop in North Africa and possibly were cultivated at al-Basra.

Wild Grasses

Avena. Oat can be cultivated for use as a fodder, but it is also commonly present as a weed in wheat fields (Salisbury 1961:112). It is not mentioned in the historical documents. Since only one seed was found in the flotation samples, it will be assumed that oat occurred as a weed at al-Basra.

Digitaria cf. *sanguinalis*. This cereal occurs as a weed or pasture grass in warm climates and is sometimes eaten like millet (Mabberley 1987:183). Only one sample (B16) contained *Digitaria*, but it constituted a large part of the sample. It is likely that this plant grew naturally in the fields or pasture lands around the city.

Lolium. Ryegrass is most often used as animal fodder (Mabberley 1987:340). There is only one example in the al-Basra assemblage, suggesting that it occurred as a weed.

Panicum cf. *miliaceum*. Also known as millet, this grass is grown as a secondary cereal in modern Morocco (Maire 1952:341). It is often processed to make flour or alcoholic drinks, or used as feed for pigs (Mabberley 1987:428). Only six seeds were found, so it is not possible to determine conclusively if *Panicum* was a cultivated crop or field weed.

Phalaris. Also known as canary grass, *Phalaris* is the most common seed recovered at al-Basra; it was found in every area of the site. *Phalaris* is often used as livestock fodder (Armstrong 1937:218). Although its abundance suggests it might have been cultivated, its high recovery rate may be due to its preservation in samples that consisted of carbonized animal dung that had been burned as fuel. In this report, I treat *Phalaris* as a wild grass, rather than a cultigen, because it was probably used as animal fodder and thus was incorporated into dung more often than most cultigens.

Setaria. Commonly known as bristle-grass, nine examples of *Setaria* were recovered from eight samples. *Setaria* could not be identified as to species, but based on their morphology, Pollock (n.d.:10ff) suggested they might represent wild varieties (*S. viridis* or *S. verticillata*). It is equally possible that they are *Setaria italica*, which commonly occurs as a weed in cultivated fields in North Africa (Maire 1952:323). *S. italica* can be grown in areas with low precipitation and on various soil types. The grains can be used for human consumption if they are boiled or made into a porridge, but they may also be used for livestock feed (Pollock n.d.:11). Overall, the evidence suggests that *Setaria* represents a wild weed rather than a cultivated crop at al-Basra.

Weedy Plants

Chenopodiaceae cf. *murale*. Chenopodium is a characteristic weed in arable land. A total of four examples of this nettle-leaved goosefoot were identified, all from industrial contexts.

Malva. Mallow is a weed that grows in fall fields, wasteland, and along streams. Three specimens were recovered at al-Basra.

Other rarely occurring weedy species at al-Basra are: *Medicago*, a perennial herb considered to be a valuable pasture plant; *Melilotus*, a weed commonly used as fodder; and *Vicia* cf. *sativa*, a small- to medium-seeded legume.

Rumex, *Bupleurum*, *Valerianella*, *Sinapis*, and *Cleome* are also represented by very small numbers. In general, they are characteristic of arable land; some may have been collected and used for either food or medicinal purposes. Pollock (n.d.:17) suggests that many of them could have been eaten by livestock and incorporated in their dung. If the dung were burned as a fuel, the seeds may have become carbonized and thus would have been preserved.

Modern Plant Remains

Silene (modern). A natural component of steppe vegetation, *Silene* can occur as a field weed in non-irrigated winter and summer crops (Zohary 1973:588). The seeds from al-Basra came predominantly from

Table 4.1. Counts of Seeds in Samples from Metalworking (F7) Contexts at al-Basra, by Genus

Excavation unit Sample number Soil floated (liters)	F7/3-1 B1 2	F7/3-3 B2 2	F7/4-1 B3 2	F7/4-2 B4 2	F7/4-3 B5 2	F7/5-1 B6 2	F7/5-2 B7 2	F7/6-1 B8 2	F7/6-1 B10 2	F7/6-2 B11 2
Cultigens										
T. aestivum/durum	-	-	-	-	1	-	-	2	-	-
T. diccocum	-	-	-	-	-	-	-	-	-	-
T. monoccum	-	-	-	-	-	-	-	-	-	-
Triticum	-	-	-	-	-	-	-	.5	-	-
Hordeum	-	-	-	-	-	-	-	-	-	-
H. vulgare	-	-	-	-	-	-	-	-	-	-
Triticum/Hordeum	-	-	-	-	-	-	-	-	-	-
Lens	-	-	-	-	1	-	-	1	1	13.5
Vicia faba	-	-	-	-	-	-	-	-	-	-
Pisum cf. sativum	-	-	-	-	-	-	-	-	-	-
Vitis vinifera	-	-	-	-	-	-	-	-	-	-
Cannabis sativa	-	-	-	-	-	-	-	-	-	-
Ficus carica	-	-	-	-	-	-	-	-	-	-
Wild grasses										
Phalaris	-	-	-	-	-	-	-	-	1.5	4.5
Avena	-	-	-	-	-	-	-	-	-	-
Setaria	2	-	-	-	-	-	-	-	-	-
Panicum	-	-	-	-	-	-	-	-	-	-
Panicum cf. maliaceum	-	-	-	-	-	-	-	-	-	-
Lolium	-	-	-	-	-	-	-	-	-	-
Poaceae	-	-	-	-	1	1	-	-	-	-
Digitaria sanguinalis	-	-	-	-	-	-	-	-	-	-
Weeds										
Chenopodium	-	-	-	-	-	-	-	-	1	1
Suaeda	-	-	-	-	-	-	-	-	-	-
Centaurea	-	-	-	-	-	-	-	-	-	-
Medicago	-	-	-	-	-	-	-	-	-	-
Melilotus	-	-	-	-	-	-	-	-	-	-
Vicia cf. sativa	-	-	-	-	-	-	-	-	-	-
Malva	-	-	-	-	-	-	-	-	-	-
Rumex	-	-	-	-	-	-	-	-	-	-
Bupleurum	-	-	-	-	-	-	-	-	-	-
Valerianella	-	-	-	-	-	-	-	-	-	-
Prunella	-	-	-	-	-	-	-	-	-	-
Sinapis sp.	-	-	-	-	-	-	-	-	-	-
Cleome	1	-	-	-	-	-	-	-	-	-
Unidentified	8	-	1	1	1	-	-	1	2	1
Noncarbonized										
F. densiflora	7	1	2	1	-	-	-	-	-	-
R. raphanistum	1	-	-	2	-	-	1	-	1	-
Boraginaceae	-	-	-	-	-	-	-	-	1	-
Erodium ciconium	-	18	-	-	-	1	-	2	11	1
Silene	5	13	1	1	4	-	2	-	-	-
Stellaria	2	-	-	-	-	-	-	-	-	-
Cyperaceae	-	-	-	-	-	-	-	-	-	-
Unidentified	-	-	-	-	-	1	1	-	17	-
No. of carbonized seeds	11	0	1	1	4	1	0	5	5.5	20
Density (No. of seeds per liter)	4.5	0	.5	.5	1.5	.5	0	1.25	2.25	10
Seed volume (ml)	<.01	0	<.01	<.01	.1	.01	0	.3	.1	.4
Charcoal volume (ml)	.2	.75	1.5	.75	2.75	2.0	.3	3.4	13	5.5

Table 4.1 (continued)

Excavation unit Sample number Soil floated (liters)	F7/7-1 B12 2	F7/7-2 B13 2	F7/8-1 B14 2	F7/8-2 B15 2	F7/9-1 B16 2	F7/11-3 B18 2	F7/12-3 B19 2	F7/13-3 B20 2
Cultigens								
T. Aestivum/durum	-	-	-	-	3	6	50	2
T. diccocum	-	-	-	-	-	-	1	3
T. monoccum	-	-	-	2	4	-	-	-
Triticum	-	1	1	-	-	-	-	-
Hordeum	-	-	-	-	3	1	2	1
H. vulgare	-	-	-	-	-	-	-	-
Triticum/Hordeum	-	-	-	-	-	-	-	-
Lens	-	-	-	1	-	-	-	-
Vicia faba	-	-	-	-	-	-	-	-
Pisum cf. sativum	-	-	-	-	-	-	-	-
Vitis vinifera	-	-	3	-	-	-	-	-
Cannabis sativa	-	-	-	-	-	-	-	-
Ficus carica	-	-	1	3	-	7	-	-
Wild grasses								
Phalaris	1.5	1	-	-	8	3	47	2
Avena	-	-	-	-	-	-	-	-
Setaria	1	-	-	1	-	1	-	-
Panicum	-	-	-	-	-	-	-	1
Panicum cf. maliaceum	-	-	-	-	-	-	-	-
Lolium	1	-	-	-	-	-	-	1
Poaceae	-	-	-	2	1	19	5	-
Digitaria sanguinalis	-	-	-	-	16	-	-	-
Weeds								
Chenopodium	1	-	1	-	-	-	-	-
Suaeda	-	-	-	-	-	1	2	-
Centaurea	-	-	-	-	-	1	-	-
Medicago	-	1	-	-	-	-	-	-
Melilotus	-	-	-	1	-	-	-	-
Vicia cf. sativa	-	-	-	-	-	-	-	-
Malva	-	-	-	-	-	-	1	-
Rumex	-	-	-	-	2	2	-	-
Bupleurum	-	-	-	-	1	-	-	-
Valerianella	-	-	-	-	-	-	-	-
Prunella	-	-	-	-	-	-	-	-
Sinapis sp.	-	-	-	-	-	-	-	-
Cleome	-	-	-	-	-	-	-	-
Unidentified	-	-	2	2	2	-	-	-
Noncarbonized								
F. densiflora	-	-	-	-	-	-	-	1
R. raphanistum	-	-	-	-	-	7	-	-
Boraginaceae	-	-	-	-	-	-	-	-
Erodium ciconium	-	-	-	1	-	-	-	-
Silene	-	-	-	-	-	-	-	-
Stellaria	-	-	-	-	-	-	-	-
Cyperaceae	-	-	-	-	-	2	-	-
Unidentified	-	-	-	3	-	-	-	-
Total no. of carbonized seeds	4.5	3	8	12	40	41	108	10
Density (no. of seeds per liter)	2.25	1.5	4	6	20	20.5	54	5
Seed volume (ml)	.1	.01	.1	.2	1.2	.8	3.75	.4
Charcoal volume (ml)	20	12	11	12	2	4	5	.5

Table 4.2. Counts of Seeds in Samples from Ceramic Kilns and Other Contexts at al-Basra, by Genus

Excavation unit Sample number Soil floated (liters)	F3W/4-1 B25 2	F3W/5-1 B26 2	F3W/8-8 B31 2	F1/5-0 303 7	F1/8-4 310 8.3	F2/7-2 311 2.5	C1/2-0 306 2.8	H1/1 302 5	I1/1-0 308 2.5
Cultigens									
T. Aestivum/durum	3	-	-	1	3	1	-	-	1
T. diccocum	-	-	-	-	2	1	-	1	-
T. monoccum	-	-	-	-	-	-	-	-	-
Triticum	-	2	2	-	2	2	-	1	-
Hordeum	-	4	1	2	13	2	-	16	-
H. vulgare	-	1	-	-	1	-	-	4	-
Triticum/Hordeum	-	-	-	1	21	8	-	4	-
Lens	-	-	-	-	-	-	-	-	-
Vicia faba	-	-	-	-	-	-	-	-	-
Pisum cf. sativum	-	-	-	-	-	-	-	-	-
Vitis vinifera	-	-	-	-	-	2	-	-	-
Cannabis sativa	-	-	-	-	-	-	2	-	-
Ficus carica	-	-	-	-	4	3	-	5	-
Wild grasses									
Phalaris	2.5	1	2	3	6	17	-	4	1
Avena	-	-	-	-	-	-	-	-	-
Setaria	-	-	1	1	2	-	-	-	-
Panicum	-	-	-	-	1	1	-	-	-
Panicum cf. maliaceum	-	-	-	-	-	-	-	-	-
Lolium	-	-	-	-	-	-	-	-	-
Poaceae	7	2	-	-	5	-	-	-	-
Digitaria sanguinalis	-	-	-	-	-	-	-	-	-
Weeds									
Chenopodium	-	-	-	-	-	-	-	-	-
Suaeda	-	-	1	-	-	-	-	-	-
Centaurea	-	-	-	-	-	-	-	-	-
Medicago	-	-	-	-	-	-	-	-	-
Melilotus	-	-	-	-	-	-	-	-	-
Vicia cf. sativa	-	-	-	-	-	-	-	1	-
Malva	-	-	-	-	-	1	-	-	-
Rumex	-	-	-	-	-	-	-	-	-
Bupleurum	-	-	-	-	-	-	-	-	-
Valerianella	-	-	-	-	-	1	-	-	-
Prunella	-	-	-	-	-	-	-	-	-
Sinapis sp.	-	-	-	-	-	-	-	-	-
Cleome	-	-	-	-	-	-	-	-	-
Unidentified	5	-	3	2	4	3	-	-	-
Noncarbonized									
F. densiflora	-	-	-	-	-	-	-	-	-
R. raphanistum	-	-	-	-	-	-	-	1	-
Boraginaceae	-	-	-	-	-	-	-	-	-
Erodium ciconium	-	-	-	-	-	-	-	-	-
Silene	-	-	-	-	-	-	1	-	-
Stellaria	-	-	-	-	-	-	-	-	-
Cyperaceae	-	-	-	-	-	-	-	-	-
Unidentified	-	24	-	-	-	-	-	-	-
Total no. of carbonized seeds	18.5	10	10	10	64	42	2	36	2
Density (no. of seeds per liter)	9.25	5	5	1.4	7.7	16.8	.7	7.2	.8
Seed volume (ml)	.1	.5	.3						
Charcoal volume (ml)	2.3	2	6						

Table 4.3. Counts of Seeds in Samples from Residential Contexts at al-Basra, by Genus

Excavation Unit	G3N/10-2	G1/4-2	G1/5-2	G1/6-2	G1/6-2	G1/12-1	G1/12-2	K1/10-0
Sample No.	B29	305	309	307	304	300	301	B27
Soil Floated (liters)	2	2.5	10	1.6	15.3	3.3	4.7	5
Cultigens								
T. aestivum/durum	-	-	-	-	2	-	-	5
T. diccocum	-	-	-	1	2	-	-	-
T. monoccum	-	-	-	-	-	-	-	-
Triticum	-	-	-	-	1	-	-	-
Hordeum	-	-	7	1	1	1	1	4
H. vulgare	-	-	-	-	-	-	-	-
Triticum/Hordeum	-	-	8	-	-	1	4	-
Lens	-	-	-	-	-	-	-	-
Vicia faba	-	-	-	-	1	-	-	-
Pisum cf. sativum	-	-	-	-	1	-	-	-
Vitis vinifera	-	-	1	-	1	-	-	-
Cannabis sativa	-	-	-	-	-	-	-	-
Ficus carica	1	-	5	-	-	8	2	2
Wild Grasses								
Phalaris	3	-	5	-	10	-	-	3
Avena	-	-	1	-	-	-	-	-
Setaria	-	-	-	-	-	-	1	1
Panicum	-	-	-	-	-	-	-	-
Panicum cf. maliaceum	-	-	2	-	2	-	-	-
Lolium	-	-	-	-	-	-	-	-
Poaceae	7	-	2	-	-	-	2	5
Digitaria sanguinalis	-	-	-	-	-	-	-	-
Weeds								
Chenopodium	-	-	-	-	-	-	-	-
Suaeda	-	-	-	-	-	-	-	-
Centaurea	-	-	-	-	-	-	-	-
Medicago	-	-	-	-	-	-	-	-
Melilotus	-	-	-	-	-	-	-	-
Vicia cf. sativa	-	-	-	-	-	-	-	-
Malva	-	-	-	-	-	-	-	1
Rumex	-	-	1	-	-	-	-	1
Bupleurum	-	-	-	-	-	-	-	1
Valerianella	-	-	-	-	-	-	-	-
Prunella	-	-	-	-	-	2	-	-
Sinapis sp.	-	-	-	-	1	-	-	-
Cleome	-	-	-	-	-	-	-	-
Unidentified	10	-	2	-	-	-	4	1
Noncarbonized								
F. densiflora	-	-	-	-	-	-	-	-
R. raphanistum	-	-	-	-	-	-	-	-
Boraginaceae	-	-	-	-	-	-	-	-
Erodium ciconium	-	-	-	-	-	-	-	1
Silene	-	-	-	-	-	-	-	-
Stellaria	-	-	-	-	-	-	-	-
Cyperaceae	-	-	-	-	-	-	-	-
Unidentified	-	-	-	-	-	-	-	-
Total no. of carbonized seeds	21	0	34	2	22	12	14	24
Density (no. of seeds per liter)	10	0	3.4	1.25	1.4	3.6	3	5
Seed volume (ml)	.1							.7
Charcoal volume (ml)	.3							2.1

Table 4.4. Identification and Weights of Hand-Collected Charcoal, by Excavation Unit

Excavation Unit	*Quercus* (g)	*Phillyrea* (g)	*Cistus* (g)	Unknown (g)	Total (g)
G1	.10	0	.10	.15	.35
G3N	2.10	0	0	2.10	4.20
F7	15.20	0	0	6.60	21.80
F1	.20	.25	0	0	.45
K1	2.00	0	0	0	2.00

deposits located just below the surface, and thus they are treated as modern inclusions.

Raphanus raphanistum (modern). Wild radish occurs as a modern field weed; it is also valued as livestock feed. A total of 13 examples were recovered, almost all of them from industrial contexts.

Erodium ciconium (modern). A large number of *Erodium* seeds were recovered from shallow deposits at al-Basra. Some *Erodium* seeds occur as weeds and are consumed by livestock; it is possible that this species represents a modern weed growing on or near the site.

Fumaria densiflora (modern), *Stellaria* (modern), Cyperaceae, *Prunella*, Boraginaceae (modern) were also present in small quantities.

Charcoal Remains

Charcoal remains (Table 4.4) were recovered by hand collection in the field and from floated material in the laboratory. Most of the charcoal studied was retrieved from excavation unit F7, located in the metal-working industrial area. This material—mostly consisting of *Quercus* or oak—is believed to have been used as a fuel to smelt iron ores. Charcoal found elsewhere on the site was identified as *Phillyrea* and *Cistus*, both of which are shrubs that form part of the palmetto scrub vegetation typically found in northern Morocco. A large portion of the charcoal could not be identified, limiting its interpretive value.

Spatial Distribution of Ethnobotanical Remains

Industrial Area (F)

The study examined ethnobotanical samples (Table 4.1) from four excavation units in the industrial sector: F1, F2, F3, and F7. Most of the samples came from F7 where they were collected systematically from each level, thus providing a good temporal sequence for the site; this unit yielded debris associated with metal-working activities. Samples from F1 and F3 were associated with the remains of ceramic kilns and those from F2 with general fill.

Metal-Production (F7)

The metal-working area, represented by excavation unit F7, yielded a large quantity of both cultivated and wild grass seeds in the lowest levels (F7/11-3, F7/12-3, F7/13-3), associated with Phase 1 (pre-Idrisid period). These levels also contained a higher density of carbonized seeds than any other deposit studied at al-Basra. As Table 4.1 illustrates, the predominant species in these deposits were wheat (*T. Aestivum/durum*) and *Phalaris* with much smaller quantities of emmer wheat, barley, fig, wild grasses (e.g., *Setaria*, Poaceae), wild radish, and weeds (e.g., *Suaeda*, *Malva*, *Rumex*). Although the deposits contained some metal slag and a worked bone, the botanical material does not appear to consist of the type of fuel (e.g., wood charcoal) needed for metal production. Instead, the high quantity of cultivars and wild grasses and weed seeds suggest that the material came from dung[3] used as a fuel or from a store of grain or fodder that was burned, possibly from a domestic context.

Samples (F7/9-1, F7/8-1 and 8-2, F7/7-1 and 7-2) from the middle levels of F7, which were most likely associated with the Idrisid period, contained large quantities of metal-working debris, including slag, iron nails, worked bone, and charcoal, the byproducts of iron smelting and smithing activities, in a loose fill deposit. The ethnobotanical remains consisted of a high proportion of weeds and wild grasses (e.g., *Phalaris*, *Digitaria sanguinalis*, *Medicago*, *Setaria*, and *Chenopodium*) and a lower proportion of cultivars

---

[3] Miller argues that when there is a wide range of domestic and weed seeds in a hearth context that remains more likely represent dung fuel than food consumed by inhabitants (Miller 1990, 1984; Miller and Smart 1984). Wild and domesticated seeds are commonly ingested by livestock and when their dung is burned as fuel, the seeds that have passed through their intestines are charred and preserved in the archaeological record.

(wheat, barley, pea, grape pips, and fig). This ratio suggests that this material may reflect the carbonized remains of dung fuel and/or domestic trash, neither one of which is particularly associated with metal production.

The upper levels of F7 (F7/6-1 and 6-2, F7/5-1 and 5-2, F7/4-1, 4/2, and 4/3), which date to Phase 3 (post-Idrisid period), were associated with debris from two collapsed structures, represented by large quantities of roof tiles, stone walls, and mudbrick. The ethnobotanical assemblage consisted of large quantities of charred wood fragments compared with the number of seeds recovered. A large proportion of the seeds were not carbonized (*Erodium ciconium, Raphanus*). There were also a large number of lentils, along with traces of wheat, wild grasses (*Phalaris, Poaceae*), and weeds (*Chenopodium*). A number of modern weed seeds and *Silene* were present. This assemblage appears to reflect carbonized and non-carbonized debris that blew into the area after it was abandoned. The topmost levels of F7 (F7/3-1 and 3-3) represent topsoil and fill. Almost all the ethnobotanical samples contained either recent or modern weeds that grow in the area immediately surrounding al-Basra and no cultivars.

Ceramic Kiln (F3)

As Table 4.2 shows, an ethnobotanical sample (F3W/8-8) from a deposit associated with the remains of the F3 updraft kiln used to fire pottery and roof tiles contained a small number of cultigens (wheat and barley), wild grasses *(Phalaris* and *Setaria)*, and weed seeds. This assemblage appears to represent the carbonized remains of dung, possibly burned as fuel for the kiln. Two samples from above the F3 kiln (F3W/5-1 and 4-1), which were taken from the lower and upper strata of a small trash pit dug into a cobble floor, contained traces of wheat, barley, and *Phalaris*, along with many unidentifiable seeds. The stratigraphic division of the pit suggests that the deposits accumulated gradually and may represent successive hearth sweepings in a domestic context.

Ceramic Kiln (F1)

As Table 4.2 illustrates, a large sample (F1/8-4) from a deposit in front of the arched entrance to the F1 updraft kiln consisted predominantly of cultivated cereals (barley, wheat), along with smaller quantities of *Phalaris*, wild grasses, and fig. The context of this sample strongly suggests that the carbonized remains reflect the use of dung as fuel for the kiln. Except for the fig seeds, the remainder represents plants that are commonly ingested by animals as fodder. A small sample (F1/5-0) taken from directly above the stacking floor of the kiln contained a similar range of botanical remains.

The Residential Area (G)

Eight ethnobotanical samples (Table 4.3) were taken from two excavation units in the residential area, both of which were associated with buildings consisting of stone walls and plaster floors, and one unit (K1) on the edge of the residential quarter. Six samples were taken during the 1980-1981 season and were analyzed by Pollock (n.d.) and two were retrieved during the 1990 season.

G1 Excavation Unit

Two samples (G1/12-1 and 12-2) from a wall and roof collapse (probable Phase 2) were recovered from a compact, red clay deposit in the G1 excavation unit. The majority of the seeds are cultigens, as one would expect to find in domestic trash. Fig seeds make up the largest portion of the sample, which also contained barley, wheat, wild grasses, and weed seeds. It seems likely that the samples represent accidentally carbonized domestic trash and/or remnants of dung fuel.[4]

Four samples from the upper levels of G1 (G1/4-1, 5-2, and 6-2), probably dating to the post-Idrisid period (Phase 3), came from a second red clay deposit representing collapsed walls and roof. The ethnobotanical material consisted of large amounts of cultivated carbonized wheat and barley seeds and smaller quantities of grape pips, fig, and *Phalaris, and* wild grasses and weed seeds. A field pea and a fava bean were also present. Although barley and *Phalaris* were likely used as fodder at al-Basra, *Phalaris*, wild grasses, and weed seeds also represent elements that could have become incorporated into animal fodder and preserved in dung. (See also footnote 4).

G3N Excavation Unit

One sample from a red pise roof collapse layer in G3N (G3N/10-2) consisted primarily of unidentified seeds, presumably weed seeds, along with fig, *Phalaris*, and one possible cultivar. The sample's small size makes it difficult to say much about its context, although it falls within the range of seeds carbonized in dung burned as fuel. (See also footnote 4).

K1 Excavation Unit

The ethnobotanical study examined an interesting sample (K1/10) recovered from a hearth context in K1, located

---

[4] Since Mahoney's study, it has become clear that the red clay (pise) deposits of collapsed wall and roofs were burned. Thus, it is possible to suggest another source for the botanical remains recovered from them. Straw and other vegetal matter from agricultural fields were often added—as tempering materials—to the packed clay (pise) used in wall and roof construction. Some of this material could have been charred and preserved when the uildings burned (see Lundquist and Benco, this volume).

on the edge of the residential sector. The hearth contained intact animal remains. The ethnobotanical material consisted of cultivars (wheat, barley, and fig) and a similar quantity of wild grasses and weeds. The density and variety of seeds, which is consistent with most other samples from residential contexts, suggests they are the carbonized remains of domestic debris swept into the hearth or the use of dung as fuel for cooking.

Subsistence Economy

The seed assemblages from al-Basra indicate that the overall proportion of cultivated plants to wild grasses and weeds is similar throughout the site. This suggests that domesticated plant use was an important feature of the city's subsistence economy. Other than two examples of hemp, there is no evidence of the important cash crops, like flax and cotton, referred to in historical texts (but see footnote 1). This absence is not surprising, since seeds of both flax and cotton are unlikely to have become carbonized and thus incorporated into the archaeological record.

The historical references to the importance of cultivated wheat and barley is borne out in the ethnobotanical study. Wheat was the predominant seed in the largest cache (F7/12-3) recovered from al-Basra. Cultivated legumes were rare, which may simply reflect human consumption patterns that do not involve burning, or carbonizing. Fig and grape seeds were also fairly common, suggesting that they were cultivated at al-Basra, although not on the same scale of wheat or barley.

Canary grass (*Phalaris*) is the most common seed recovered from the site. It was probably used as fodder for cattle, sheep, and goat. Because it was recovered in such quantities, it is possible that *Phalaris* was deliberately cultivated for animal fodder. Its near ubiquity throughout the urban site suggests either that the grass was brought into the walled city to feed animals or, more likely, that it came into the city in the form of animal dung, which was then used as a fuel for cooking, heating, and possibly ceramic production. Overall, the large proportion of wild grasses in the seed assemblages suggest that dung was used as a source of fuel at al-Basra.

Industrial Economy

The industrial areas of the site (F) contained the highest densities of both seeds and charcoal (Figure 4.1). The average density in the industrial units amounted to 9.4 seeds per liter; in the residential/commercial sector it was 2.5 seeds per liter. The volume of charcoal (2.8 ml per liter of floated material) was also considerably higher in industrial contexts than in residential areas (less than 1 ml per liter).

In addition, the seed to charcoal ratio (Figure 4.1) in samples from the residential area (8.3:1) is more than twice that in samples from the industrial area (3.4:1), despite the fact that seed densities are lower in the residential sector. This further supports the theory that dung fuel was a predominant fuel source for domestic cooking and heating. The large quantities of charcoal recovered from industrial contexts associated with large amounts of iron slag provide strong evidence that charcoal was used in the industrial area, primarily for smelting iron.

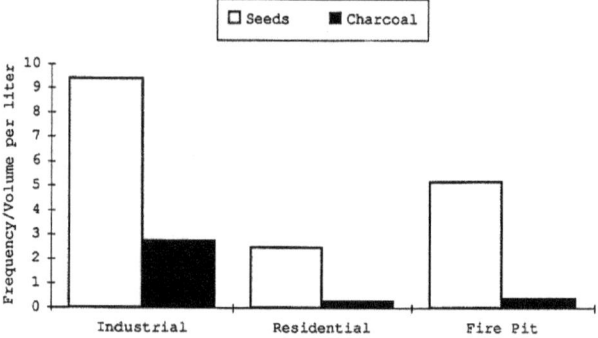

Figure 4.1 Density of seeds (number per liter) and charcoal (volume per liter), by area.

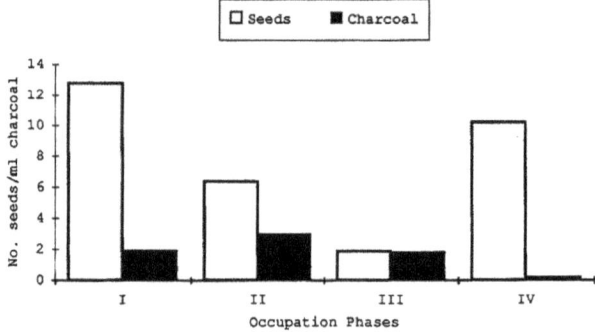

Figure 4.2 Density of seeds (number per liter) and charcoal (volume per liter), by occupation phase.

Temporally, Phase 1 marks the period with the highest density of seeds (Figure 4.2). The relative proportion of charcoal volume to seed counts is the lowest found at al-Basra, suggesting that little fuel was consumed for industrial purposes at this time. The archaeological remains also indicate that metal production was insignificant during the early settlement. This phase exhibits the highest density of wild grasses and weeds, which suggests that dung fuel was commonly used for domestic activities and/or ceramic production.

Phase 2 witnesses an increase in the proportion of charcoal volumes to seed counts, indicating that wood and/or charcoal became more important sources of fuel

(Figure 4.2). This correlates with the archaeological evidence of a growth in industrial activities, especially metal production, in the urban center at this time.

Although these relative proportions continue through Phase 3, there is a notable decrease in the density of both seed remains and charcoal (Figure 4.2). This pattern suggests that either a population decline or a shortage of wood resources occurred, resulting in an increase in the use of dung as fuel. The seed assemblages from Phase 4 contexts are believed to be mixed with modern material.

Conclusions

The archaeobotanical analysis shows that wood or charcoal was used as a fuel for metalworking activities at al-Basra. In addition, the carbonized remains of plants and weeds commonly used for fodder found in both industrial and residential contexts indicate that dung was an important fuel source, especially in domestic contexts. Over time, dung appears to have replaced wood as the primary source of fuel. This may reflect significant changes in the city's economy and environment toward the end of its occupation in the eleventh or twelfth centuries. It is possible that after more than 300 years of local consumption and regional industrial activities, the wood resources around the urban center had become depleted. This environmental degradation could have been compounded by political and economic marginalization during its late occupation period (see Ennahid, this volume). Thus, it is possible that a combination of political and environmental factors led to al-Basra's economic decline and, eventually, to the abandonment of the urban center.

Acknowledgments

The thesis that was the basis of this article could not have been completed without the support and guidance of Nancy Benco and Naomi Miller. Nancy Benco deserves all of my thanks for taking the time to extract this article from my thesis research. Funding for the archaeobotanical analysis was generously provided for by a Cotlow Research Grant from the Department of Anthropology, George Washington University.

References Cited

al-Bakri, Abu-Ubayd (died ca. A.D. 1094)
 1965 *Description de l'Afrique septentrionale*. Edited and translated by M. de Slane. 3rd ed. Adrien-Maisonneuve, Paris.

Armstrong, S. F.
 1937 *British Grasses and their Employment in Agriculture*. Cambridge University Press, Cambridge.

Benco, N. L.
 1987 *The Early Medieval Pottery Industry at al-Basra, Morocco*. BAR International Series 341. British Archaeological Reports, Oxford.
 2002 1990 Archaeological Investigations at al-Basra, Morocco. *Bulletin d'archéologie marocaine* 19:293-340.

Brignon, J., A. Amine, B. Boutaleb, G. Martinet, and B. Rosenberger
 1967 *Histoire du Maroc*. Hatier, Paris.

Dennell, R. W.
 1978 *Early Farming in South Bulgaria from the VI to the III Millennia B.C*. BAR International Series 45. British Archaeological Reports, Oxford.

Horne, L.
 1982 Fuel for the Metal-Worker. *Expedition* 25(1):6-13.

Ibn Hawqal (died ca. A.D. 988)
 1842 *Description de l'Afrique*. Translated by M. de Slane. Journal Asiatique (3rd ser) 13:153ff.

Leo Africanus (died ca. A.D. 1548)
 1896 *The History and Description of Africa*. Hakluyt Society, London.

Lewicki, T.
 1974 *West African Food in the Middle Ages*. Cambridge University Press, Cambridge.

Mabberley, D. J.
 1987 *The Plant Book: A Portable Dictionary for Higher Plants*. Cambridge University Press, Cambridge.

Mahoney, N.
 1994 Economy and Environment at al-Basra: An Archaeobotanical Analysis of a Medieval Islamic Urban Center. M.A. Thesis, Department of Anthropology, George Washington University.

Maire, R.
 1952 *Flore de l'afrique du nord*, vol. 1. Paul Lechevallier, Paris.

Mikesell, M. W.
 1961 *Northern Morocco: A Cultural Geography*. University of California Press, Berkeley.

Miller, N. F.
 1990 Clearing Land for Farmland and for Fuel. In *Economy and Settlement in the Near East*. Edited by N. F. Miller. Museum Applied Science Center for Archaeology, University Museum, University of Pennsylvania, Philadelphia.
 1984 The Use of Dung as Fuel: An Ethnographic Example and an Archaeological Application.

Paléorient 11(2): 71-79.

Miller, N.F., and T. L. Smart
  1984 Intentional Burning of Dung as Fuel: A Mechanism for the Incorporation of Charred Seeds into the Archaeological Record. *Journal of Ethnobiology* 4(1):15-28.

al-Muqaddasi, M. (died ca. A.D. 990)
  1950 *Description de l'occident musulman au IVe-Xe siècle*. Edited and translated by C. Pellat. Editions Carbonel, Algiers.

Nuttonson, M.
  1961 *An Introduction to North Africa and a Survey of the Physical Environment and Agriculture of Morocco, Algeria, and Tunisia with Special Reference to their Regions Containing Areas Climatically and Latitudinally Analogous to Israel*, vol. 1. American Institute of Crop Ecology, Washington, D.C.

Perry, D.
  1999 Macrobotanical Remains from al-Basra. Ms. on file, Department of Anthropology, George Washington University, Washington, D.C.

Pollock, S.
  1983-1984 Progress Report on Plant Remains from Badis, al-Basra, Nakur, and Qsar es-Seghir. *Bulletin de l'archéologie marocaine* 15:355-360.
  n.d. Macrobotanical Remains from Four Medieval Urban Sites in Northern Morocco. Unpublished manuscript on file, Department of Anthropology, George Washington University.

Renfrew, Jane
  1973 *Paleoethnobotany*. Columbia University Press, New York.

Salisbury, E.
  1961 *Weeds and Aliens*. Collins, London.

Watson, A. M.
  1983 *Agricultural Innovation in the Early Islamic World*. Cambridge University Press, Cambridge.

Zohary, M.
  1973 *Geobotanical Foundations of the Middle East*. Gustav Fischer, Stuttgart.

Craft Production

Chapter 5

POTTERY AND ETHNIC CHANGE AT AL-BASRA

Jennifer F. Hembree

This chapter explores the temporal changes in two technological styles of pottery making at the medieval Islamic site of al-Basra. The goal is to suggest reasons why these changes in manufacturing techniques occurred. The study includes a discussion of clay composition, paste preparation techniques, vessel formation, decorative techniques, and firing methods. By viewing ceramic technologies as indicative of style and by placing them within their temporal contexts, this chapter shows how technological style can be used to investigate ethnicity, population movement, and pottery production practices at a large, urban center.

Technological Style

The debate on how technology can be used to examine ethnicity and social boundaries within the archaeological record has metamorphosed within the Americanist arena in recent decades. Accompanying the processualist conceptualization of culture as an adaptive system, change—including stylistic change—is attributed primarily to external forces. Within this framework, style is considered an effect—a passive product (Jones 1997:113). Similarly, artifact manufacture, use, and sometimes even form are viewed as adaptive strategies (Gosselain 1998; Hegmon 1992; Jones 1997). Technologies, as well, are believed to be governed by both ecological and physical constraints.

Recent archaeological theory, however, has provided an alternative view. Within the post-processualist framework, humans are given agency in the material culture they produce. Material culture not only structures human agency but it is also a product of that human agency (Hodder 1986; Jones 1997). Furthermore, all aspects of material culture must be considered because "structures of meaning are present in all the daily trivia" (Hodder 1982:213). Technologies and production, which generate artifacts, are the results of human agency and human cognition, and thus have style (Hegmon 1992:529; Lechtman 1977:5).

Various methods and theories have been developed for use in the study of how technological style emerges. Sackett (1990) suggests the concept of isochrestic variation or technical choice, in which technical variation results from a choice made between technologically equivalent alternatives. In this sense, technological style is thought "to reflect learned and ingrained behavior" (Goodby 1998:161), as opposed to being the result of a manipulative procedure. Stemming from the work of Leroi-Gourhan, the French archaeological tradition has focused on the *chaîne opératoire*, the manufacturing sequence of artifacts (Stark 1998:2). *Chaînes opératoires* are viewed as "deeply embedded operational sequences . . . comprising the foundation of a society's technology" (Stark 1998:5, citing Leroi-Gourhan 1993:305, 319). Similarly, the use of Bourdieu's theory of practice and the concept of the habitus has been promoted. Within the habitus ("a system of durable dispositions"), techniques, like other patterns of social actions, are formed (Dietler and Herbich 1998:245-246). All of these approaches suggest that techniques are not "products," but neither are they "intentionally added on in order to signal group identity" (Dietler and Herbich 1998:247). Techniques are the result of "decision-making behavior" (Stark 1998:6). Technological style is, therefore, a reflection of both conscious and unconscious elements of technical choices internalized by the artisan (Stark 1998:6).

Case Study: Cream Ware and Buff Ware Pitchers from Al-Basra

Of more than 13,000 potsherds studied in the al-Basra ceramic assemblage (Table 5.1), 87 percent have been coded by ware (paste composition). The most frequent ware types are buff wares, cream wares, and handmade wares, and the less common types are coarse and reddish-brown wares. This study focuses on the two most common, locally made wares—cream wares and buff wares.

Table 5.1. Counts and Percentages of al-Basra Pottery, by Ware Type

Ware type	No.	%
Buff	7984	59.0
Cream	1923	14.2
Handmade	1006	7.4
Coarse	236	1.7
Other	2375	17.6
Total	**13,524**	**99.9**

Cream Wares

Cream wares make up 14.2 percent of the coded potsherds (Table 5.1). They are fine-textured and white or cream in color, with hues ranging from light olive and light brown to orange. Cream wares contain numerous fine calcite and hematite inclusions (Benco 1987:67). Because of their highly calcareous chemical composition, they are soft, porous, and powdery to the touch (Benco 1987:103). A small proportion (11 percent) are painted with simple lines or circles. The iron-oxide paint varies in color from red to reddish-brown to brown, depending on the amount of oxidization during firing (Figure 5.1).

Figure 5.1 Fragments of al-Basra cream ware pottery with painted motifs.

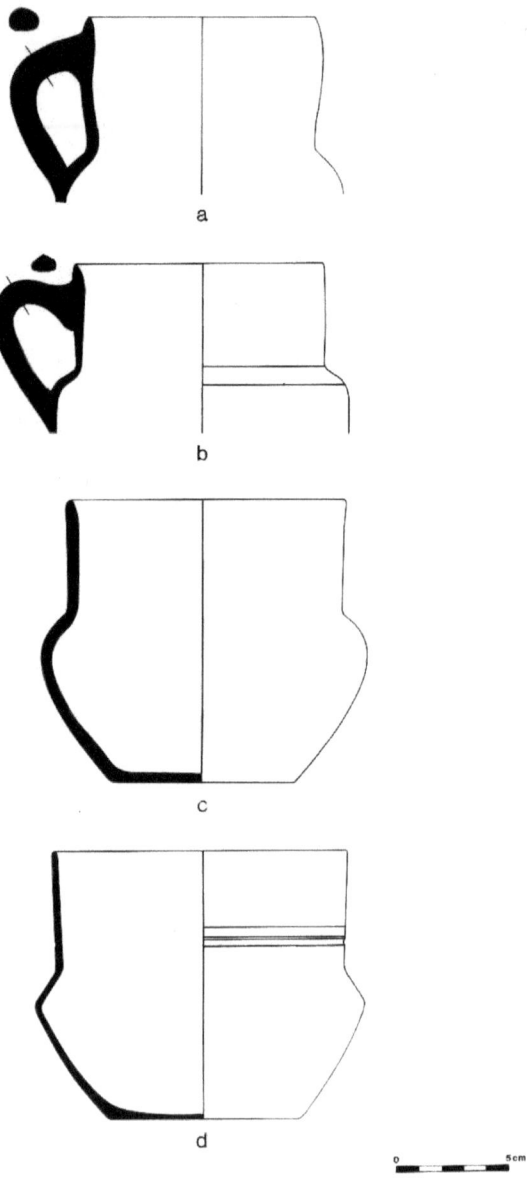

Cream wares are most often found in the form of a pitcher, a small spoutless vessel with a rounded or slightly beveled lip (Figure 5.2). The neck of the vessel is nearly vertical and its shoulder is rounded. The handles, if present, are usually attached directly to the rim (Benco 1987:67, 79; Rezek 1996:21-22). It is likely that cream ware pitchers were made by hand, using a simple tournette, as female potters do today in Morocco (Benco 1989). The faint traces of irregular rilling on the surfaces may have been produced by a cloth as the potter turned the vessel by hand, rather than on a quickly rotating wheel (Rye 1981:60, Figure 62). Cream ware pitchers were probably fired at temperatures between 850°C and 1000°C. At these temperatures, calcareous clays develop into shades of pink, yellow, or olive (Rice 1987:336; Matson 1971:66-67). Despite their high calcium content, the vessels did not fracture or spall after firing because of the fine size of the calcite particles (Rice 1987:98).

Figure 5.2 Al-Basra pitcher styles. (a) and (c): cream ware pitchers with rounded shoulders; (b) and (d): buff ware pitchers with sharply carinated shoulders.

Cream ware pitchers appeared to have been utilized to store, carry, or serve water. Contemporary Moroccan potters prefer this kind of clay for water containers because it makes the water taste sweet (Nancy Benco, personal communication 2000).

Vessels characterized by cream-colored pastes and iron-oxide painted motifs have been described as "Berber wares" both ethnographically and archaeologically in North Africa and Spain (Bel 1914; van Gennep 1911; Velázquez Bosco 1912; Zozoya 1969). Similar vessels have been documented in ethnographic studies of potters in the Rif Mountains (see Benco n.d.b.; van Gennep 1911; Vossen and Ebert 1986). They have also been found archaeologically at Islamic-period sites in both

Spain and North Africa. Such vessels first appear in Muslim Spain in the early ninth-century (Zozoya 1980:312), around the time that Abd al-Rahman I, accompanied by Arab and Berber troops, established the Ummayid dynasty in Andalusia (Benco 1987:17). In addition, they have been found at the tenth-century Ummayid palaces at Medina az-Zahra and Medina Elvira (Velázquez Bosco 1912:Plate 39; Zozoya 1980:Figures 2-4). In North Africa, they have been recovered from the tenth- to eleventh-century site of Tlemcen in Algeria, among other sites (Bel 1914:Figure 40). At al-Basra, the concentration of these wares in the early occupation levels coincides with and supports the historical record that the city of al-Basra was built on the site of an earlier Berber settlement (Benco 1987:20; Eustache 1970-1971:119).

Buff Wares

Buff wares constitute nearly 60 percent of the coded wares at al-Basra (Table 5.1). These potsherds are buff or grayish in surface color, are relatively dense (with a hard surface), and can be categorized as sandy, fine, or very fine, depending on the size and density of quartz inclusions (Benco 1987:103). Some of the clay may have been levitated in simple settling pits, thereby creating a very fine paste (Nancy Benco, personal correspondence 2000). Buff wares are made on a wheel, as the rilling (compression ridges) on both interior and exterior surfaces indicate. According to refiring tests, buff wares were fired in kilns at temperatures between 800°C and 1000°C (Benco n.d.a.). The variations in sherd color (buff to gray) indicate that the firing atmosphere was not well-controlled but that vessels in different parts of the kiln were subjected to various oxidizing conditions. Buff wares are usually undecorated, although some are incised with linear or wavy combing. They appear in a variety of forms, including carinated jars, large and small storage jars, bowls, and pitchers (Benco 1987).

Unlike the round-shouldered cream ware pitchers, the buff ware pitchers generally have sharply carinated shoulders. Handles, if they are present, are usually attached below the rim rather than on the rim as they are on cream ware pitchers (Rezek 1996:26). About 12 percent of buff ware pitchers are incised below the lip and less than 1 percent are painted.

Temporal Changes in Pitcher Wares

The relative frequencies of these two technologically different pitcher types change during al-Basra's occupation (Table 5.2). During the earliest occupation phase (Phase 1, ca. A.D. 600-800), cream ware vessels constitute nearly one quarter (24 percent) of the ceramic assemblage. By the third and final urban phase (ca. A.D. 980-1100), they represent only 14 percent of the assemblage. Phase 4 components, which represent the post-urban phase at the site and are characterized by mixed deposits, are not included in this analysis. During the same period at the urban center, buff wares increase steadily from Phase 1, when they make up 63 percent of the assemblage, to Phase 3, when they constitute 71 percent.

The changing relationship between cream and buff wares can best be viewed through the prism of the pitcher. Unlike some other vessel forms, pitchers remain a constant presence in the al-Basra assemblage. They make up 9 percent of the ceramic assemblage and remain close to this proportion throughout the city's history (Table 5.3).

Table 5.2. Counts and Percentages of al-Basra Wares, by Occupation Phase[1]

Occupation phase		Buff	Cream	Hand-made	Coarse	Others	Total
4 (post-urban)	No.	296	73	23	28	31	549
	%	66.0	16.0	5.0	6.0	7.0	100.0
3 (post-Idrisid)	No.	1357	268	153	61	73	1912
	%	71.0	14.0	8.0	3.0	4.0	100.0
2 (Idrisid)	No.	1400	373	209	24	65	2071
	%	68.0	18.0	10.0	1.0	3.0	100.0
1 (pre-Idrisid)	No.	809	304	130	15	25	1283
	%	63.0	24.0	10.0	1.0	2.0	100.0

[1] Only pottery collected from units excavated to the earliest occupation phase are included.

Table 5.3. Counts and Percentages of al-Basra Pitchers, by Occupation Phase

Occupation phase	All sherds	Pitchers N	%
4 (post-urban)	549	47	8.6
3 (post-Idrisid)	2398	243	10.1
2 (Idrisid)	2860	299	10.4
1 (pre-Idrisid)	1577	149	9.4
Total	**7384**	**738**	**99.9**

Over 700 pitcher rim fragments from excavation units spanning all three phases were analyzed in this study. As Figure 5.3 indicates, the relative proportions of cream ware and buff ware pitchers change through time. During Phase 1, pitchers are predominantly made of cream wares. Cream ware pitchers constitute 60 percent, or nearly twice that of buff ware pitchers. By Phase 2, the proportion of cream ware pitchers has decreased to 40 percent, while that of buff ware pitchers has increased to 58 percent. A more pronounced decline in cream ware pitchers occurs during Phase 3. Their relative frequency drops to 19 percent while buff ware pitchers increase to 77 percent of the assemblage.

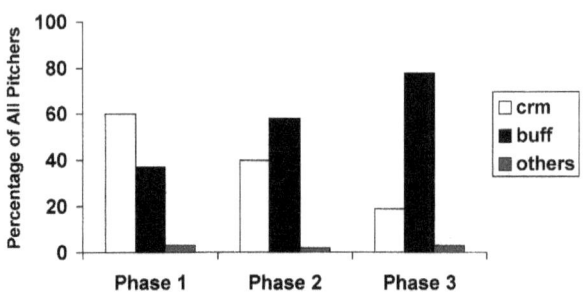

Figure 5.3 Relative frequencies of al-Basra pitchers, by ware and occupation phase.

Interpreting Technological Change in Pottery

As discussed earlier, technological styles are learned and ingrained behaviors and thus are considered conservative and resistant to change (Rice 1984:252). A transformation in the technological style requires a change in the manufacturing process (Stark 1999:29), which means either a new technical choice or an alteration of "dispositions" among the producers and craftspeople. At al-Basra, the pitcher assemblage indicates that different technical choices, or manufacturing processes, existed side-by-side. It also shows that the predominance of these technical choices relative to each other shifted over time. In order to examine why these developments occurred, I have drawn on a number of ethnographic, historical, and archaeological analogies from Islamic North Africa.

One possible explanation is that al-Basra's early potters simply decided to adopt a new technological style. They began to exploit new clay sources (i.e., from highly calcareous, cream-firing clays to non-calcareous, buff-firing clays) and changed their forming and decorating techniques (i.e., from red-painted to plain or incised wares and rounded to carinated shoulder forms, and from hand-thrown to wheel-turned vessels). Modern ethnographic studies of pottery production in the Maghreb, however, suggest this scenario was unlikely. According to Balfet's extensive research among traditional potters, pottery technology in the Maghreb is very conservative in nature. "The procedures have not changed... and the painted geometric decoration is more or less the same as it was two millennia ago" (Balfet 1966:169). As an extensive inventory of contemporary potters in Morocco (Vossen and Ebert 1986) shows, cream wares similar to those found archaeologically at al-Basra are still produced by Berber tribal potters in the provinces of Kenitra, Chefchaouen, and Taounate near al-Basra.

A second, and more likely, explanation is that some of the early al-Basra potters were replaced by other potters who were accustomed to a different way of making pottery. The historical record supports this possibility. According to Eustache (1955:234), the Idrisid city of al-Basra may have originally been built on the site of an existing Berber settlement. The new city attracted not only Berbers but also Arabs from other parts of North Africa. In the ninth century, it probably received an influx of new immigrants from southern Spain. Historical documents indicate that large numbers of Spanish Muslims (*muwalladun*) migrated to the Maghreb during the early part of the ninth century after revolts broke out in Cordova in A.D. 818 and again in A.D. 826 (Dozy 1972; Lévi-Provençal 1944). The Spanish immigrants were mostly craftsmen and farmers (Glick 1979). Thus, it is possible that the Spanish artisans, some of whom may have been potters, brought their technological traditions, or styles, with them. The potters would have chosen clay deposits and forming, decorating, and firing techniques that they were most familiar with. Over time, their way of making pottery might have proved superior to that of the Berber potters and a growing population of Spanish immigrants in the town might have further increased the demand for their pottery.

This scenario is also supported by archaeological evidence from al-Basra. Cream ware pitchers with rounded shoulders, associated with a Berber pottery-making tradition, are predominant in the pitcher assemblage from the first occupation phase (ca. A.D. 600-800). Large quantities of buff-fired vessels, especially very fine buff wares, begin to appear only in the second occupation phase. The buff ware pitchers exhibit sharply carinated shoulders and different handle attachments in this phase. During the third occupation phase, the trend toward proportionately fewer cream ware pitchers and more buff ware vessels continues.

Berber pottery traditions do not completely disappear from the urban scene. Cream ware vessels are present throughout the three urban phases at al-Basra, although in decreasing quantities as time passes. The Berber preference for a utensil that sweetened the taste of water may explain the persistence of cream ware pitchers.

Discussion and Conclusions

While the indigenous potters of al-Basra did not change their way of making pottery, a new technological style appears to have been introduced from the outside by artisan immigrants. Thus, two technological styles—one exploiting cream-firing clays and hand-building and the other buff-firing clays and wheel-throwing—were employed at al-Basra. Two groups of potters—indigenous Berber potters and Spanish *muwalladun*—coexisted at the urban center. Each group made different culturally induced choices during the pottery production sequence. They chose different clay deposits (cream firing vs. buff firing), preparation techniques (sifting vs. levigation), forming processes (handmade vs. wheel-turned), decorating styles (paint vs. incising or nothing), and very likely different firing methods.

As Dietler and Herbich (1998:26) note, technological style may be the product of the habitus, ingrained and resistant to change. Clearly, the al-Basra potters, both indigenous and immigrant, had choices in the way they produced pottery. Either group could have changed its technological style, but neither group did. The choices potters made at al-Basra may have been what Stark (1999:41) calls "an internalized understanding." In the Berber case, this was an understanding of what Berber pottery is and how it should be produced. The Berber potters chose to perpetuate this understanding, despite the appearance of a new tradition. In the case of Spanish immigrant potters, this meant continuing a technological style in a new environment and with new resources.

References Cited

Balfet, H.
  1966 Ethnographical Observations in North Africa and Archaeological Interpretation: The Pottery of the Maghreb. In *Ceramics and Man*, edited by F. R. Matson, pp. 161-177. Methane and Co., London.

Bel, A.
  1914 *Un atelier de poteries et faïences du Xe siècle de J.-C. découvert à Tlemcen*. Barham, Constantine.

Benco, N.
  1987 *The Early Medieval Pottery Industry at al-Basra, Morocco*. BAR International Series 341. British Archaeological Reports, Oxford.
  1989 Morphological Variability: An Approach to the Study of Craft Specialization. In *A Pot for All Reasons: Ceramic Ecology Revisited*, edited by C. Kolb and L. Lackey, pp. 57-72. Temple University Press, Philadelphia.
  n.d.b. Chemical and Mineralogical Analyses of Early Islamic Pottery from Al-Basra. Ms. on file, Department of Anthropology, George Washington University, Washington, D.C.
  n.d.a. Traditional Pottery Production in Morocco. Ms. on file, Department of Anthropology, George Washington University, Washington, D.C.

Dietler, M., and I. Herbich
  1998 Habitus, Techniques, Style: An Integrated Approach to the Social Understanding of Material Culture and Boundaries. In *The Archaeology of Social Boundaries*, edited by M.T. Stark, pp. 232-263. Smithsonian Institution Press, Washington, D.C.

Dozy, R.
  1972 *Spanish Islam: A History of the Moslems in Spain*. Translated by F. G. Stokes. Frank Cass, London.

Eustache, D.
  1955 El-Basra, capitals idrissite, et son port. *Hesperis* 42: 218-238.
  1970-71 *Corpus des dirhams idrisites et contemporaries*. Banque du Maroc, Rabat.

Glick, T. F.
  1979 *Islamic and Christian Spain in the Early Middle Ages*. Princeton University Press, Princeton.

Goodby, R. G.
  1998 Technological Patterning and Social Boundaries: Ceramic Variability in Southern New England, A.D. 1000-1675. In *The Archaeology of Social Boundaries*, edited by M. T. Stark, pp. 161-182. Smithsonian Institution Press, Washington, D.C.

Gosselain, O. P.
  1998 Social and Technical Identity in a Clay Crystal Ball. In *The Archaeology of Social Boundaries*, edited by M. T. Stark, pp. 78-106. Smithsonian Institution Press, Washington, D.C.

Hegmon, M.
  1992 Archaeological Research on Style. *Annual Review of Anthropology* 21:517-536.

Hodder, I.
  1982 *Symbols in Action: Ethnoarchaeological Studies of Material Culture*. Cambridge University Press, Cambridge.
  1986 *Reading the Past: Current Approaches to Interpretation in Archaeology*. Cambridge University Press, Cambridge.

Jones, S.
  1997 *The Archaeology of Ethnicity*. Routledge, London.

Lechtman, H.
  1977 Style in Technology: Some Early Thoughts. In *Material Culture: Styles, Organization, and Dynamics of Technology*, edited by H. Lechtman and R. S. Merrill, pp. 3-20. West Publishing, New York.

Leroi-Gourhan, A.
  1993 *Gesture and Speech (Le geste et la parole)*. Translated from the French by A. B. Berger. MIT Press, Cambridge.

Lévi-Provençal, E.
  1944 *Histoire de l'espagne musulmane*, vol. 1. L'institut francais d'archéologie orientale du Caire, Cario.

Matson, F.
  1971 A Study of Temperatures Used in Firing Ancient Mesopotamian Pottery. In *Science and Archaeology*, edited by R. H. Brill, pp. 65-79. MIT Press, Cambridge, Massachusetts.

Rezek, R.
  1996 An Analysis of the Changing Pottery Industry of the Medieval Islamic City of al-Basra, Morocco. Senior Thesis, Department of Anthropology, George Washington University, Washington, D.C.

Rice, P.
  1984 Change and Conservatism in Pottery-Producing Systems. In *The Many Dimensions of Pottery* edited by S. E. van der Leeuw, pp. 231-293. Universiteit van Amsterdam, Amsterdam.
  1987 *Pottery Analysis: A Sourcebook*. University of Chicago Press, Chicago.

Rye, O.
  1981 *Pottery Technology: Principles and Reconstruction*. Taraxacum, Washington, D.C.

Sackett, J. R.
  1990 Style and Ethnicity in Archaeology: The Case for Isochresticism. In *Uses of Style in Archaeology*, edited by M. Conkey and C. Hastorf, pp. 32-43. Cambridge University Press, Cambridge.

Stark, M.
  1998 Technical Choice and Social Boundaries in Material Culture Patterning: An Introduction. In *The Archaeology of Social Boundaries*, edited by M. T. Stark, pp. 1-11. Smithsonian Institution Press, Washington, D.C.
  1999 Social Dimensions of Technical Choice. In *Material Meanings: Critical Approaches to the Interpretation of Material Culture*, edited by E. S. Chilton, pp. 24-43. University of Utah Press, Salt Lake City.

van Gennep, M.
  1911 *Etudes d'ethnographie Algerienne: révue d'ethnographie et de sociologie*. E. Leroux, Paris.

Velázquez Bosco, R.
  1912 *Medina Azzahra y Alamiriya*. Madrid.

Vossen, R., and W. Ebert
  1986 *Marokkanische töpferei: töpferorte und -zentren eine landesaufnahme (1980)*. Dr. Rudolf Habelt GmbH, Bonn.

Zozoya, J.
  1969 Red-Painted and Glazed Pottery in Western Europe: Spain. *Medieval Archaeology* 13:133-136.
  1980 Essai de chronologie pour certain types de céramique califate andalouse. In *La céramique médiévale en Méditerranée occidentale: Xe-XVe siècles*, edited by G. Demains d'Archimbaud and M. Picon, pp. 311-315. Editions du Centre Nationale de la Recherche Scientifique, Paris.

Chapter 6

VIEW FROM THE ROOF TOPS:
CLAY TILES AND ROOF CONSTRUCTION AT AL-BASRA

Lance Lundquist
Nancy L. Benco

Clay roof tiles, rather than potsherds, are the most common artifacts, by weight, found at the large urban site of al-Basra. More than 11,000 kg of tiles, almost four times the weight of pottery, have been recorded. Despite their predominance at many Islamic sites, roof tiles have rarely been described or discussed in the archaeological literature.[1]

In this chapter, we present the results of research on roof tile manufacture, stylistic variation, and use at al-Basra. The data for this study come from roof tiles excavated during the 1995, 1998, and 1999 field seasons[2] in the residential and industrial zones. During fieldwork, all roof tile fragments recovered from below the modern surface were collected, weighed using a 7-kg spring scale to the nearest 0.1 kg, and then discarded. The few whole or nearly whole tiles that were recovered were weighed, measured, and in some cases retained as samples for further study. Of the total 11,222 kg of tiles weighed, 2,944 kg were documented in 1995, 2,717 kg in 1998, and 5,561 kg in 1999.

Roof Tile Shapes and Sizes

The roof tiles at al-Basra are similar in shape and size, but vary in thickness and weight. In general, the roof tiles are curved and trapezoidal in shape, with a wide front end and a narrow back end (Figure 6.1). Their average length is 44 cm, with a range of 43.5 to 44.5 cm. The frontal width averages 22 cm, with a range of 20.5 to 24 cm. The frontal height varies from 6 to 7.5 cm. The back width averages 12.5 cm, with a range of 12 to 13 cm. The back height varies from 3.5 to 5 cm. The narrow range of these dimensions suggests that a standardized tile size was important, possibly because roof tiles were reused over time. The tiles vary, however, in thickness, ranging from at least 1.1 to 1.9 cm, even within the same tile. This variation in thickness affects their weight, which goes from 1.9 to 2.8 kg, with even heavier tiles (up to 3.2 kg) possible. Given the substantial variation in thickness and weight, the other tile dimensions at al-Basra appear remarkably standardized.

Although the excavations and reconstructions of complete roof collapses (see below) indicate that the city's roofs were constructed of two overlapping layers of roof tiles, the tiles used for the top and bottom layers appear to differ only in their placement on the roof.

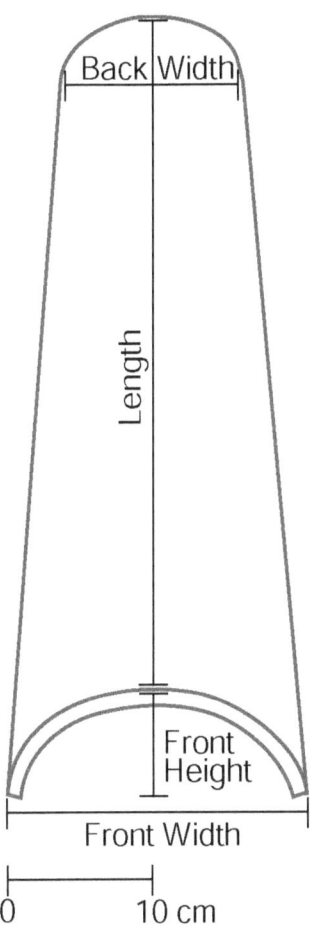

Figure 6.1 Generalized shape and dimensions of a typical roof tile at al-Basra.

Roof Tile Manufacture

Information about the manufacture of roof tiles at al-Basra comes from an analysis of the tiles themselves and from the excavation of an updraft kiln.

---

[1] Cressier et al. 1998:329 and Mohamedi et al. 1991 are notable Islamic exceptions. Roof tiles have been treated in depth in other regions and for other time periods (e.g., see Schneider 1991; Wikander 1988).
[2] Roof tiles were not collected or weighed during the first two field seasons in 1990 and 1994.

Figure 6.2 Three nearly complete roof tiles found in the F3 kiln at al-Basra. They belong to Type A.

Selection of Raw Materials

The tiles were produced from a calcareous clay that contained various mineral inclusions, including calcite, hematite, sand, and grit (Benco n.d.). A form of vegetal matter, such as chaff or straw, was added to the mixture, as evidenced by the presence of elongated voids on the tile surfaces and cores. The tiles range in color from yellowish pink to pale olive white and deep rose.

The tiles were almost certainly made from local materials and fired in or near the urban center. Their abundance, large size, bulky weight, and relatively low rooftop visibility would have made it highly desirable to acquire raw materials and produce the tiles in or near the center. In addition, the tiles have a chemical composition that is similar to that of local clays, as well as of some al-Basra pottery.[1] The presence of abundant overfired tile fragments (tile wasters) in debris associated with an updraft kiln (F3) in the city's industrial zone confirms that at least some of the tiles were fired in the urban center.

Forming Roof Tiles

The standardized width and length of the al-Basra tiles strongly indicate that they were fashioned in a mold. It is possible that the mold was simply the upper (convex) surface of another roof tile. The tile mold would have been sprinkled with a separating agent, such as straw or sand. A lump of clay would have been spread on top of the convex mold and then smoothed down along its surfaces and edges with a tool or the tile maker's hand. Alternatively, the mold may have been a flat wooden frame, with the dimensions of either a single tile or a flat rectangular sheet, placed on the ground (Schneider 1991:199). If the mold were in a sheet form, the clay would have had to be cut into trapezoidal forms before continuing; either way, the end product would have involved a transfer to a semi-round mold for drying.

After they were formed, some tiles were decorated by drawing a tool, or fingers, through the wet clay to create parallel or zigzag lines. Tiles would have been allowed to dry on the mold, probably lying on or near the ground. One tile fragment recovered from al-Basra contained the print of a dog paw on its surface, suggesting that a dog had stepped on it while it was still drying. After drying, tiles would have been lifted from their convex molds. This action would have been facilitated by the presence of the separating agent, which left a roughened surface on the concave side of the newly formed tile.

Firing Roof Tiles

After drying, the tiles were placed in a kiln for firing. Normal firing temperatures ranged between 750 to 1000°C, as the presence of calcium spalling on many tile surfaces suggests (Rye 1981:33). Two complete and four broken roof tiles were found nestled together and resting in a rectangular-shaped updraft kiln (F3) in al-Basra's industrial zone (Figure 6.2). These partially blackened tiles had baked but had subsequently fallen into the fire box when the floor collapsed.

---

[1] Chemical analyses (atomic absorption spectroscopy) of tile fragments indicate that their chemical composition is similar to that of the locally made al-Basra pottery (Benco n.d.).

A substantial number of tiles could have been fired at one time. The F3 kiln, which measured 3.5 m by 4 m in size, would have provided about 14 m² of surface area. This would have allowed about 150 average-sized al-Basra tiles to be placed side-by-side on the kiln floor, with many more if they were stacked on top of each other. Assuming a minimum tile weight of 2 kg, the weight load for a single layer of tiles would have been at least 300 kg, and up to 600 kg for a double layer and 900 kg for a triple layer. This potential weight load helps to explain the size of the four large, vaulted arches below the kiln floor. These sturdy arches were 55 cm thick and ran across the 3.5 m width of the kiln floor (Benco 2002).

Stratigraphically, the F3 kiln was located in the lowest levels of the site (Benco 2002; this volume). Chronometrically, the kiln dates to the pre-Idrisid period. A radiocarbon assay (Beta-39976) of wood charcoal from the kiln debris yielded a radiocarbon age of 1380 ± 80 B.P., which calibrates to A.D. 540-790 at a 95 percent (2 sigma) probability. This range falls into the period just prior to the historically documented founding of al-Basra by the Idrisid dynasty in A.D. 800. Additional support for an early date for the F3 kiln comes from an archaeomagnetic study (Rimi et al., this volume).

Stylistic Variability of Roof Tiles

During the 1998 field season, a pilot study was conducted to define and record the different styles of roof tiles at al-Basra. A bag of about 5 kg of randomly selected large tile fragments was collected from each provenience unit. These tiles were washed in water, cleaned with a brush, and allowed to dry. The study defined five main tile types, which are labeled as Types A, B, C, D, and E (Figure 6.3).

Tile Types

Type A is characterized by long, parallel grooves that run the length of the tile. The grooves are 1 cm to 1.5 cm

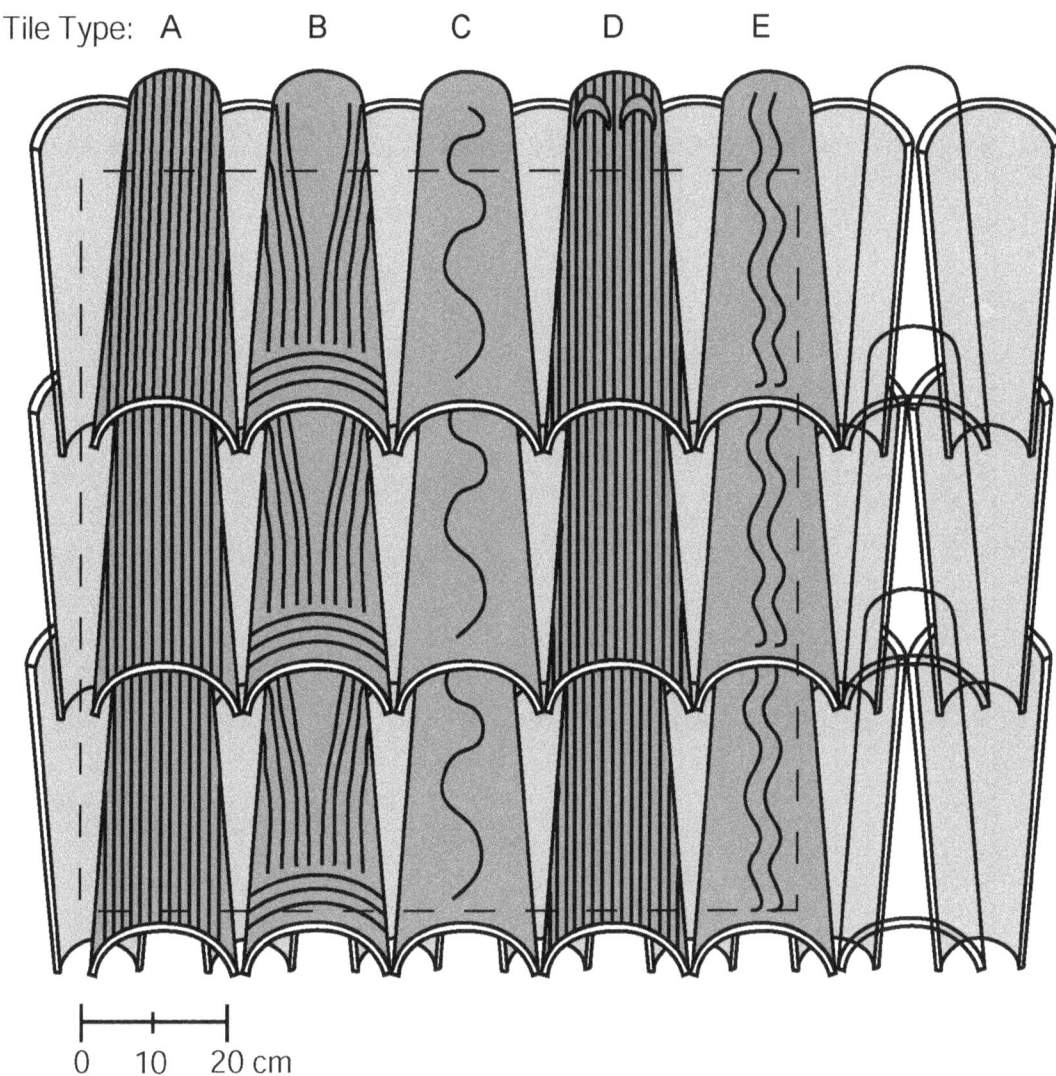

Figure 6.3 Schematic drawing of a tiled roof, illustrating five typical al-Basra tile types (A, B, C, D, and E). Cutaway (on right) shows the probable method of layering top and bottom tiles. Dashed lines represent 1 m² area. Drawing is based on data collected from excavation unit G4S10E0 roof collapse.

apart and are 1.4 cm to 2 cm wide. Along the sides the grooves have been smoothed as much as 3 cm wide on each side. Type A tiles are relatively common at al-Basra. They were found in both the residential (G) and industrial (F) zones. Type A tiles were found in the collapsed debris of the F3 kiln, suggesting they had been fired there (Figure 6.2). Type A tiles appear more frequently in the earlier and middle phases at al-Basra, but more sampling is needed to verify this pattern.

Type B is distinguished by two sets of grooves on the top surface of the tile. One set consists of one to three parallel grooves that run perpendicular to the length the tile; these grooves are located at the front, or broader, end of the tile. The other set consists of four parallel grooves that start from the perpendicular lines and run toward the back of the tile. The narrow back end remains undecorated, suggesting that the decoration was meant to be seen. Type B tiles are also fairly common. They were found only in the residential (G) area and were primarily associated with a large flagstone-paved courtyard. Type B tiles are more frequent in the later periods at al-Basra but, like Type A, there are exceptions and more data are required to resolve the issue.

Type C is relatively rare. This type is characterized by a single S-shaped curve on the top surface. The curve was made by dragging a finger through the soft clay. Type C tiles were found in the residential (G) zone but are best represented in the upper levels of the industrial (F) zone.

Type D is represented by a single tile. Similar to Type A, it has horizontal grooves running lengthwise along the tile. On the narrow end are two deeply incised, curved semicircles that look like half moons. The purpose of these semicircles is unknown. They would have been covered by an overlapping tile and thus not visible on the roof. They may have served to stabilize the tile in some way, or may have been a maker's mark. This tile was found in an upper level of the residential (G) area.

Type E is also rare at al-Basra. It is characterized by two parallel wavy lines (finger drag marks) that run the length of the tile and is somewhat similar to Type C. Tiles with this simple design have been found in the southwestern Iberian Peninsula (James Boone, personal communication 2000). In the Iberian examples, the lines terminate before reaching the narrow back end of the tile, suggesting that the marks were intended to be seen. In the al-Basra cases, the tiles were fragmentary and the length of the lines could not be determined. Samples were recovered from the middle levels of the residential (G) zone.

In summary, the 1998 pilot study shows that, although the vast majority of al-Basra roof tiles are plain and undecorated, a small number (less than 5 percent) feature simple motifs that may be sensitive indicators of time and function. The most common, Type A, is generally found in the lower and middle levels of the site, including the early period updraft kiln (F3). They are present in both the industrial and residential areas. The second most common, Type B, tends to occur in the upper levels of the residential area. Type C tiles are most common in the upper levels of the industrial zone. Tile types D and E are found in the residential zone, with Type D associated with an upper level and Type E with a middle level. In addition, the study shows that Types A and C tend to be concentrated in the industrial area while Types A, B, D, and E occur in the residential zone, hinting at the possibility of spatial or functional differentiation in tile types.

Reasons for Tile Decoration

Why were some of the roof tiles decorated? Two possibilities seem likely: Either the decoration served as a maker's mark or it was meant to enhance the appearance of a roof. Because the decorative motifs were largely placed on portions of the tile that would have been visible (i.e., the wider front portion rather than the narrower back portion) and because relatively few tiles were treated in this way, it seems more likely that the motifs served a decorative purpose. Type B tiles support this hypothesis. Their motifs are located near the wider front end and along the body, but terminate before reaching the narrower back end, which was probably covered by another tile. They are mainly found in conjunction with a building complex (G4-G5) that is centered around a well-built flagstone pavement in the residential area. This is likely a high-status complex and the use of new (rather than reused) and decorated tiles would have given it even more distinction.

Studies of roof tiles elsewhere suggest that some tile designs are temporally sensitive indicators. In the Iberian Peninsula, Boone (personal communication 2000) has established a rough chronological sequence of roof tile motifs for the Late Roman, Islamic, and Christian periods. A particular finger-made zigzag design occurs on Roman imbrex tiles. The same design is present on tiles from the Islamic period, but it disappears abruptly in the mid-thirteenth century at the beginning of the Christian medieval period. Islamic tiles are also occasionally impressed with Arabic words or phrases. This sequence indicates continuity in tile production between the Late Roman and Islamic periods. It also has allowed Boone to use roof tile designs to assign sites to specific periods (e.g., Late Roman, Islamic, and Christian) in the Iberian Peninsula.

Roof Construction Techniques

The tile study has also allowed us to reconstruct the roof construction techniques that were commonly used in the buildings at al-Basra. This reconstruction was based on data collected from several in situ roof collapses excavated at the site (Table 6.1).

Table 6.1. Counts and Weights of Roof Tiles and Pottery from Ten Roof Collapses at al-Basra

Excavation unit	Area (m^2)	Tile weight (kg)	Ave. tile weight (kg)	Estimated number of tiles	Estimated number of tiles/m^2	Pottery weight (kg)	Occupation phase
G4S10E0	5.60	344.4	2.2	156.5	27.9	2.30	2B/2A
G4S23W6/10	1.95	158.0	2.8	56.4	28.9	2.44	2B
G4S23W6/4	3.00	188.0	2.2	85.5	28.5	8.12	2B/2A
G4S9W25/ G4S4W28	26.75	1490.6	2.2	677.5	25.3	2.78	2B/2A
G4N5W20	10.00	369.8	2.2	168.1	16.8	11.57	2B
G4S4W28	14.00	314.0	2.2	142.7	10.2	12.86	2B/2A
G5S	16.00	306.0	2.2	139.1	8.7	80.80	3B
G4S23W6/1	17.50	321.0	2.2	145.9	8.3	8.37	2B
G4N	16.00	221.2	2.2	100.5	6.3	30.19	2B
G4SE	11.00	149.0	2.2	67.7	6.2	12.40	2B

Identifying In Situ Roof Collapses

For the most part, roof collapses could be easily identified during excavation. They consisted of a thick layer (up to 50 cm or more) of densely packed roof tile fragments, which tended to be fairly large in size. The roof tiles were embedded in a reddish-colored clay (pisé), which had once formed part of the roof as well as the upper part of the building's walls. Scattered throughout the red clay were small fragments of charred wood, which represented the remains of wooden beams that had supported the roof. In a few cases, relatively large fragments (up to 5 cm long) of the beams were preserved. The red clay also contained high quantities of iron nails, which were used to hold the beams together. The densely packed tiles and clay rested directly on top of an occupation surface, which usually consisted of packed earth but, in some cases, of a well-constructed pebble or flagstone floor.

The collapse of buildings as a result of fire appeared to be a citywide event at the end of the middle occupation period (Phase 2). Roof collapses with charred wood fragments appeared in nearly every excavation unit dug at the site. The widespread collapse seems to have occurred after most residents had abandoned their homes. Little, if any, cultural material was found between the fallen roof debris and the occupation surface, suggesting that the rooms had been vacated before the building collapsed. In only a few cases were nearly intact pottery vessels or a thin lens of sand found between the roof debris and floor. The blaze that destroyed the buildings must have consumed them quickly. In one roof collapse, excavators recovered the complete skeleton of a domestic cat (*Felis*), which evidently had been trapped on the hot tile roof.

This widespread collapse of the city likely took place at the end of the Idrisid period (Phase 2) in the late tenth century. Historical documents indicate the city was destroyed in ca. A.D. 979-980 during a conflict between the Ummayids of Spain and the Fatimids of Ifriqiya (Tunisia) for control of northern Morocco. Radiocarbon assays of charred wood from debris associated with the building collapses have produced dates mostly from the tenth century.

Analyzing Roof Collapses

The method used to examine the roof collapses and reconstruct the typical roof style used at al-Basra involved: (1) carefully observing the horizontal and vertical position of roof tiles during excavation, (2) calculating the surface area covered by the tile collapse, (3) determining the weight of tile fragments removed from the area, and (4) using the dimensions of actual or typical al-Basra tiles. The typical tile had an average length of 44 cm, an average frontal width of 20.5 cm, an average surface area of roughly 902 cm^2, and an average weight of 2.2 kg. Given these dimensions and assuming the tiles were laid side by side (edge to edge), one would need 11.09 tiles to cover a flat roofed area of 1 m^2 (10,000 cm^2 /902 cm^2 = 11.09 tiles).

Placement of Tiles on Roof

The tiles were likely placed in an overlapping fashion on a slightly sloped roof (Figure 6.3). Based on data obtained from several well-documented roof collapses (Table 6.1), the tiles appear to have overlapped one another by about 20 percent. For example, in Unit G4S10E0, the roof collapse consisted of a double layer of densely packed tiles in red clay. A total of 344.4 kg of tiles, the equivalent of 156.5 complete tiles (344.4 kg /2 kg = 156.5), were removed from an area of 5.6 m². This represents an average of 27.9 tiles per m² for a double layer, or 13.98 tiles per m² in each layer (156.5/5.6 = 27.9 tiles; 27.9/2 = 13.98 tiles). If 11.09 tiles could be laid side by side within 1 m², then 13.98 tiles would have required a 20.7 percent overlap (11.09/13.98 = 79.3 percent exposed, 20.7 covered). Figure 6.3 shows a schematic drawing of a tiled roof with a 20 percent tile overlap. The area inside the dashed lines represents 1 m², with 28 roof tiles lying in two layers.

Three other examples of undisturbed roof collapses were recorded at al-Basra (Table 6.1). In Unit G4S23W6, locus 10, 158 kg of roof tiles were recovered from a 1.95 m² area (it was only partially exposed). Using the measurements of a complete tile (weight 2.8 kg, length 44.5 cm, and frontal width 24 cm) found in the debris, the roof fall would represent an estimated 28.9 tiles per m², nearly identical to that above. The tiles rested on a 20 cm layer of red clay containing iron nails and the whole collapse lay on top of a plastered floor.

Just a few meters south in the same excavation unit, G4S23W6, locus 4, a total of 188 kg of tiles was removed from a 3 m² area. Based on a typical tile weight (2.2 kg), this collapsed roof would also have consisted of about 28 tiles per m², representing a 20 percent overlap. This collapse lay directly above an earthen surface with an intact ceramic vessel still lying on it.

By far the largest collapse, which extended across two contiguous excavation units (G4S9W25 and G4S4W28), yielded a remarkable 1,490.6 kg of tiles from a 26.75 m² area. Using an average tile weight (2.2 kg), this collapsed roof would have consisted of 25.3 tiles per m², just slightly less than the others. Below this tile collapse was a layer of red clay containing iron nail fragments and charred wood, all of which rested on top of a pebbled courtyard floor.

Six other heavy roof collapses that were analyzed, however, differed from these four in several important ways (Table 6.1). They had much lower tile densities, ranging from 6.2 to 16.8 tiles per m², and were associated with much higher quantities of pottery, strongly suggesting that they were disturbed as a result of post-depositional activities. It is possible that some roof tiles had been removed from these collapses, perhaps for reuse in construction, and that broken pottery had been subsequently dumped into these areas.

The al-Basra tiles were most likely arranged in two overlapping layers on the roof top. As the tile cutaway on the right side of Figure 6.3 shows, tiles in the bottom layer were placed topside down on the roof with their narrower ends facing toward the upper part of the slope. The tiles on the top layer were placed above these, with their topside up and their broader ends facing toward the lower part of the slope. In other words, the bottom tiles were rotated 180° in relation to the top tiles. This technique would have "locked" a top tile into two bottom tiles, based on the "V" shape of the two bottom tiles. This arrangement would have provided good rain drainage as well as have secured the top layer of tiles to the roof.

Use of Wood Beam Supports

The tile roofs at al-Basra were probably supported by wooden beams that were laid across the narrow width of each room. The rooms were relatively long (ca. 9 m) but had a narrow width (ca. 2.5 m). The widths of rooms may have been restricted in size by the length of wooden beams that could be cut from trees growing in the region.[1] The poles were nailed or lashed together. A layer of clay and mortar may have been placed between and over the wood poles, as is the custom today in Morocco. The clay-mortar mixture would have helped to secure the curved tiles to the roof.[2] This roof construction method is supported by the archaeological evidence. Most of the in situ roof collapses at al-Basra had up to 20 cm of red clay located below the fallen tiles. This material likely came from the collapsed roof, although some of it may have derived from the upper part of the walls. In any case, the use of a clay-mortar lining on the roof would have helped to insulate the building during the cool rainy winters and hot dry summers.

Pitch of Roofs

The al-Basra roofs appear to have been sloped toward one side rather than flat or gabled. Some slope would be needed to allow water to drain down the tiles. While a flat roof with a 20 percent tile overlap (Figure 6.3) uses about 28 tiles per m², a sloped roof requires more tiles, depending on the angle. Figure 6.4 shows the number of tiles needed for a range of roof slopes, from a 5 to 28° angle, calculated for a building excavated in Unit G4S10E0. A slope of less than 5° would not provide adequate drainage, while a slope of more than 28° would require more tiles than were present in the roof collapse. A minimally sloped roof with a 10° angle and a 20 percent tile overlap, for example, would require slightly

---

[1] A study of the ethnobotanical remains from al-Basra (Mahoney 1994) showed the presence of holly oak (*Quercus ilex*) and/or cork oak (*Quercus suber*) along with *Phillyrea* and *Cistus*, both of which form part of the palmetto scrub vegetation in northern Morocco. These trees and bushes are typically not tall.

[2] The use of a simple mortar-and-clay layer to secure tiles with no nail holes has also been suggested for roof construction during the Early Helladic and Mycenaean periods in the Mediterranean (Wikander 1988:208).

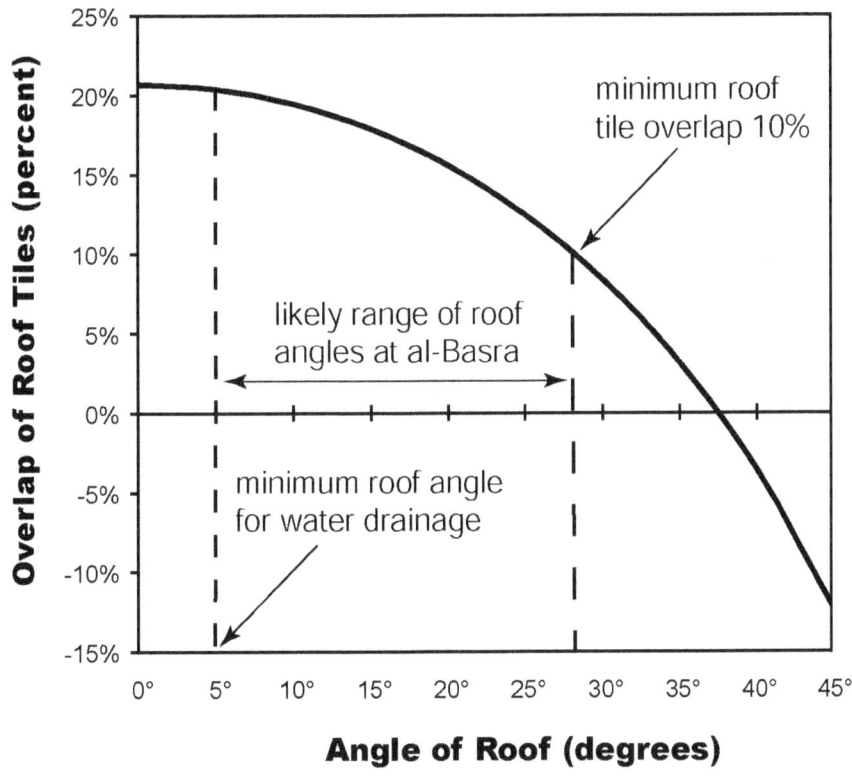

Figure 6.4 Roof slopes (in degrees) and tile requirements, derived from excavation unit G4S10E0 roof collapse.

more than 28 tiles per m², which is close to the al-Basra average. A 45° roof slope with the same overlap would require almost 40 tiles per m², well above the amount associated with any structure at al-Basra. A reconstructed Islamic house from Setif (Mohamedi et al. 1991, cover picture) shows a pitched roof (around 14°) slopeddownward toward an open inner courtyard. Although the tiles at al-Basra are curved rather than flat (as they are at Setif), it is likely that the roofs at al-Basra were structurally similar (Boone and Benco 1999:59).

Conclusions

Although ceramic roof tiles are an often-ignored category of material culture at most archaeological sites, they represent a potentially rich source of information. Variations in tile shape, size, and paste composition can be used to reconstruct manufacturing techniques, while different decorative treatments can provide good temporal markers. Finally, the archaeological context can be used to understand how tiled roofs were constructed and ultimately collapsed.

References Cited

Benco, N. L.
1987 *The Early Medieval Pottery Industry at al-Basra, Morocco*. BAR International Series 341. British Archaeological Reports, Oxford.

2002 1990 Archeological Investigations at al-Basra, Morocco. *Bulletin d'archéologie marocaine* 19:293-340.

n.d. Chemical and Mineralogical Analyses of Early Islamic Pottery from al-Basra. Ms. on file, Department of Anthropology, George Washington University, Washington, D.C.

Boone, J. L., and N. L. Benco
1999 Islamic Settlement in North Africa and the Iberian Peninsula. *Annual Review of Anthropology* 28:51-71.

Cressier, P, A. El Boudjay, H. El Figuigui, J. Vignet-Zunz
1998 Hajar al-Nasr, 'capitale' idrisside du Maroc septentrional: archéologie et histoire (IVe H./Xe ap. J.-C.). In *Genèse de la ville islamique en al-Andalus et au Maghreb occidental*, edited by P. Cressier and M. García-Arenal, pp. 305-334. Casa de Velázquez, Madrid.

Mohamedi, A., A. Benmansour, A. Amamra, and E. Fentress
1991 *Fouilles de Sétif (1977-1984)*. Agence Nationale d'Archéologie et de Protection des Sites et Monuments Historiques, Algiers.

Mahoney, N.
1994 Economy and Environment at al-Basra: An

Archaeobotanical Analysis of a Medieval Islamic Urban Center. M.A. Thesis, Department of Anthropology, George Washington University, Washington, D.C.

Rye, O.
  1981 *Pottery Technology: Principles and Reconstruction*. Taraxacum, Washington, D.C.

Schneider, P.
  1991 Zur Herstellung eines archaischen Tondaches. In *Bautechnik der Antike*, edited by A. Hoffmann, pp. 197-207. Zabern, Mainz.

Wikander, Ö
  1988 Ancient Roof-Tiles–Use and Function. *Opuscula Atheniensia* 17:15, 203-216.

Ideological Perspectives

Chapter 7

SPEAKING STONES: ISLAMIC BURIAL PRACTICES AT AL-BASRA

Rachel Kluender

Islam constitutes a religious culture in the fullest sense (Arnaldez 1999:94), permeating every aspect of a believer's life from birth to death. In this chapter, I explore how Islamic beliefs about death are made tangible in the archaeological record. My study focuses on one of two ancient cemeteries located outside the city walls of al-Basra in northern Morocco. It draws on documentary and ethnohistorical information about Islamic mortuary traditions along with the city's own history to describe the cemetery's construction, layout, use, and meaning during medieval Islamic times.

According to the eleventh-century geographer Abu-'Ubayd al-Bakri, the city of al-Basra had two cemeteries at the time that he wrote: "The principal cemetery is on a hill to the east of the city; the western cemetery is named *Macbera Codaa*" (al-Bakri 1965:216). The remains of the cemetery analyzed for this study are believed to be those of al-Bakri's western cemetery, although its precise dating has not yet been confirmed.

The ancient cemetery occupies the top of a ridge overlooking the broad Mda River valley. It is located about 200 m northwest of the city's enclosing wall (Figures 7.1-7.2) and covers an area of about 5,500 m². Despite the recent installation of an electrical transformer tower, which disturbed the graves in the southeastern part of the cemetery, most of the cemetery's stone features remain relatively well preserved.

Methodology

The cemetery was mapped during the 1999 field season at al-Basra. Of a total of 108 stone features recorded, 103 were graves and five were possible structures (Figure 7.3). Although other graves and/or structures are visible, only stone features for which at least one dimension (either length or width) could be accurately determined were mapped. Documentation of the graves consisted of recording each grave's dimensions, orientation, shape, type(s) of stones used in construction, presence/absence of marker stones, and any unusual characteristics of the feature. These features represent a non-random sample of an estimated 60 to 80 percent of the total number of graves present. The small size of the cemetery in relation to al-Basra's substantial population of about 10,000 (Redman 1983:365) may be explained by the townspeople's use of multiple cemeteries.

Cemetery Location

In accordance with Islamic tradition, which prescribes human burial outside the city walls (Brown 1991:123-124; Simpson 1995:243), al-Basra's cemetery was located about 200 m northwest of the city's enclosing wall (Figure 7.2). The other known cemetery lies on top of a small hill to the southeast of the city. It is possible that other locations for the disposal of the dead also existed around the urban center. At the medieval city of Fez, which was established at the same time as al-Basra, several cemeteries were known to lie outside the city walls. The Arab historian Leo Africanus (1963:473) noted that in sixteenth-century Fez many fields outside the city had been given by noblemen for the burial of the dead.

At some point in time, individuals were also buried within the city walls of al-Basra. Several Islamic burial clusters have been discovered archaeologically within the ancient walls, but these burials are located stratigraphically in the uppermost levels of the site, suggesting that they were placed within the ruins of al-Basra after the city had been abandoned.[1] A small cluster of Islamic graves was found outside the western wall of the city during the excavation of Unit E2.

Grave Construction

Muslim burial customs typically prescribe that graves are dug between 1 m and 1.5 m deep, depending on the sex (Simpson 1995:242) and the height of the deceased. Ideally, graves should be shallow enough to permit the interrogation of the deceased by the angels (Insoll 1999:169; Simpson 1995:242). According to ethnographer Edward Westermarck (1926:498), a grave should be just deep enough to prevent the release of "obnoxious emanations" and to protect the body from scavengers.

Although none of the graves in al-Basra's western cemetery were excavated, it is likely they were fairly shallow. A human bone was found exposed on the surface of at least one of the graves. In addition, the soil on the

---

[1] A similar pattern has been discovered at the ancient Roman site of Volubilis, where Islamic graves were discovered buried within the ruins of the former Roman city. According to Islamic custom, however, these graves were located outside the enclosure wall of the Islamic settlement (Akerraz 1985).

Figure 7.1 View of a rectangular grave (foreground) in the western cemetery, looking eastward toward al-Basra's city walls.

hill is very rocky and would have been difficult to dig deeply. Further down the hill where five post-urban burials were excavated next to a late-phase stone structure (Unit E2), the burials were located just 13 to 75 cm below the surface.

The graves in the western cemetery were constructed with stones that were placed at or slightly above ground. The fact that the stones are flush with the ground indicates that very little erosion or deposition has occurred since the graves were built and suggests that the surface record is a fairly accurate reflection of the original appearance of the cemetery. It also indicates that the graves were constructed according to the Islamic injunction of *taswiyah al-qubur*, or equalization of tombs with the surrounding ground (Sourdel-Thomine 1978:352; Westermarck 1926:499). This type of construction is explained by Westermarck (1926:459) in his classic ethnography on Morocco: "In order to prevent the earth [on top of the grave] from sliding down, the mound is surrounded with a ring of stones. These stones must be put side by side and none on the top of another." He further notes that this construction method—an oval or elliptical ring of stones—is peculiar to the Maghreb and may be an "ancient Berber custom" (Westermarck 1926:500).

Nearly all of the graves in the western cemetery were constructed exclusively of angular blocky stones or of smooth rounded cobbles. In only a few cases were both types of stone used in the same grave. Of 103 graves, forty-seven were marked with angular stones and forty delineated with rounded cobbles, while four graves were constructed of both angular and rounded stones (Figure 7.4). The construction method for twelve graves could not be determined. This nearly bimodal distribution suggests that different types of stone may have been used to indicate some aspect of the deceased's persona, such as sex, age, or tribal affiliation. During his ethnographic work, Westermarck (1926:500-501) noted the practice of placing stones in different directions to denote the deceased's sex. It is possible that differently sized or shaped stones accomplished the same purpose.

Head and Foot Markers

According to Islamic tradition, ornamentation or decoration of graves is frowned upon (Simpson 1995:247). Insoll (1999:169) notes that, traditionally, the only place that may be commemorated with a marker

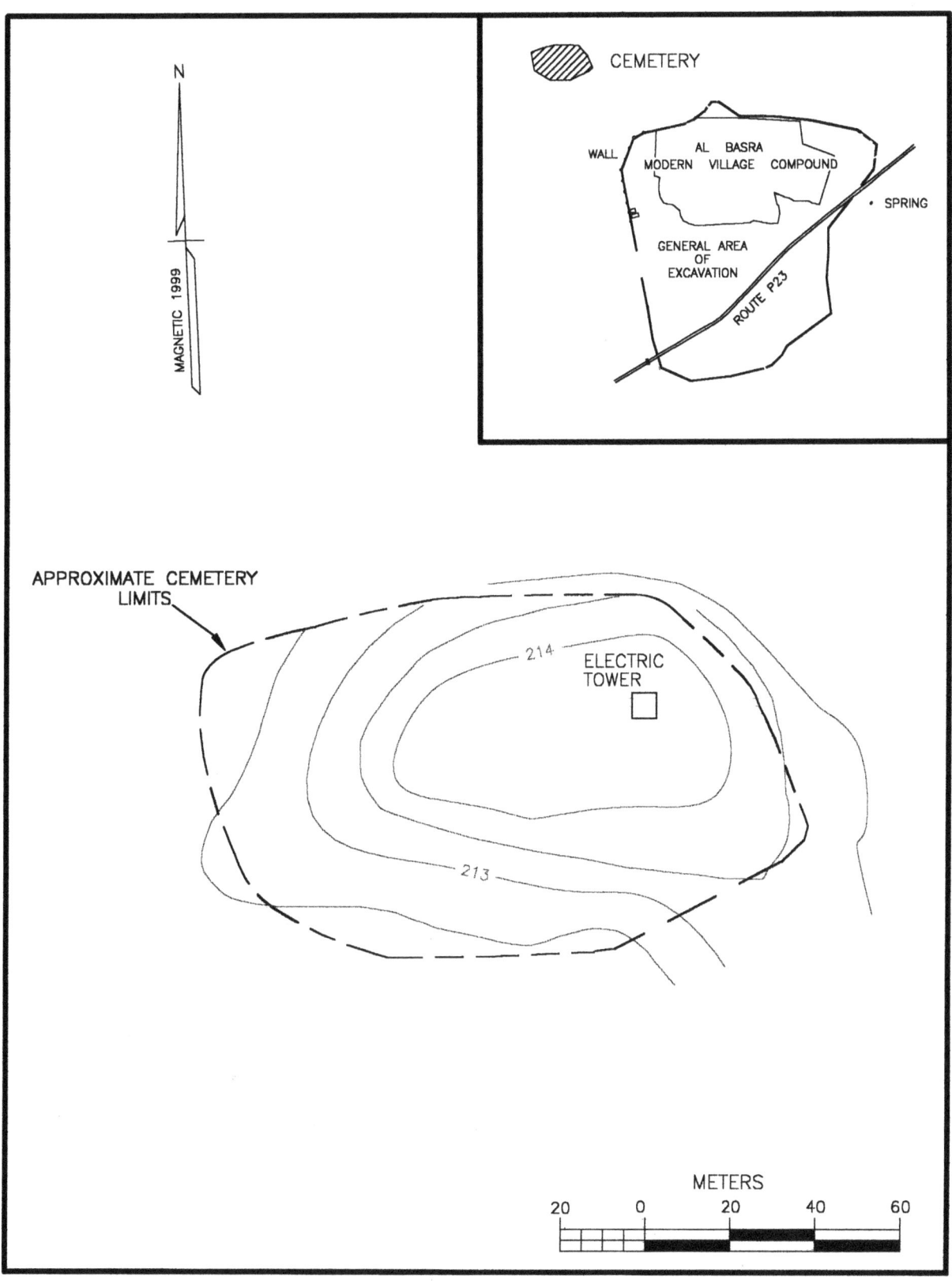

Figure 7.2 Map showing the location of the western cemetery outside al-Basra's city walls.
Map prepared by James E. Franklin.

Anatomy of a Medieval Town

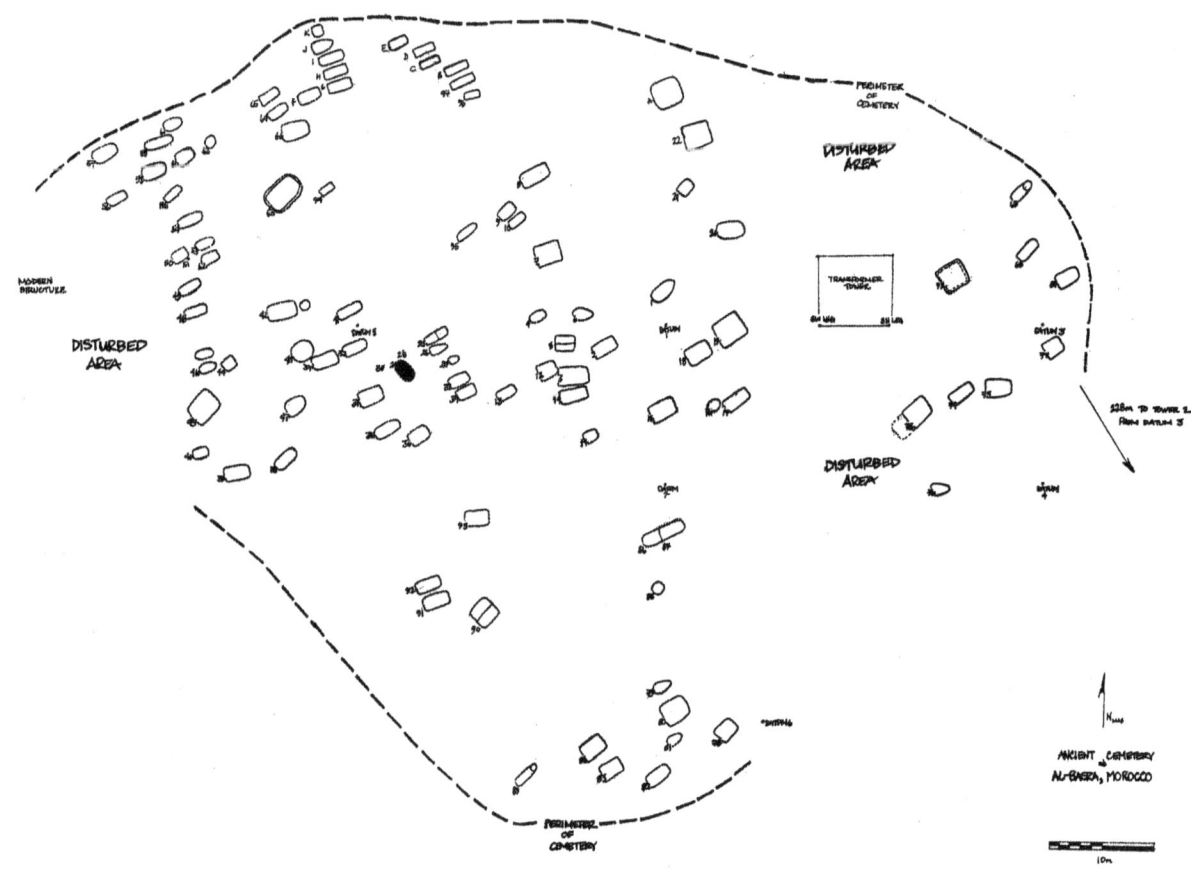

Figure 7.3 Map showing location and orientation of 108 graves and structures in al-Basra's western cemetery. Map prepared by Rachel Kluender.

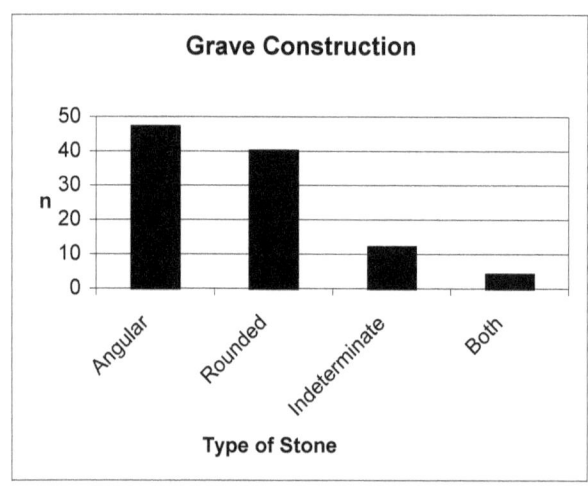

Figure 7.4 Distribution of graves, by shape of construction stone.

stone or piece of wood (*shahid*) is where the head of the deceased is laid. In reality, however, the use of grave markers varies widely, depending on the Islamic legal school or sect followed and the geographic area. According to the sixteenth-century Arab historian Leo Africanus (1963:474), when a nobleman or an important citizen was buried, one stone was laid over his head and another was placed over his feet and one of these might be engraved with an epitaph. Westermarck (1926:460) observed this tradition ethnographically in twentieth-century Morocco: "An upright stone, or sometimes a board, is placed at the head of the grave, and very frequently another one at the foot; such a stone or board, or that at the head only, is called…*l-meshäd* or *š-šâhed*, 'the witness'."

Although the vast majority of graves at al-Basra do not have a head or foot stone, twelve graves (8 percent of the total) have one or the other (eight with a head stone and four with a foot stone) and one grave (1 percent) has both. In all cases, the marker stones are very large angular stones placed upright at either the head or the foot of the grave. These stones are three to four times larger than other stones used in the construction of the grave. None of the head or foot stones contain any evidence of inscriptions. Based on historical and ethnographic observations, it is possible that the presence of head and foot stones on a small proportion of the graves indicates that these few individuals may have possessed some special status during their lifetimes (Leo Africanus 1963:474; Westermarck 1926:501).

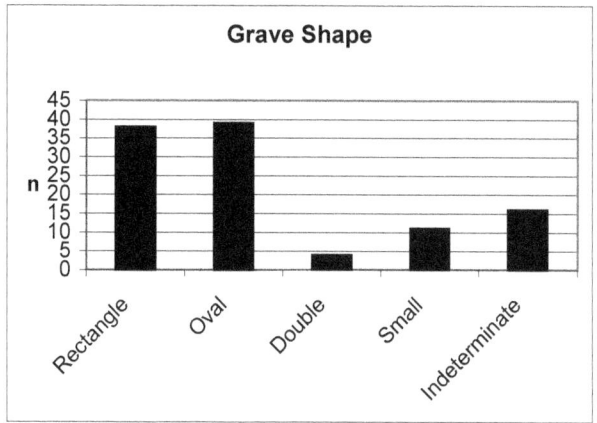

Figure 7.5 Distribution of graves, by general shape.

Table 7.1. Relationship between Grave Shape and Type of Construction Stone

Grave shape	Angular stone (no.)	Rounded stone (no.)	Total no.[1]
Rectangular	23	17	40
Oval	8	17	25
Total	31	34	65

[1] Total includes only those graves for which both shape and stone construction could be determined. Chi-square = 4.01008. Degrees of freedom: 1. p is less than or equal to .05. Distribution is significant.

Grave Shapes

The graves in al-Basra's western cemetery fall into five shape categories: rectangular graves, with corners that are clearly right angles; oval or elliptical graves, with corners that are rounded and sometimes taper to a point at the foot; double graves; small round graves; and graves with an indeterminate shape. Of 103 graves, thirty-eight (35 percent) are rectangular and thirty-nine (36 percent) are oval (Figure 7.5). Four are double graves (4 percent) and eleven (9 percent) are small round graves. The shape of eleven graves could not be determined. There is a statistically significant correlation between the shape of a grave and the shape of the stones used in its construction (Table 7.1). Angular stones were used significantly more often in the construction of rectangular graves than in oval graves, while rounded cobbles were used equally for the two most common grave shapes (note that this analysis excludes double graves, small graves, structures, and all graves for which either shape or construction elements could not be determined).

In other parts of the Islamic world—Jordan (Granqvist 1965), Egypt, and Iran (Simpson 1995:248)—different grave shapes, or construction stones, are used to indicate the gender of the deceased. It is possible, based on the correlation between stone type and grave shape, that these construction methods were used as indications of the gender of the deceased.

Double Graves

The four double graves are large and rectangular in shape, with a very clear line of stones running down the center of the grave. The graves range in size from 1.86 m long and 1.05 m wide to 2.20 m long and 2.43 m wide. In two cases, half of the double grave was constructed of large angular stones and the other half was built of rounded cobbles. In a third case, a rectangular-shaped grave had an oval-shaped grave attached to it. The construction materials used in the fourth double grave could not be determined because of the high number of missing stones. Double graves have not been reported in the English-language literature on Islamic burial traditions. However, residents of the modern village of Jouana-Basra, which is situated on the ancient site, have suggested that double graves may belong to husbands and wives. If true, this explanation would support the hypothesis that grave shape and stone type were employed to denote the deceased's sex.

Small Graves

The eleven small graves at al-Basra are circular or oval, rather than rectangular, in shape. It is likely that these graves belong to infants or children. Five of the small round graves are located adjacent to the foot of a larger grave. These graves may contain infants and their mothers, who may have died during or shortly after childbirth, or they may contain infants who were interred next to one of their parents, regardless of the circumstances of death.

In some Islamic countries, infants and children are buried in separate cemeteries, sometimes located within the walls of the city (see Near Eastern examples in Granqvist 1965:58; others in Simpson 1995:244). In Egypt, neonates may be interred anywhere, but infants more than three days old must be given individual graves unless they died at the same time as an adult, in which case they may share a grave (Fakhry 1950, cited in Simpson 1995:244).

Grave Clusters

Although it is difficult to determine the number of grave clusters in the western cemetery because of surface disturbances, at least one major concentration can be distinguished along the northern perimeter (Figure 7.3). This grave group consists of approximately ten graves. The graves are both physically close to each other, usually with less than half a meter separating them, and uniform in their size and rectangular construction. Precisely what the spatial grouping of graves may represent probably varies. According to some Islamic scholars (Brown 1991:124; Simpson 1995:244), grave clusters represent different lineal groups. They also may reflect different construction periods, i.e., graves built during a short period of time, perhaps by the same group, possibly indicating the loss of a number of people due to disease or warfare.

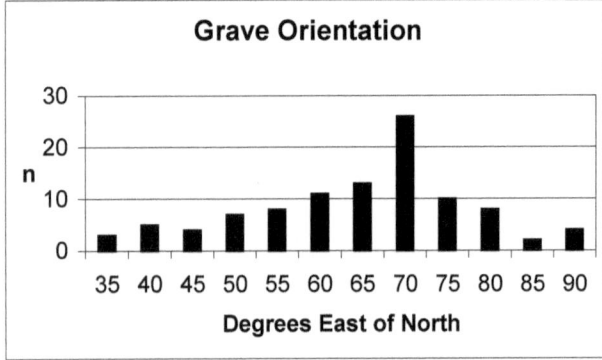

Figure 7.6 Distribution of graves, by their compass orientation.

Cemetery Structures

The western cemetery at al-Basra has at least five large stone alignments that appear to be actual structures rather than graves. Four of these are square or rectangular in shape and one is circular. These structures are much larger in size—up to 3 or 4 m across—than the graves. In two cases, the walls are two stones wide. The structures contain enough stone rubble to suggest that they stood several courses above ground level. They appear in every respect to be contemporaneous with the graves.

Although their precise purpose is unknown, several possibilities exist. They may have served as above-ground tombs, a use that would be difficult to demonstrate without the presence of human remains. They may have been used for commemoration, veneration, and/or prayer (Brown 1991:124; Insoll 1996:22-23, 24). In North Africa, it is common for people to visit and pray in cemeteries (Brown 1991:124; LeTourneau 1961:68; Westermarck 1926:479-483, 511; also Sakr 1995:83 in general); even fairly crude or symbolic structures like those at al-Basra could have served to localize such activities.

Grave Orientation

Islamic burial customs require that the deceased be buried "with the head in the direction of the *qiblah*, so that it lies on its right side with the face towards Mecca. . ." (Insoll 1999:168-69; also Sakr 1995:77; Simpson 1995:241, 245; Westermarck 1926:458, 497). With one exception, the graves in al-Basra's western cemetery follow this precept.

Although the al-Basra cemetery was not excavated, it is possible to determine the position of the buried individuals by the general orientation of the graves. As Figure 7.6 shows, most of the graves are aligned at about 70°, with the head-to-foot alignment at 250°-to-70° azimuth (reading from north).[1] If individuals were buried on their right side with their heads facing Mecca, as Muslim custom dictates, they would face a direction that was at a 90° angle to their head-to-foot orientation; this direction would be 160° azimuth (Figure 7.7). It is important to note that the actual direction toward Mecca in northern Morocco is 97° azimuth.[2]

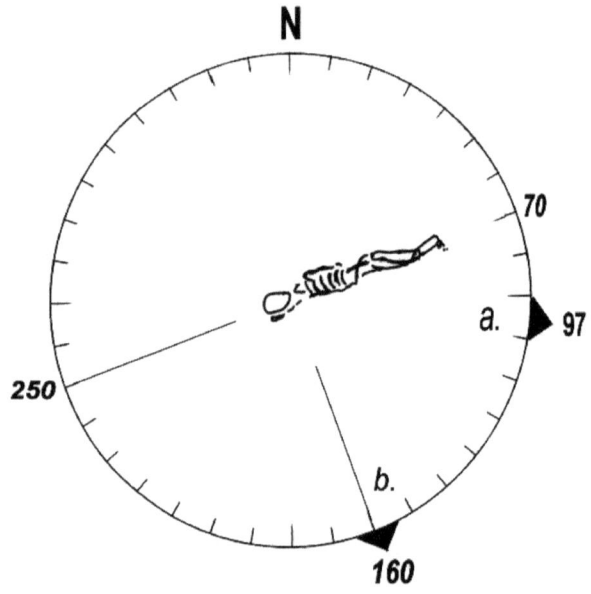

Figure 7.7 Orientation of (b) a typical al-Basra grave (facing 160° azimuth) compared (a) with actual *qibla* direction in northern Morocco (97° azimuth).

There is one exception—a grave that is aligned almost due north-south (see Figure 7.3, black grave) but that, in other respects, appears to be contemporary with the rest of the cemetery. In Islam, graves may be oriented differently due to circumstances of death, such as suicide, or to characteristics of the individual—for example, one might expect separate treatment for thieves or adulterers (Simpson 1995:243, 245). Perhaps a more likely

---

[1] The al-Basra grave orientations are based on magnetic north in 1999.
[2] Although the "correct" direction from northern Morocco to Mecca is about 97° azimuth, medieval Moroccan *qibla* orientations vary considerably and through time (Bonine 1990:51-55). For example, the quiblas of the ninth-century, Idrisid-period Qarawiyyin and Andalousian mosques in Fez are oriented at 163° and 151° azimuth, respectively. Although there are no known qibla readings for the eleventh-century Almoravid period, those for the twelfth-century Almohad period range from about 155° to 159° azimuth (Bonine 1990:Table 1). The gazes of the individuals buried in al-Basra's western cemetery (ca. 160° azimuth) thus fall within the range of the prevailing qibla directions for the ninth through the twelfth century in medieval Morocco, despite the fact that they all diverged by 50° to 60° from the actual direction to Mecca.

explanation for the anomalous grave at al-Basra is that it belongs to a non-Muslim. As a regional center of trade and production (Benco 1987:26-27; Boone and Benco 1999; Boone et al. 1990:643; Redman 1983; Ennahid, this volume), al-Basra would have attracted numerous merchants and travelers, some of whom may have been non-believers. If they had died at al-Basra, they may have been buried in the local cemetery, but with their graves oriented in a manner consistent with their own beliefs.

Discussion and Conclusions

The western cemetery at al-Basra exhibits generally strict compliance with traditional Islamic mortuary practices. The location of the cemetery outside the city wall, the forms of the individual graves, their method of construction, orientation towards Mecca, and limited ornamentation in the form of head- and foot-stones all follow the precepts of the Quran and *hadiths*. Even strong, long-standing mortuary traditions are subject to change, however, and the variability visible in this cemetery raises some intriguing questions for future research. The medieval Moroccan observance of Muslim traditions was, like elsewhere in the Islamic world, flexible and locally specific. Westermarck (1926:490) describes Moroccan funeral rites as "largely in agreement with the tenets of Islam; but there are also many customary rites which are not prescribed by the religious law, and some which are actually prohibited by it." Excavation of these graves would undoubtedly expand the archaeological understanding of medieval al-Basra's adherence to Islamic practice, but at the considerable cost of violating the strong Islamic injunctions against grave disturbance.

In a recent book on Islamic archaeology, Insoll has written of Islamic burial ritual that "the treatment of the corpse prior to burial, the procedures for its actual interment, and its position within the grave, are fairly uniform and vary little throughout the Muslim world. . . . It is above ground that ideals and realities diverge" (Insoll 1999:169). Cemetery surface records offer a glimpse of that above-ground sphere of behavior.

References Cited

Abdesselem, M.
　1990　Mawt. *Encyclopaedia of Islam*, New Edition, vol. 6. E. J. Brill, Leiden.

Akerraz, A.
　1985　Note sur l'enceinte tardive de Volubilis. *Histoire et archéologie de l'Afrique du Nord; actes du IIe colloque international réuni dans le cadre du 108e Congrès National des Société Savantes, Grenoble, 5-9 avril 1983*, pp. 429-438. Paris.

Arnaldez, R.
　1999　Religion, Religious Culture, and Culture. In *Religion and Culture in Medieval Islam*, edited by R. G. Hovannisian and G. Sabah, pp. 93-102. Cambridge University Press, Cambridge.

al-Bakri, A. (died ca. A.D. 1094)
　1965　*Description de l'Afrique septentrionale*. Edited and translated by M. de Slane. 3rd edition. Adrien-Maisonneuve, Paris.

Benco, N. L.
　1987　*The Early Medieval Pottery Industry at al-Basra, Morocco*. BAR International Series 341. British Archaeological Reports, Oxford.

Bonine, M. E.
　1990　The Sacred Direction and City Structure: A Preliminary Analysis of the Islamic Cities of Morocco. *Muqarnas* 7:50-72.

Boone, J., and N. L. Benco
　1999　Islamic Settlement in North Africa and the Iberian Peninsula. *Annual Review of Anthropology* 28:51-71.

Boone, J., J. E. Myers, and C. L. Redman
　1990　Archaeological and Historical Approaches to Complex Societies: The Islamic States of Medieval Morocco. *American Anthropologist* 92:630-646.

Brown, K. L.
　1991　Makbara [cemetery]. *Encyclopaedia of Islam*, New Edition, vol. 6. E. J. Brill, Leiden.

Campbell, S., and A. Green (editors)
　1995　*The Archaeology of Death in the Ancient Near East*. Oxbow Monograph 51. Oxbow Books, Oxford.

Granqvist, H.
　1965　*Muslim Death and Burial: Arab Customs and Traditions Studied in a Village in Jordan*. Centraltryckeriet, Helsinki-Helsingfors.

Insoll, T.
　1996　*Islam, Archaeology, and History: Gao Region (Mali) ca. AD 900-1250*. International Series 647. Cambridge Monographs in African Archaeology 39.
　1999　*The Archaeology of Islam*. Blackwell, Oxford.

Leo Africanus (died ca. A.D. 1548)
　1963　*History and Description of Africa and of the Notable Things Therein Contained*. Translated by J. Pory and edited by R. Brown. Burt Franklin, New York.

LeTourneau, R.
　1961　Fez in the Age of the Marinids. Translated by B.

Clement. University of Oklahoma Press, Norman, Oklahoma.

Redman, C. L.
 1983 Comparative Urbanism in the Islamic Far West. *World Archaeology* 14:355-377.

Sakr, A. H.
 1995 *Death and Dying*. Foundation for Islamic Knowledge, Lombard, Illinois.

Simpson, J.
 1995 Death and Burial in the Late Islamic Near East: Some Insights from Archaeology and Ethnography. In *The Archaeology of Death in the Ancient Near East*, edited by S. Campbell and A. Green, pp. 240-252. Oxbow Monograph 51. Oxbow Books, Oxford.

Sourdel-Thomine, J.
 1978 Kabr [tomb]. *Encyclopaedia of Islam*, New Edition, vol. 6. E. J. Brill, Leiden.

Westermarck, E.
 1926 *Ritual and Belief in Morocco*. Macmillan and Co., London.

Chapter 8

URBAN WOMEN IN EARLY ISLAMIC MOROCCO

Hannah Dodd

As a constructed cultural space, [architecture] is a defined context where people undertake particular activities at particular times. People move through its confines and do things at appropriate places. Hence, meaning is realized through social practices. Such contingency allows redefinition of space without necessarily altering its physical properties. (Pearson and Richards 1994:40)

From India to the Maghreb, medieval Islamic cities featured a strikingly similar array of structures within the boundaries of their massive city walls. A mosque was typically located in the center of the city. Marketplaces (*suqs*) were located near the mosque and/or city gates. Bathhouses (*hammams*) were located in association with both the mosque and the residential quarters of the city. Simple house facades lined the maze-like streets of the residential quarters. Comfortable rooms and courtyards were concealed behind their solid doors and screened windows. Industrial areas that produced smoke and fumes were commonly located on the periphery of the city and away from the institutions and houses in the city's core (Hakim 1988; Insoll 1999; Redman 1986).

Archaeologists expect to encounter these structures when excavating medieval Islamic cities. These expectations are based in part on historical accounts written by early Arab chroniclers such as Ibn Khaldun, al-Bakri, and al-Idrisi. These men traveled across most of the Islamic world between the ninth and the fourteenth century documenting the people and places they encountered. Much has also been written on the subject of Islamic urbanism by modern-day historians and anthropologists (Hakim 1988; Hassan 1972; Ismail 1972; Southall 1998; von Grunebaum 1955). These studies have focused on the division of urban space into religious, governmental, commercial, and residential regions and structures.

Abu-Lughod (1987:167-169) argues that a more complete understanding of the Islamic urban environment requires a further subdivision of space into male and female "turf." Among the principal aims of Islamic architecture and urban planning is the prevention of undesired contact between the sexes and the protection of "visual privacy." Islamic laws (*shari'ah*) and traditions establish male and female social spaces, denying the respective sexes access to certain structures and regulating their access and behaviors within others. In effect, these laws and restrictions superimpose gendered social space on the general physical area of the city. Residents navigate the physical space differently, depending on the social rules that apply to their gender.

This chapter explores the manner in which the female inhabitants of al-Basra, a medieval Moroccan city, navigated the physical space of their urban surroundings. Ethnographic and historical accounts concerning the lives and practices of Muslim women will be discussed in order to illustrate the existence and uses of gendered space. This information will then be used, along with direct historical analogy, to build and support a hypothesis that the same gendered use of space is evident in the physical remains that make up the archaeological record of the site (Wylie 1992:27).

Urban Women: Ethnographic and Historical Evidence

Islamic literary and religious texts offer two conflicting characterizations of women. They are portrayed, sometimes simultaneously within the same account, as both maintainers of social stability and instigators of social upheaval (Kruk 1998). As these seemingly contradictory roles coexist within the same texts, they also coexist within the Islamic social milieu. They permeate the expectations and restrictions placed on Muslim females by their communities.

The family is the most important social unit of Islamic society (Bourdieu 1962:97). Women keep the order and safety of their family unit by supporting their husbands, bearing and raising children, and living by and upholding the teachings of the Islamic faith. Women who maintain their families in such a way are seen to be preserving social order and stability (Kruk 1998:103).

The characterization of women as maintainers of social stability can be traced back to the origins of Islam. The *hadith* is a record of the life and practices of the Prophet and his family after whom all Muslims, males and females, are to model their behavior. The wives and daughters of Mohammad are discussed at length in these religious texts. They were not only devoted to their husbands but were also among the earliest and most dedicated converts to Islam. The practices of seclusion and veiling were their exclusive privileges, earned by virtue of their character and place in society (Ahmed 1992:53-55). Because they were beautiful and recognizable public figures, they attracted a great deal of unwanted attention from the community, and from men in particular. Veiling and seclusion protected them from this undesired scrutiny.

Given the recently growing popularity of Islamic fundamentalism and the resulting institution of severe restrictions and penalties against Muslim females, the alternate characterization of woman as the source of social upheaval is the one most commonly discussed in recent media and scholarship (El Guindi 1999; Mernissi 1987). Women are depicted by Islamic society and its literature as highly sexual beings who manipulate their sexuality to distract and seduce men (Kruk 1998; Mernissi 1987:27-34). Men, on the other hand, are represented as far less capable of controlling their sexual appetites. They are, therefore, helpless to resist the sexual advances and temptations of unrelated women. Their judgment is hampered and morals relaxed.

In this light, women are perceived to be the destroyers of families, and thus of social stability. If permitted, they bring about social discord (*fitna*) and a great many moral evils, adultery being the most feared and despised of these. For this reason, women are kept away from the direct gaze of men. Related males must guard their virginity and chastity, for they are matters of family honor (Davis 1983; Insoll 1999; Mernissi 1987).

Gendered Space in Islam

Ethnographic studies, Islamic literature, and religious texts all suggest that Islamic women led lives almost entirely apart from general male society, even when sharing the same physical space (Ahmed 1992; El Guindi 1999; Insoll 1999; Mernissi 1987; Seng 1998). The maintenance of this sexual separation within the confines of a populous city involved the careful and purposeful navigation of the city's social spaces with the appropriate gendered behaviors in mind. This was the case for both male and female inhabitants. Space was conceptually divided into male-dominated and female-dominated contexts. These areas were commonly demarcated by structure walls that divided street from building and room from room. As the sexes crossed boundaries from one context to the other, their behavior changed accordingly.

Individual households, for example, were generally understood as "female-dominated" contexts. Women spent most of their time within the walls of the house. Non-familial males were, therefore, strictly limited in their access to this space. Once permitted to enter, unrelated males were restricted in their movements and behaviors within the house.

By contrast, most contexts outside of the household were considered "male-dominated" space. While women did have considerable access to this space, they were expected to conduct themselves in a very specific manner that again promoted distance and privacy from general male society (Mernissi 1987:97). They commonly veiled themselves, covering most of the body including the face and/or hair. This allowed them to see without being seen (El Guindi 1999). In effect, they transported their privacy with them as they moved through the community.

Muslim women were only permitted to have unveiled and/or unmonitored social contact with male family members, including fathers, fathers-in-law, brothers, husbands, sons, step-sons, and nephews (El Guindi 1999:86). Even veiled females' contact with unrelated men was highly restricted (Davis 1983; Insoll 1999). Any extended social contact with unrelated males had to occur in the presence of a related male. When women encountered unfamiliar males by accident or necessity, they were expected to lower their gaze in order to avoid undesirable and/or suggestive eye contact.

The Home

Ethnographic and historical accounts of Morocco confirm that most women spent the majority of their time overseeing household affairs (Davis 1983). Even within the household, however, female social interactions were restricted. The ideal Islamic house was modeled after the Prophet's house (Insoll 1999:62). Space was divided into different zones of social interaction (Figure 8.1). The front half of the house was called the *salamlik* (Ismail 1972:115). It represented the more public, male-oriented region of the household. Here, the men of the house greeted unrelated males. Relatives or close male friends were permitted to penetrate further into the inner courtyards and guest rooms located in the *salamlik*.

The women of the house spent the bulk of their time working and socializing with female friends in the rear and most private area of the house, the *haramlik* or *haram* (Ismail 1972:115). Often a rear door led directly into this region so that the women and their friends might come and go without passing through the front, semi-public region of the house. In houses that were either too small or too narrow to contain separate male and female courtyards and rooms, the same segregation was accomplished by designating gendered floors or hanging curtains between male and female space. The only men permitted to enter the private regions of the house were members of the immediate family. In many cases, the *haramlik* was the most comfortable and attractive space in the house as it was the region in which both the women and men of the house spent the majority of their time (Ahmed 1992:117).

The privacy of the family within the house was further guarded by architectural features that restricted vision from the street. Entryways were built with a bent axis so that passing or visiting males were denied an accidental or

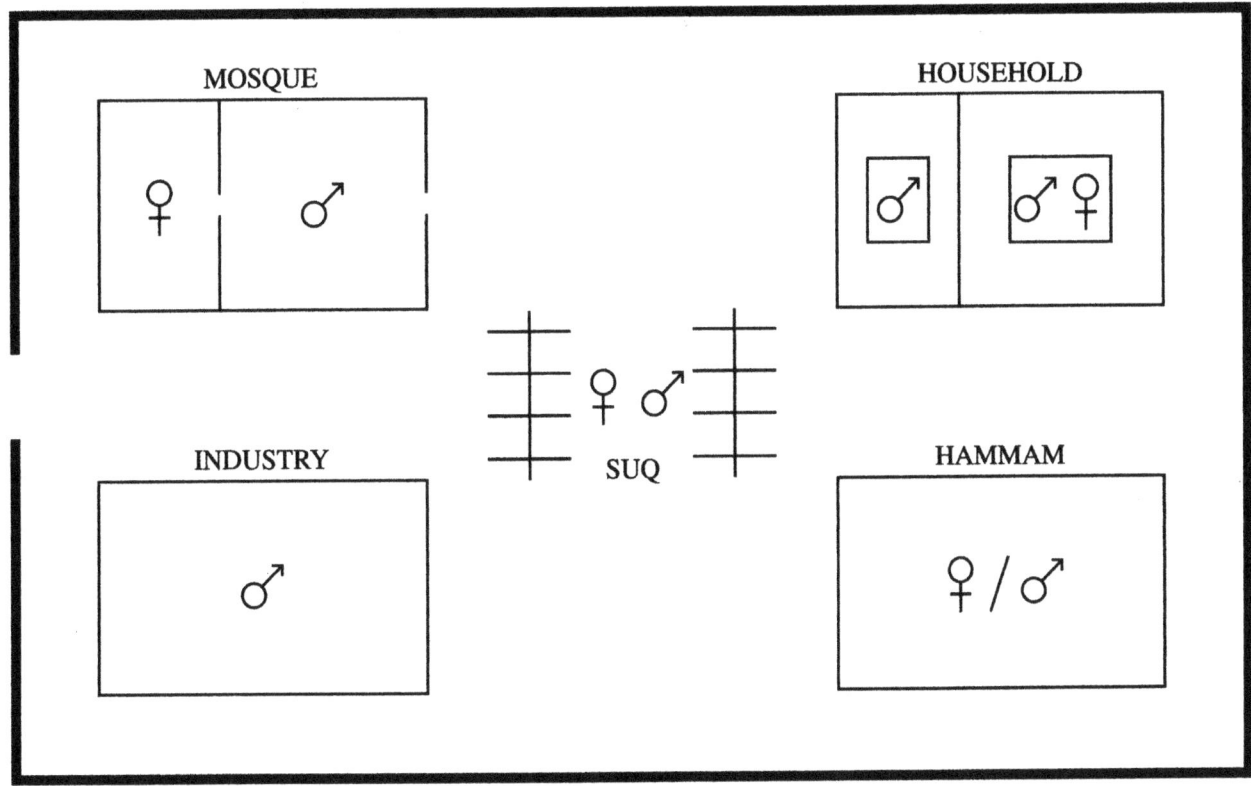

Figure 8.1 Schematic drawing of male and female spaces within a mosque, industry, suq, household, and hammam within an idealized Islamic city.

intentional view of the interior of the house unless invited to enter by a member of the household (Redman 1986). The windows of the house were commonly screened by lattice structures called *mashrabiyyahs* (Abu-Lughod 1987:167; El Guindi 1999:99; Ismail 1972:115). These allowed women to observe the community outside without being viewed by unrelated males on the street. Islamic law also dictated that the windows of facing buildings in an urban context had to be offset from each other so that lines of sight between households might not threaten the privacy of either family (Abu-Lughod 1987:167).

The duties of women within the household varied depending on their social status. The wealthiest women had servants to attend to the household chores and the raising of children (Seng 1998). Because they had help, they never needed to leave the protection of the house unless there was a social function (e.g., wedding, birth, funeral) to attend. Most women, however, were much more active. They were responsible for maintaining the house, cooking the meals, raising the children, and often overseeing the family finances (Bourdieu 1962; Davis 1983). If the family was poor, the women also took up household industries such as textile production or potting.

The Community

A woman's status was commonly measured by her family's ability to provide for her so that she might remain concealed and protected within her house. Some women, however, could not afford to remain at home. Widows, divorcees, and women from impoverished families were often left with no choice but to take jobs to supplement the income of their husbands and/or sons (Davis 1983; Zarinebaf-Shahr 1998:308). Among the more honorable of these were jobs that could be carried out within the house, such as small-scale clothing and handmade pottery production. Bathhouse (*hammam*) attendant was another relatively desirable position for women because the female attendant only worked during the hours set aside for female bathing (Davis 1983:72). The job, therefore, did not require contact with men.

These positions were few, however, and many women were forced to take jobs that led them into closer proximity with men. The physical nature of many of these jobs also necessitated less modesty in dress. Women who took these positions were commonly considered lower class and less honorable. Dancers, field laborers, and prostitutes all belonged to this lowest class of female workers (Davis 1983:75). There is no evidence to suggest, however, that even the poorest of women took work in male-dominated industries such as large-scale metal and wheel-made ceramic production.

While a woman's leaving her home and entering the community to work was discouraged, not all forays beyond the walls of the home were reputation-damaging. Among the urban settings that respectable women were permitted to enter under the proper circumstances were the *mosque*, the *hammam*, and the *suq* (Figure 8.1).

The Mosque

The practice of Islam plays a critical role in the lives of all inhabitants of Islamic cities (Hassan 1972:110; Ismail 1972:117). Muslims are expected to pray five times a day and attend the congregational prayer that occurs every Friday. These types of worship took place in different religious structures within the medieval Islamic city (Insoll 1999:28). The *jami* mosque, the largest and most central, housed the congregational Friday prayer (Hakim 1988:67; Ismail 1972:117). *Masjids*, which were smaller, simpler structures located throughout the city, were used for ablutions and daily prayer by small groups of worshipers (Hakim 1988:74; Insoll 1999:28).

In certain communities, during certain historical periods, women were prohibited from attending the mosque (Hakim 1988:67; Insoll 1999:29). Women who did not, or could not, go to the mosque prayed on prayer mats facing Mecca wherever they happened to be at the designated time (often within their own houses). Most Islamic communities, however, allowed women to attend the mosque. The space within the mosque was divided into male and female areas of worship (Davis 1983:113; Insoll 1999:29). Males prayed at the front of the building and women were positioned either at the back or on a balcony above. In some mosques women were assigned a separate area to perform ablutions (Insoll 1999:57). This arrangement allowed men and women to remain focused on prayer without being distracted by members of the opposite sex. Although the mosque represented a single public religious space, it was spatially divided into two gendered social spaces (Figure 8.1).

The Hammam

Women were also permitted to enter the *hammam*, or community bathhouse, which was found in most Islamic cities because of its critical role in Muslim ritual ablutions (Hakim 1988:88; Ismail 1972:123). The *hammam* functioned as a focal point of Islamic society where both men and women went regularly to bathe, relax, and socialize. While some communities featured separate *hammams* for male and female bathers, most bathhouses were patronized by both men and women. Separate male and female days and hours were scheduled to accommodate both sexes while avoiding undesired contact (Abu-Lughod 1987:168; Hakim 1988:88; Ismail 1972:122). Here, in the presence of exclusively female members of the community, women were able to be completely open. They bathed, received massages, and exchanged gossip, all in a public context (Ahmed 1992:122; Davis 1983:41). The bath was also the site of many ceremonies, including the preparation of a bride before her wedding (Davis 1983:32). The community bathhouse is a good example of a single physical space that was used by both sexes, but at different times (Figure 8.1).

The Suq

The *suq*, or marketplace, was the one urban setting where men and women coexisted without obvious spatial or temporal divisions of social space (Figure 8.1). The *suq* was typically made up of row after row of small stalls facing onto pedestrian streets, both open and covered (Hakim 1988:80; Lane 1954:313). The rows of stalls were organized according to the wares offered. For example, food dealers occupied one row, textile dealers another, and leather dealers another. Although women have been prevented from visiting the *suq*, as well as the mosque, during certain historical periods and in certain places, within most communities they have been allowed to carry out their family shopping (Davis 1983:41). Historical accounts document that clothing, textile, and jewelry stalls were the most popular among female shoppers (Ahmed 1992:118).

Women from high-status households often avoided this foray into the community by sending the men of the house or servants to the *suq* to make the desired purchases. In other cases, they were visited by peddlers who came directly to their homes where they could inspect and buy the goods inside the *haramlik*, with male family members present, or in the area outside of their homes, where neighbors could witness the transaction. Middle and lower-class women who lacked servants often looked forward to the weekly visit to the *suq* because it provided them with a change of scene and the opportunity to socialize (Davis 1983:41). While at the *suq*, women were expected to abide by the rules of modesty but they were allowed to move about relatively freely.

Urban Women at Al-Basra: Archaeological Evidence

Site of al-Basra

The Islamic city of al-Basra was probably built on top of a pre-existing Berber village by the Idrisids around A.D. 800 (Benco 1987:20). It served as a thriving commercial and administrative center until about A.D. 979 when it was destroyed. The Idrisid city boasted a large

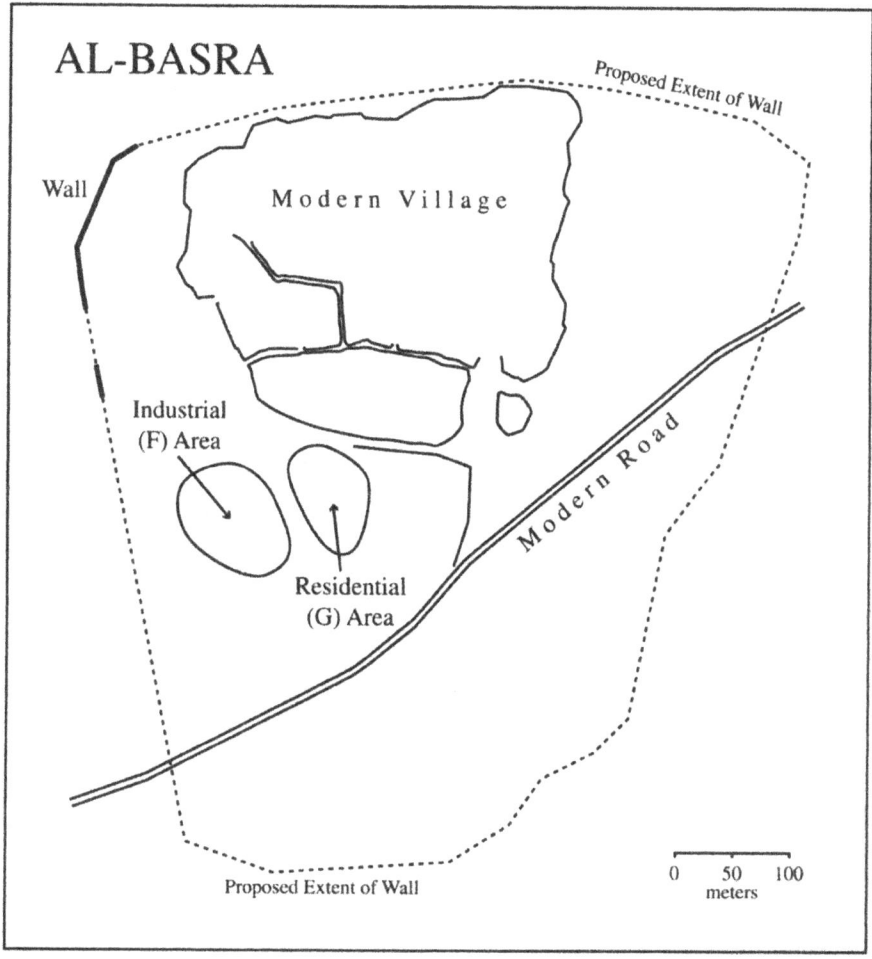

Figure 8.2 Map of al-Basra, showing residential and industrial areas. (Adapted from Benco 1987: Figure 4.1)

population, an enclosure wall, a mosque, and two hammams. It participated in an elaborate trade network and produced numerous items, including flax, wheat, cattle, ceramics, and metal.

Historical texts suggest that al-Basra, as well as Fez, its larger contemporary neighbor (Benco 1987:59), were spatially organized in a similar way, with a densely populated residential and commercial core surrounded by a lower density area where industrial structures were located. Excavations at al-Basra have focused on two areas: the residential quarter (Area G) in the center of the walled city and the industrial zone (Area F) near the western wall (Figure 8.2). The remains of the residential sector of the city are characterized by cut-stone wall foundations that form a maze of rooms and courtyards. The industrial area is distinguished by the presence of two large updraft pottery kilns and metalworking facilities.

Spatial Distribution of Artifacts

The analytical study examined archaeological evidence that likely dates to the Idrisid period, the first urban florescence at al-Basra. The artifacts were recovered from three 4-m-by-4-m units in the F area (F3W, F7, and F8) and three 4-meter-by-4-meter units in the G4 area (G4, G4N0W20, and G4N5W20).

The comparative study focused primarily on the presence and/or absence of "female possessions" (Insoll 1999) in these two areas. This class of artifacts includes objects associated with the production and application of *kohl*, a dark eye-makeup commonly used by Islamic women (Insoll 1999; Lane 1954); these objects include applicators, small glass containers, and small chunks of antimony, the mineral from which kohl is derived (Figures 8.3-8.4). Although these objects could have had other uses in other contexts, their close spatial association in the archaeological record is taken to indicate their use as a kohl set by women. Other objects believed to be "female possessions" (Insoll 1999; Lane 1954) are pieces of jewelry, including copper earrings and beads predominantly made of glass and shell, but also of agate, jet, carnelian, lapis, and gold (Figures 8.5).

There is a sharp contrast between the types of artifacts recovered from the residential G4 units and the F units, where metal and ceramic production activities took place

(Table 8.1). The vast majority of female possessions were recovered from residential units, while they were almost completely absent in industrial units. A full 100 percent of the beads, copper earrings, kohl applicators (both spatulas and probes), and pieces of kohl mineral were found in the residential units analyzed. In addition, 94 percent of the delicate glass fragments were found in the residential context.

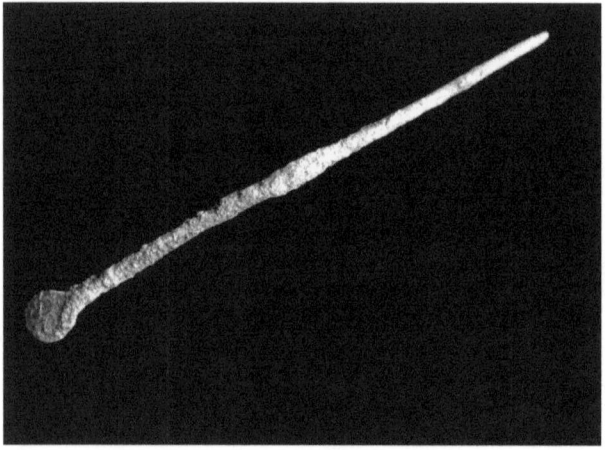

Figure 8.3 Photo of copper applicator, probably used for kohl.

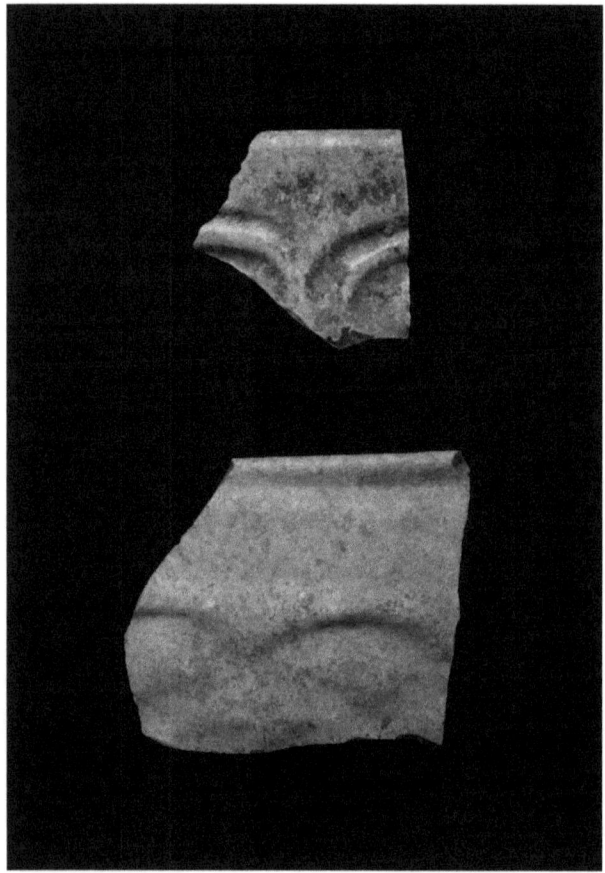

Figure 8.4 Photo of glass vessel rim.

Figure 8.5 Photo of polished stone beads.

The artifacts found in the industrial units assume a very different pattern. The most abundant materials recovered from these contexts are the byproducts of large-scale metal (e.g., slag) and ceramic (e.g., wasters) production. In addition, a large number of worked bone tools were recovered from these contexts (Benco, Ettahiri, and Loyet 2002). In fact, only one of 70 bone tools included in this analysis was found outside the industrial units.

Use of Ethnographic and Historic Analogy in Archaeological Interpretation

Archaeologists routinely grapple with the problem of deriving patterns of behavior from evidence that is strictly material in nature. The excavation of a city reveals walls and the spaces they define, but archaeologists must piece together the behaviors that took place within these physical spaces from the artifact assemblages and their contexts. Ethnographic analogy informs many of these interpretations of behavior. In the case of direct historical analogy, the ethnographic examples are drawn from the same region and/or culture that the archaeologist is attempting to interpret. The availability of ethnographic and historical records of urban Islam allow us to interpret the behavior that produced the pattern of artifacts witnessed in the archaeological record of al-Basra.

The data reveal distinct trends in the deposition of objects considered to belong to women. The vast majority were found in rooms and courtyards associated with the residential (G) zone. By contrast, virtually no female objects were recovered in the industrial (F) zone. This

Table 8.1. Counts and Percentages of Female Artifacts in Residential and Industrial Areas

Area	Beads (no.)	(%)	Copper earrings (no.)	(%)	Kohl applicators (no.)	(%)	Mineral fragments (no.)	(%)	Glass fragments (no.)	(%)	Bone tools (no.)	(%)
Residential (G)	185	100.0	5	100.0	5	100.0	2	100.0	130	100.0	1	1.0
Industrial (F)	0	0.0	0	0.0	0	0.0	0	0.0	8	6.0	69	99.0
Total	185	100.0	5	100.0	5	100.0	2	100.0	138	100.0	70	100.0

pattern supports the expectations established by ethnographic and historical data suggesting that urban women spend most of their time in the residential area of the city and little or no time participating in large-scale industry.

While the analogy of women in urban Islam can be used to build and support a gendered interpretation of al-Basra, there may be alternative interpretations for the observed pattern of artifact distribution. The spatial pattern may be a result of function rather than gender. Women within the workplace would have behaved differently than women within the home. This differing behavior might have produced the same varied distribution of female possessions despite the presence of women in both contexts.

This possibility does not, however, invalidate the interpretation of gendered space in the archaeological record of al-Basra. The ethnographic and historical accounts suggest that gender and function are intimately connected in Islamic society. The function of a space is, therefore, often determined by the gender of its occupants and vice versa. Because of their interrelatedness, it is often difficult to distinguish function from gender in the archaeological record of Islamic societies. Further research may help to clarify whether the differences between industrial and residential artifact distributions are a result of function, gender, or a combination of the two.

Extensive excavations at the site of al-Basra have revealed only the residential and industrial zones sampled in this study. The mosques, hammams, and suqs all remain buried and unexplored but, once they are found, they could be invaluable in the elaboration of our understanding of gendered space within urban al-Basra.

For example, while not many artifacts are carried into and/or left within a mosque, the structure's layout could provide significant evidence on which to base an interpretation. The presence of a balcony or a feature of demarcation between front and back areas (e.g., a banister or row of columns) could indicate a segmentation of the group, potentially along gender lines. The existence of a second room for ablutions would further corroborate a hypothesis of gendered space within the mosque.

Key to the interpretation of a *hammam* structure would be the identification of typically male possessions in the ethnographic and historical records. The discovery of two *hammams*, each containing artifact assemblages typical of a single gender would be highly suggestive of separated gendered social space. A single *hammam* containing an artifact assemblage of both male and female possessions would indicate a shared social space, although the nature and conditions of this sharing (e.g., scheduling) would be difficult, if not impossible, to sort out archaeologically.

The highly public marketplace or *suq* would likely be the most difficult to interpret. Stalls that catered to women might be detectable by leftover merchandise, such as earrings, beads, perfume vials, and the like. The complete absence of such items could mean one of two things: either the stalls were swept regularly and cleaned out completely upon abandonment leaving no artifacts behind or women did not enter the marketplace and peddlers responded by taking female wares to individual households.

Gendered Social Space at Islamic Sites

This chapter has used ethnographic and historical accounts to inform a gendered interpretation of the archaeological site of al-Basra. The physical space of both historical and modern-day Islamic cities can be subdivided into social spaces that are used differently by men and women. By direct historical analogy, different areas of the archaeological city of al-Basra were identified as either male- or female-dominated contexts. The artifact assemblages of some of these contexts were then compared to support the hypothesis of a gendered use of space. This analysis confirms that it is difficult, but not impossible, to define the nature of social space in the archaeological record where all evidence is physical rather than behavioral.

While the results of this study only detail a small portion of a single site, they suggest that further exploration of gendered spaces in urban Islamic settings may yield some valuable results. In the future, careful excavation of Islamic urban structures and spaces with questions of gender in mind may reveal nuances of spatial use never before considered.

References Cited

Abu-Lughod, J. L.
1987 The Islamic City: Historic Myth, Islamic Essence, and Contemporary Relevance. *International Journal of Middle East Studies* 19:155-176.

Ahmed, L.
1992 *Women and Gender in Islam: Historical Roots of a Modern Debate*. Yale University Press, New Haven.

Benco, N. L.
1987 *The Early Medieval Pottery Industry at al-Basra, Morocco*. BAR International Series 341. British Archaeological Reports, Oxford.

Benco, N. L., A. Ettahiri, and M. Loyet
2002 Worked Bone Tools: Linking Metal Artisans and Animal Processors in Medieval Islamic Morocco. *Antiquity* 76(292):447-57.

Bourdieu, P.
1962 *The Algerians*. Translated by A. C. M. Ross. Beacon Press, Boston.

Davis, S. S.
1983 *Patience and Power: Women's Lives in a Moroccan Village*. Schenkman Publishing, Cambridge, Mass.

El Guindi, F.
1999 *Veil: Modesty, Privacy, and Resistance*. Berg, Oxford.

Hakim, B.
1988 *Arabic-Islamic Cities: Buildings and Planning Principles*. Kegan Paul International, London.

Hassan, R.
1972 Islam and Urbanization in the Medieval Middle-East. *Ekistics* 195:108-112.

Insoll, T.
1999 *The Archaeology of Islam*. Blackwell, Oxford.

Ismail, A. A.
1972 Origin, Ideology and Physical Patterns of Arab Urbanization. *Ekistics* 195:113-123.

Kruk, R.
1998 The Bold and the Beautiful: Women and 'Fitna' in the 'Sirat Dhat Al-Himma': The Story of Nura. In *Women in the Medieval Islamic World: Power, Patronage, and Piety*, edited by G. R. G. Hambly, pp. 99-116. St. Martin's Press, New York.

Lane, E. W.
1954 [1860] *An Account of the Manners and Customs of the Modern Egyptians*. Dover Publications, New York.

Mernissi, F.
1987 *Beyond the Veil: Male-Female Dynamics in Modern Muslim Society*. Indiana University Press, Bloomington.

Pearson, M. P., and C. Richards
1994 Ordering the World: Perceptions of Architecture, Space and Time. In *Architecture and Order: Approaches to Social Space*, edited by M. P. Pearson and C. Richards, pp. 1-37. Routledge, New York.

Redman, C. L.
1986 *Qsar es-Seghir: An Archaeological View of Medieval Life*. Academic Press, Orlando.

Seng, Y. J.
1998 Invisible Women: Residents of Early Sixteenth-Century Istanbul. In *Women in the Medieval Islamic World: Power, Patronage, and Piety*, edited by G. R. G. Hambly, pp. 241-268. St. Martin's Press, New York.

Southall, A.
1998 *The City in Time and Space*. Cambridge University Press, Cambridge.

von Grunebaum, G. E.
1955 Islam: Essays in the Nature and Growth of a Cultural Tradition. *Memoirs of the American Anthropological Association* 81. Washington, D.C.

Wylie, A.
1992 The Interplay of Evidential Constraints and Political Interests: Recent Archaeological Research on Gender. *American Antiquity* 57:15-35.

Zarinbaf-Shahr, F.
1998 Women and the Public Eye in Eighteenth-Century Istanbul. In *Women in the Medieval Islamic World: Power, Patronage, and Piety*, edited by G. R. G. Hambly, pp. 301-324. St. Martin's Press, New York.

Beyond the City

Chapter 9

BEYOND AL-BASRA: SETTLEMENT SYSTEMS OF MEDIEVAL NORTHERN MOROCCO IN ARCHAEOLOGICAL AND HISTORICAL PERSPECTIVE

Said Ennahid

Archaeologists investigating medieval Moroccan state societies have at their disposal a wide variety of documentary sources that provide them with an unparalleled insight into these societies. Recent research conducted in Morocco has shown the promise of using documentary sources in formulating anthropologically oriented research questions and interpretive models (Benco 1987, 2001, 2002; Boone et al. 1990; Boone and Benco 1999; Cressier 1992; Cressier and Garcia-Arenal 1998; Redman 1983, 1983-1984, 1986).

This study moves beyond the boundaries of the city of al-Basra in order to achieve a broader understanding of Moroccan medieval life. It focuses on what lies "beyond the city" since al-Basra was far from being a closed microcosm with no links to its hinterland communities and neighboring cities. This research utilizes data derived from textual evidence, mainly chronicles and geographic descriptions of medieval Morocco, to shed light on the settlement systems in northern Morocco between the ninth and fifteenth centuries A.D. Theoretically, it is based on a conceptual model that was formulated a decade ago by Boone et al. (1990) and tested in my doctoral dissertation.[1]

Documentary Evidence as an Aid to Archaeological Research

The use of historical data to address archaeological questions requires the application of screening devices, such as identifying the author's sources and checking his background (i.e., political/religious partisanship) to sift through errors, discrepancies, exaggerations, fallacies, and bias-induced statements. In medieval Arabic texts, the number of errors and inconsistencies is often proportional to how distant in time and/or space the author was from the event and/or location he described. More scrutiny is required to evaluate a chronicler's account of an event that occurred centuries before his lifetime than of one that took place during his lifetime. The same thing is true for a geographer's description of a place that is located hundreds of miles away from his place of residence.

Another common type of distortion in medieval documentary evidence is personal or political bias.

Several Arab geographers and chroniclers were known to have had close ties to the political elite. In fact, some of them held high offices within the state bureaucracy, for example, the ninth-century geographer Ibn Khurdâdhbah who served as director of the Post and Intelligence Department (*Sahib al-barîd wa 'l-khabâr*)[2] for the 'Abbasids of Baghdad. Several passages in the chroniclers' texts praise the caliph in power or promote the state's ideology. More important, the information they gathered was often collected for administrative and intelligence purposes. Ibn Khurdâdhbah, al-Ya'kûbî, and Ibn Hawqal had close shî'îte ties, a fact that helps to evaluate their favorable statements toward the shî'îtes (e.g., Ibn Hawqal's sympathizing attitude toward the Fatimid movement).

The medieval Islamic texts fall into two main categories: historical chronicles and geographical accounts. Of more than 20 medieval Arab geographers and historians used in this research, the contributions of five geographers were most instrumental: (1) Ibn Hawqal, died ca. A.D. 988, (2) al-Muqaddasî, died ca. A.D. 990, (3) Abû 'Ubayd al-Bakrî, died in A.D. 1094, (4) al-Idrîsî, died in A.D. 1166, and (5) Leo Africanus, also known as al-Hasan al-Wazzân, died in A.D. 1548.[3] In addition, works of al-Muqaddasî, Ibn Hawqal, and al-Idrîsî feature a series of maps (Ibn Hawqal 1967; al-Idrîsî 1957; al-Muqaddasî 1950, 1994). While these maps are undoubtedly valuable sources of information for the study of medieval Arab cartography, their utility for regional settlement studies is limited to showing the general distribution of large medieval settlements.

Overall, the documentary sources vary a great deal in terms of the resolution and the relevance of the information they provide. The earliest descriptions of medieval Morocco, especially those written by Arab geographers from the Middle East, are too brief and vague to be of any real value for settlement studies (e.g., Ibn Khurdâdhbah, A.D. 885; Ibn al-Faqîh, A.D. 903; and al-Istakhrî, A.D. 951).[4] Not surprisingly, the geographers and chroniclers who lived in Morocco or al-Andalus (Muslim Spain) wrote more detailed accounts than their

---

[1] Political Economy and Settlement Systems of Medieval Northern Morocco: An Archaeological-Historical Approach. British Archaeological Reports, International Series No. 1059, Oxford, 2002.

[2] The system of transliteration of Arabic words is adapted from the *Encyclopedia of Islam*.

[3] 3 For an extensive overview of medieval textual sources on Morocco, see Siraj (1995). For a detailed overview of medieval Arab geographic literature, see Miquel (1967-1968).

[4] A notable exception is the ninth-century description by al-Ya'qûbî (1937) of a medieval itinerary in northern Morocco.

Anatomy of a Medieval Town

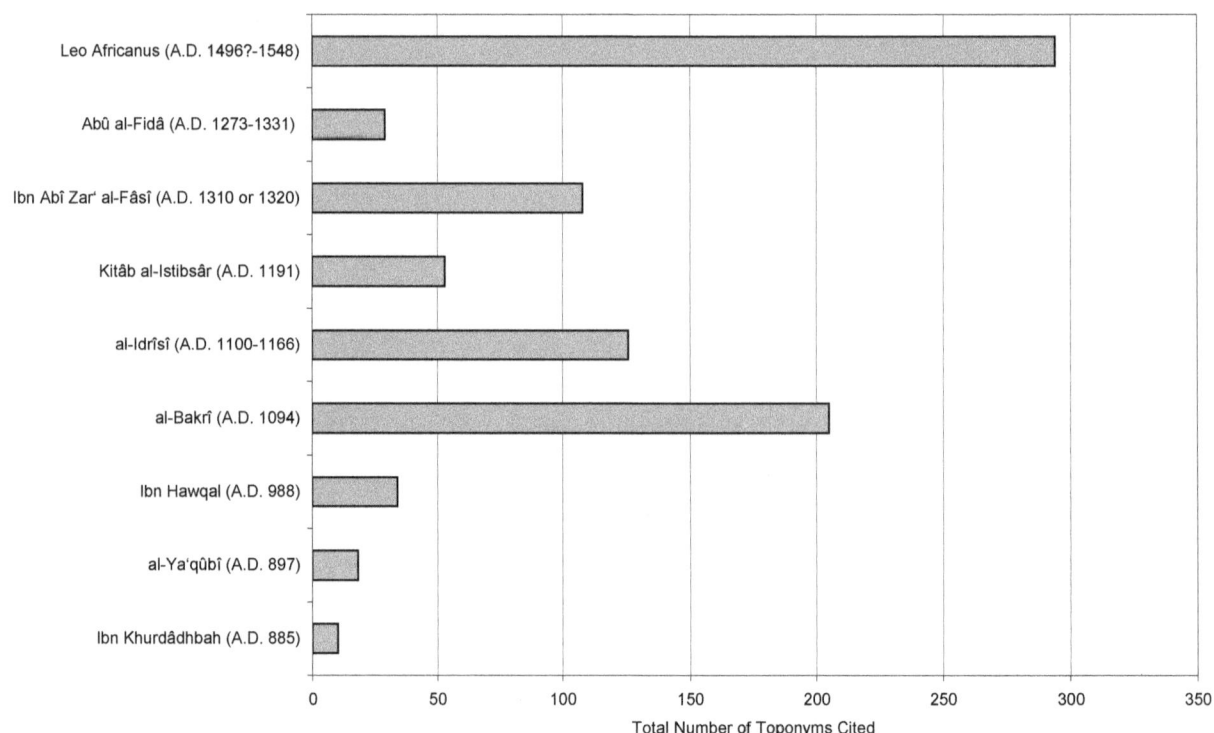

Figure 9.1 Number of toponyms cited in textual evidence, by name of chronicler. (Based on Massignon 1906:46-47)

distant contemporaries because they were more closely acquainted with the political, economic, and geographic conditions of the country. As Figure 9.1 shows, the contribution of eastern geographers (Ibn Khurdâdhbah, al-Ya'qûbî, Ibn Hawqal, and Abû al-Fidâ) in terms of toponymic information is modest compared with that of geographers who lived in Morocco or al-Andalus; eastern geographers provided the lowest numbers of toponyms for medieval Morocco.

The geographers' accounts contain several categories of settlement information. The number and order of these categories vary from one source to another. As the schematic drawing in Figure 9.2 shows, the main categories in a typical description of a medieval settlement can be arranged hierarchically. The account begins with a general description of the province or the district in which the settlement is located and may include a list of all settlements in the district (e.g., al-Muqaddasî's description of the district of Fez). A more specific description follows, with details on settlement toponymy, location, chronology, size, typology, anatomy, and population. Although toponymies and locations are relatively clear, information on settlement chronology, size, and type is generally less explicit. Chronological data such as foundation dates are usually indicated in broad terms, for example, *madîna awwaliyya* (old city), *madîna azaliyya* (ancient city), and *madîna hadîtha* (modern city). These terms allow only gross distinctions to be made between pre-Islamic and Islamic settlements. Information on site size is also given in broad terms, for example, *madîna 'âmira,* or prosperous city; *madîna âhila,* or populous city; and *madîna mutawassita,* or middle-sized city. Of course, this information acquires greater value when it is linked with other textual data, such as population size or tax payments. The terminology used to describe settlement types is relatively more specific but also more diverse, with at least forty different terms employed. Al-Muqaddasî was the first to establish a well-defined settlement terminology by consistently using a number of specific terms to convey specific meanings, for example, *iqlîm,* or province; *misr,* or metropolis; and *qasaba,* or provincial capital.[5] His work helped to standardize medieval Arab geographical literature.

The last category of settlement information provided by documentary sources deals with the anatomy of the site and the city's political, economic, and sociocultural history. While information on site anatomy (e.g., description of public monuments and houses, a sketch of the city, etc.) is used primarily in site-specific studies, information on population size, tax payments, and public facilities—in terms of their number and size—is used by archaeologists to establish settlement hierarchies, an important variable in regional settlement system studies. It should be noted that these categories of settlement data are provided only for prominent settlements, such as metropolises and capitals. Descriptions of small towns rarely exceed a few lines of text.

---

[5] Al-Muqaddasî (1994:50-51) compared metropoles (*amsâr*) to kings, provincial capitals (*qasabât*) to chamberlains, cities (*mudun*) to armies, and villages (*qurâ*) to foot soldiers.

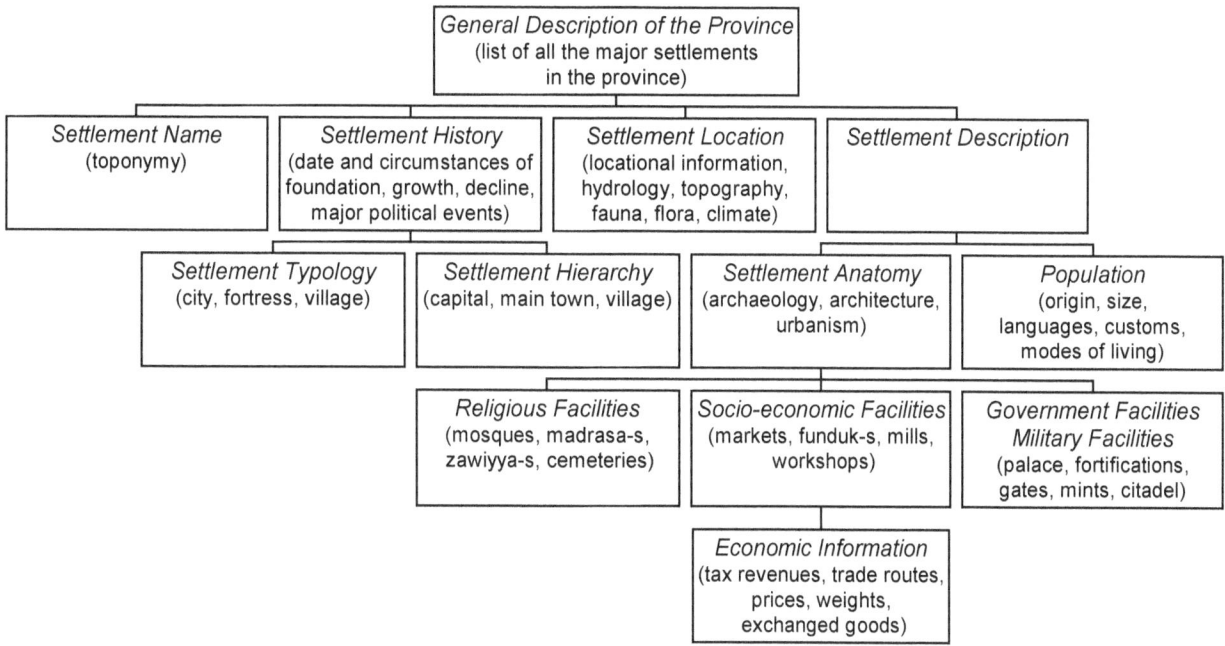

Figure 9.2 Schematic classification of settlement data found in textual evidence.

The archaeological identification of historically documented settlements, of course, is enhanced when the texts provide detailed and specific information. In northern Morocco, the number of historically known settlements that have been identified archaeologically is slightly lower than the number of those that have not yet been located (Figure 9.3). Moreover, the number of unidentified sites is higher in the earlier period. More than half of the Idrisid sites known to exist historically (25 out of 43) are not yet identified. Two possible explanations for this pattern can be proposed: that earlier settlements were smaller than later ones, and thus less visible on the ground, or that earlier towns were built with less durable construction materials than later ones.

Political Economy and Settlement Systems: A Conceptual Model

The theoretical framework of this project is drawn from a model formulated by Boone et al. (1990). Figure 9.4 illustrates the main premises of this model. For purposes of this study, the political economy and settlement systems of medieval northern Morocco are divided into two major phases: (1) an early phase consisting of the Idrisid state, ca. A.D. 789-974, and (2) a later phase consisting of subsequent dynasties—the Almoravid empire, ca. A.D. 1073-1147; the Almohad empire, ca. A.D. 1130-1276; and the Marinid empire, ca. A.D. 1258-1420. In the Idrisid state, the political economy was primarily agrarian-based and the settlement system was multitiered and hierarchical. Provincial capitals (e.g., al-Basra) were located in rich agricultural lands and were surrounded by smaller sites in the hinterland[6] (Figure 9.5). Fez, the capital of the Idrisid state, was the largest city within the system. Below this city were the provincial capitals, which formed self-sufficient and semi-independent politico-economic entities (Eustache 1970a, 1970-71)[7] and were in control of important agricultural and/or mining resources. Smaller towns and villages surrounded provincial capitals. Trade activities operated at two levels: (1) a local level involving the provincial capital and its hinterland, and (2) a regional level involving the provincial capital, nearby coastal entrepôts, and a number of provincial towns/mints.[8]

The city of al-Basra represents a model Idrisid provincial capital with its own coastal entrepôt (Mûlây Bû Salhâm or medieval Buhayrat Aryagh) and its own mint (Eustache 1955, 1970-71). Other examples of Idrisid cities and their ports include Qasr 'Abd al-Karîm and Tushummush, Hajar al-Nasr and Asîla, Nakûr and al-Mazamma, and Aghmât and Kûz (Cressier 1992; Cressier and Garcia-Arenal 1998; Rosenberger 1967).

---

[6] In order to investigate al-Basra's local exchange system and interaction with its hinterland, I recently conducted an archaeological survey in the region around the urban center and identified a number of sites. Ceramic samples from 15 of those sites have been subjected to instrumental neutron activation analysis (INAA) to determine if al-Basra's pottery was distributed to hinterland communities.

[7] The Idrisid principalities reflected the territorial divisions of the state after the death of Idrîs II. Each of his eldest sons became the head of a provincial capital.

[8] For details on Idrisid mints and mining resources, see Eustache (1970b, 1970-71); Garcia-Arenal and Manzano Moreno (1995:31); and Rosenberger (1964, 1970a, 1970b).

Anatomy of a Medieval Town

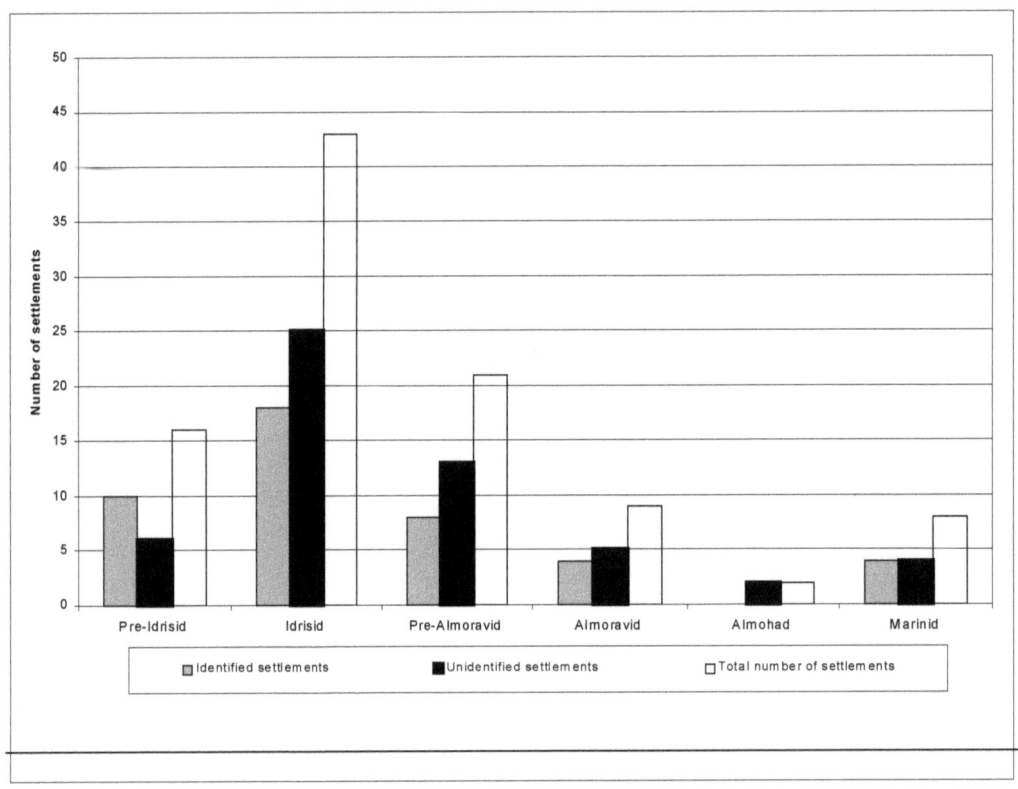

Figure 9.3   Number of archaeologically identified and unidentified settlements that are historically documented in northern Morocco, by time period.

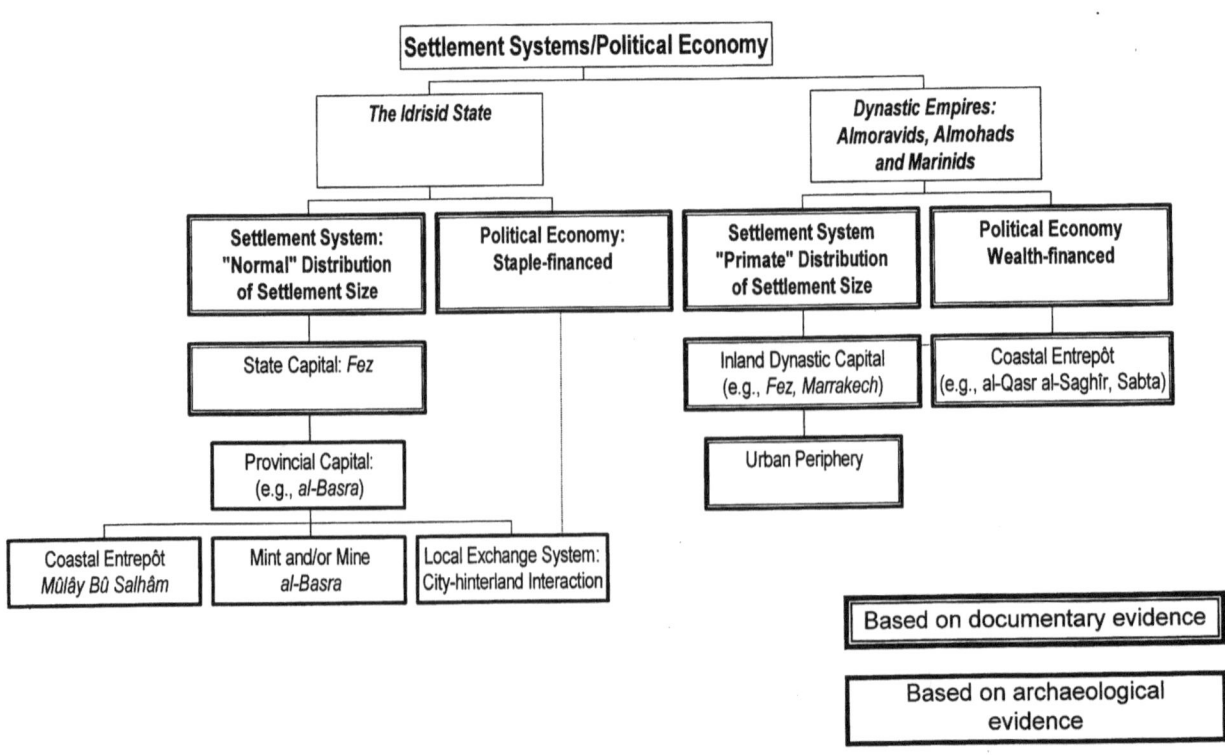

Figure 9.4   Schematic drawing of the main premises of the conceptual model used in this research.
(Based on Boone et al. 1990)

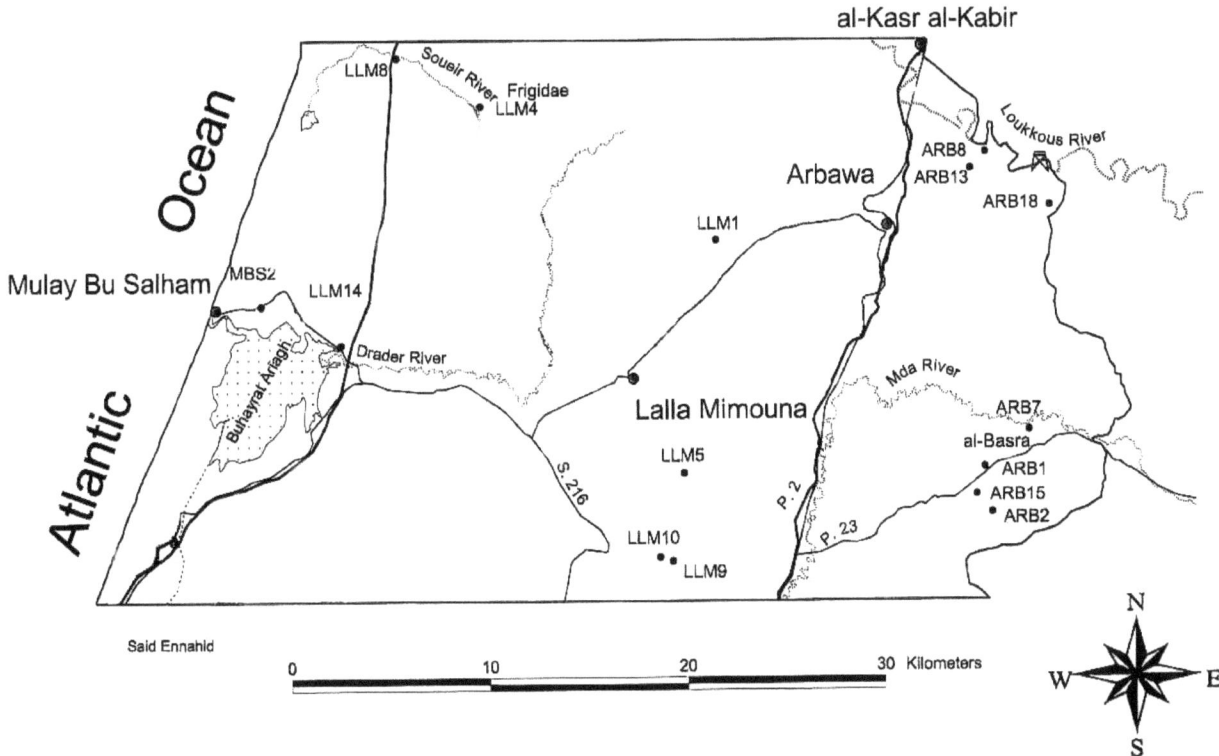

Figure 9.5 Map showing survey area in region of al-Basra and the location of identified archaeological sites (LLM, ARB, and MBS). Potsherds collected from the surface of these sites were analyzed using instrumental neutron activation analysis (INAA).

The Idrisid period came to a close as new economic horizons began to open for medieval Morocco. The trans-Saharan gold traffic gradually shifted from an easterly direction (Niger to Tunisia and Egypt)[9] to a northerly one (Niger to Morocco and the western Mediterranean Basin), with a positive economic impact on Morocco. The Berber tribal groups living on the northern fringes of the Sahara quickly took advantage of the lucrative Saharan trade (Devisse 1972a, 1972b, 1988; Devisse and Hrbek 1988; Vanacker 1973). One of these groups, the Almoravids, eventually took control of the long-distance trade. The emergence of the Almoravid empire in the eleventh century marks the beginning of the second phase. The Amoravid political economy relied on revenues from long-distance trade. The new economy gave rise to a "primate" settlement system, in which the capitals of the interior (especially Fez and Marrakech) became substantially larger in size (at least three times larger) than other urban centers (Boone et al. 1990:640).

According to the model proposed by Boone et al. (1990), urban growth occurred along three principal "discontinuities" that separated distinct economic spheres. The first discontinuity operated in inland Morocco and triggered the growth of inland capitals, which functioned as hubs of long-distance trade between *Bilâd al-Sûdân* (sub-Saharan West Africa), Morocco, and the rest of the Mediterranean Basin. The second discontinuity was at the geographic periphery of the dynastic empires: the Atlantic coast, the Mediterranean coast, and the northern fringes of the Sahara. The urban centers that developed along this periphery were mostly coastal entrepôts involved in transshipment activities. The last discontinuity divided the urban and rural economies, which were much smaller economic spheres.

According to the model, the growth and long-term survival of a medieval Moroccan city depended on two factors: (1) the degree of economic integration that developed between a city and its hinterland and (2) the extent of the city's political and economic involvement with the state (Boone et al. 1990:641-642). Two types of urban centers succeeded in this regard: (1) inland dynastic capitals that, in addition to their role in long-distance trade, developed strong economic ties with their immediate hinterland, and (2) coastal entrepôts whose mercantile activities were strong enough to survive the withdrawal of state management and to flourish on their own.

The main premise of the Boone et al. model is that there was a shift in the medieval Moroccan political economy from a "staple finance" system to a "wealth finance" system. As defined by D'Altroy and Earle (1985:188), a

---

[9] According to Ibn Ḥawqal, "The route from Egypt to Ghana went over them but the winds blew continually upon the caravans, heavy and light, and more than one heavy caravan was annihilated and light one exterminated; also the enemy attacked them and annihilated them on more than one occasion. So they abandoned this road and left it for [that of] Sijilmâsa" (Levtzion and Hopkins 1981:45; see also Ibn Ḥawqal 1967:61).

staple finance system involves "obligatory payments in kind to the state of subsistence goods, such as grains, livestock, and clothing." State personnel collect these staples either as tax on private land or as produce from state-owned land through corvée labor. This revenue is used to support state personnel and attached craft specialists. A staple finance system is most suitable for small agrarian states, such as the Idrisid dynasty. A wealth finance system, on the other hand, is characterized by the manufacture and/or acquisition of precious goods, such as sub-Saharan gold. The acquisition of wealth is achieved through a variety of means: the state collects it either directly as tax payment or indirectly as goods manufactured by attached specialists. Wealth is used by the state to pay its personnel (administrators and craftsmen) and to finance state projects (D'Altroy and Earle 1985:188).

These two systems are not mutually exclusive. In the Inca political economy of South America, staple finance was used as a financial base to support provincial administrators, whereas wealth finance was used to support representatives of the central authority (D'Altroy and Earle 1985:188). Likewise, in early medieval Morocco the Idrisid economy, although essentially agrarian-based, was supplemented with revenues from mining (mostly silver for minting purposes) and long-distance trade (Garcia-Arenal and Manzano Moreno 1995:31, 1998:279, 282). While the Almoravid finance system was primarily based on revenues from long-distance trade (wealth finance), it also depended on agricultural and craft production to supply the raw materials and finished goods to exchange with sub-Saharan West Africa.

Settlement Systems: Insights from Textual Evidence

An analysis of textual evidence from the works of medieval geographers shows that there was, in fact, a shift in regional settlement systems from a multitiered pattern (the Idrisid period) to a primate pattern (later dynastic periods). In this section, I will evaluate the Boone et al. model in light of newly gathered textual data and explore some new directions. Boone et al. (1990) based their model on textually derived evidence drawn from the work of Vitorino Magalhaes Godinho (1947), an economic historian of the Annales School. While this evidence supported the model's settlement shift, it was inconclusive for two reasons. First, the bulk of Godinho's textual data is derived from two sources—al-'Umarî and Leo Africanus—whose works date to the fourteenth and the sixteenth century, respectively (Leo Africanus 1956; al-'Umarî 1927). The settlement information provided by these two geographers is more detailed and more reliable for the Marinid period, which is at the end of the model's second phase, than for earlier periods.

Second, and most important, Godinho's evidence lacks settlement size figures for the Idrisid and pre-Almoravid periods. His earliest figures (Godinho 1947:135) extend from the beginning of the Almoravid period to nearly the end of the Almohad period (A.D.1060-1217). This limitation is particularly serious because the phase during which the settlement shift occurred is not documented textually. Although Boone et al. (1990:641) acknowledge this shortcoming: "[the textual data they present] may only represent the tail end of a more radical shift in settlement size distribution," their documentary evidence represents only the aftermath of the phenomenon under investigation.

In order to obtain documentary evidence covering the entire period (the ninth to the fifteenth century), I examined the works of more than 20 medieval Arab geographers and historians. From these texts, I identified 99 medieval sites in northern Morocco. For each site, I recorded three categories of settlement-related information: (1) settlement type, (2) settlement size, and (3) settlement chronology.

Settlement Types and Sizes

One of the most important texts I analyzed was the tenth-century geographer al-Muqaddasî's description[10] of medieval Morocco. This account offers the most detailed and systematically organized descriptions of the Idrisid's settlement system (Figure 9.6). According to al-Muqaddasî, the province of al-Maghrib was composed of North Africa (except Egypt), al-Andalus, and Sicily. It contained two metropoles (*amsâr*, sing. *misr*) and six districts (*kuwar*, sing. *kuwra*). The metropoles were al-Qayrawân (Kairouan) and Qurtuba (Cordoba). The districts were Sijilmâsa, Fez (also known as al-Sûs al-Adnâ), Sûs al-Aqsâ, Barqa, Ifrîqiya, and Tâhart. Only the district of Fez (i.e., northern Morocco)[11] will be discussed here since the other districts are beyond the geographic scope of this research.

The city of Fez was the capital (*qasaba*) of the district of Fez. This district was composed of two territories or *nawâhî* (sing. *nâhiya*)—Tanja[12] and al-Zâb[13]—and 41 main cities. The 41 main cities, as listed by al-Muqaddasî, are: al-Basra, Zalûl, al-Jâhid, Sûq al-Kutâmî, Wargha, Sabû, Sanhâjâ, Huwwâra, Tîzâ [Tâzâ], Matmâta, Kazannâya, Salâ, Madînat Banî Qarbâs, Mazhâhiyya,

---

[10] Al-Muqaddasî's book is known as *Ahsan al-taqâsîm fî ma'rifat al-aqâlîm* (the best divisions for knowledge of the provinces). It was written in A.D. 985.
[11] In the description of al-Muqaddasî, the district of Fez also comprises parts of southern Tunisia and all of southern Algeria (al-Muqaddasî 1950:76, note 9).
[12] The territory of Tanja is, geographically, the equivalent of Roman *Mauretania Tingitana*. This territory was composed of 10 cities: Walîla [Volubilis], Madraka, Matrûka, Zaqqûr, Ghuzza, Ghumîra, al-Hâjir, Tâjarâjarâ, al-Baydâ`, and al-Khadrâ` (al-Muqaddasî 1950:9). Tanja was also mentioned as a city: "Tanja that town so remote" (al-Muqaddasî 1994:198).
[13] Al-Zâb territory is composed of Msîla, which is the capital of the territory, Maqqara, Tubna, Biskra, Badîs [Badès], Tahûdha, Tawlâqâ, Jamîla, Bantiyûs, Adna, and Ashîr (al-Muqaddasî 1950:9).

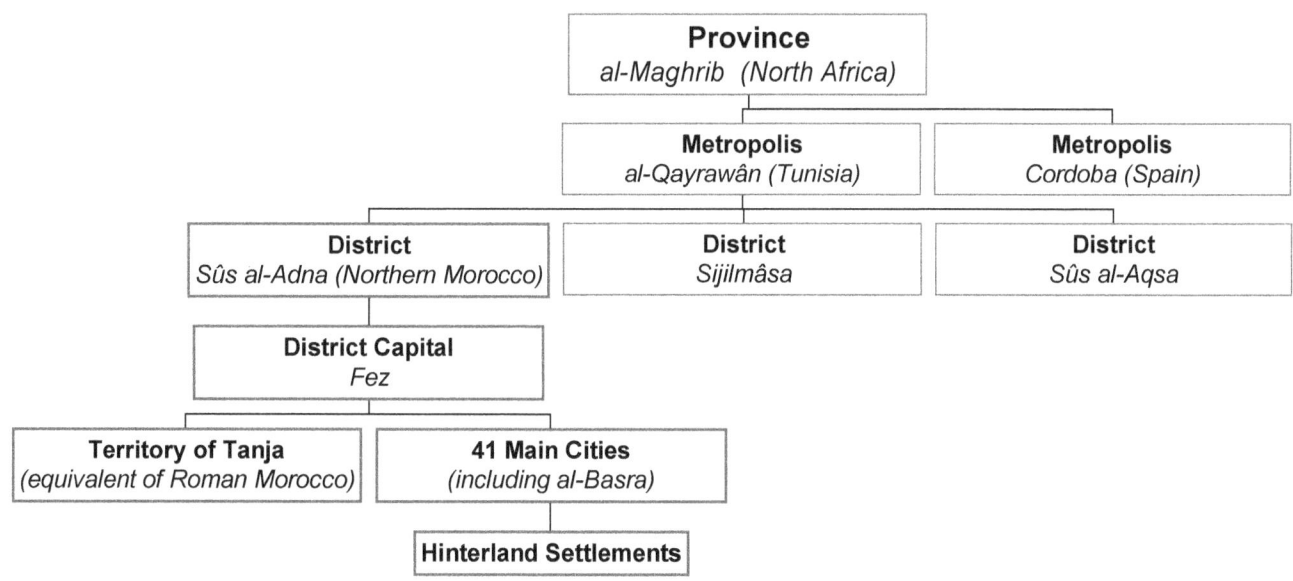

Figure 9.6 Hierarchy of urban settlements in early medieval Morocco. (Based on al-Muqaddasî 1950)

Azîlâ, Sabtâ [Ceuta], Balad Ghumâr,[14] Qal'at an-Nusûr, Nakûr, Balash, Marnîsa, Tâbarîdâ, Sâ', Miknâsa [Meknès], Qal'at Shamît, Madâ`in, Burj n-Ûzikî, Tayûnû, Maksîn, Amlîl [Melilla], Amlâh Abî l-Hasan, Qastîna, Nafzâwa, Niqâwûs, Biskara, Qabîsha, Mâdînat Banî Zahhîq, Luwâta 'Abd Allâh, Luwâta Barkiyya, Akdhâr Ibn Shirâq, and Mâdînat Jabal Zâlâgh (al-Muqaddasî 1950:7-9).

Al-Muqaddasî's Idrisid settlement system was clearly multitiered and hierarchical (Figures 9.4 and 9.6). The city of Fez, the capital of both the state and the district, figured prominently within the Idrisid settlement system. Below Fez were the provincial capitals. This second level consisted of mid-sized cities located in rich agricultural and/or mining areas. Al-Muqaddasî listed 51 cities: 41 within the district of Fez and 10 within the territory of Tanja. In addition to provincial capitals, mid-sized settlements included the smaller towns surrounding them. The smallest unit of settlement in al-Muqaddasî's hierarchy is represented by the villages or *qurâ* (sing. *qarya*) located in the hinterlands of various cities.

Chronological Change in Settlement Sizes

Although al-Muqaddasî's description strongly points to a normal distribution of settlement sizes during the tenth century, his work does not record the shift to a primate distribution that occurred a century later. In order to obtain this information, I looked at the size of each of the 99 historically documented settlements for each chronological period and assigned it to one of six settlement size classes:[15]

Class I:	more than 100,000 inhabitants
Class II:	50,000-100,000 inhabitants
Class III:	25,000-50,000 inhabitants
Class IV:	10,000-25,000 inhabitants
Class V:	2,000-10,000 inhabitants
Class VI:	less than 2,000 inhabitants

Data on settlement size was derived from documentary evidence, either directly in the form of population estimates expressed in numbers of cooking hearths (*mawâqid*)[16] or indirectly by examining information on settlement typology and anatomy (i.e., categories of settlements and the number and size of their public facilities).

Figure 9.7 illustrates the distribution of settlement size classes by dynastic period. As the model predicted, there was a radical shift in the number of mid-sized settlements (Class V) between the Idrisid and Almoravid periods. The number dropped by nearly 70 percent (from 54 to 17 settlements) and continued to fall more gradually during later periods. The historical documents attribute this decrease to the large-scale destruction that usually accompanied the emergence of a new dynastic empire and the collapse of an old one (e.g., Almoravids,

---

[14] Balad Ghumâr (Ghumâra) was a territory of a tribal group rather than an urban center in the strict sense of the word.

[15] For the sake of compatibility, I used the same values for settlement size classes as Godinho's (1947:134-135).

[16] In medieval texts, population size is indicated by the number of cooking hearths or *mawâqid* (sing. *mawqid*). A hearth is the equivalent of a household. Godinho (1947:134) estimated the average size of the medieval family to be five persons. In order to convert the number of cooking hearths into actual numbers of inhabitants, Godinho multiplied the number of hearths by five.

Anatomy of a Medieval Town

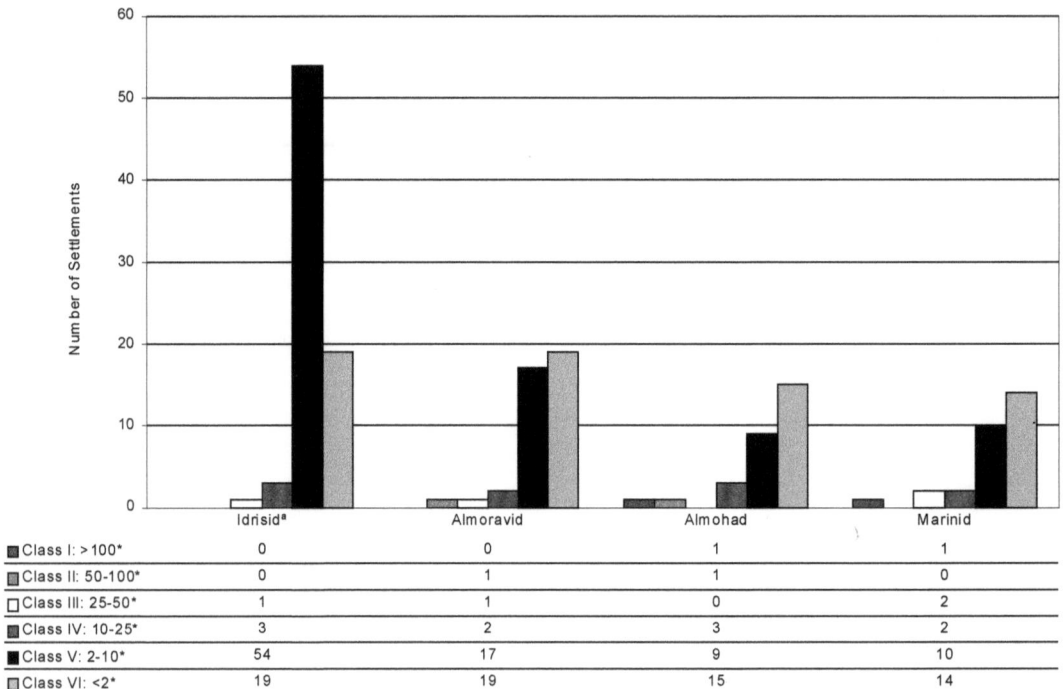

	Idrisid[a]	Almoravid	Almohad	Marinid
Class I: >100*	0	0	1	1
Class II: 50-100*	0	1	1	0
Class III: 25-50*	1	1	0	2
Class IV: 10-25*	3	2	3	2
Class V: 2-10*	54	17	9	10
Class VI: <2*	19	19	15	14

*Population Size (in thousands of inhabitants)
[a] pre-Idrisid, Idrisid, and pre-Almoravid periods combined.

Figure 9.7 Distribution of settlement size classes, by dynastic period.

Almohads). Al-Basra is a typical example of a mid-sized city that might have succumbed because of warfare related to dynastic succession. Several mid-sized and small cities were destroyed because they did not have sufficient military manpower and/or defensive features to counterattack dynastic troops. Others were simply abandoned because their fragile economy was negatively affected by the prevailing political instability. Figure 9.7 also shows a more gradual decrease in the number of Class VI cities (less than 2,000 inhabitants), mostly during the Almohad and Marinid periods. The number of large settlements of more than 10,000 inhabitants (Classes I, II, III, and IV) remained low throughout the Middle Ages.

During the Idrisid period when it served as the state capital, Fez was not significantly larger than the rest of the Idrisid cities (Boone et al. 1990:641). During the Almoravid period, when it achieved primacy over all settlements, its population reached more than 100,000 inhabitants. By the Almohad period, it had become a true metropolis. In the fourteenth century, under the reigns of al-Mansûr and his son al-Nâsir, Fez featured 785 mosques, 122 public fountains, 93 public baths (hammâm), 472 mills, and, most important, 89,236 households (Ibn Abî Zar' 1843:25-26, 1860:57-58). Using Godinho's formula (1947:134), I converted the household number to a population size of close to 450,000 inhabitants. Although these numbers should be treated with caution, it is clear that Fez was by far the largest city in northern Morocco during the Almohad period. According to other research conducted by Godinho (1947:131-140), "the two largest cities in Morocco [Fez and Marrakech] were at least three times larger than the next-largest city class of 25,000-50,000" (Boone et al. 1990:640).

Tax Payment Information

Based on the hypothesis that larger cities paid more taxes than smaller ones, one would expect to find in the case of a primate settlement system: (1) a significant gap between the tax payment of the largest cities and that of the next-largest ones, and (2) a strong correlation between tax payments and settlement size.

To test the first component of this hypothesis, I used data derived from the work of al-'Umarî (1927:171), a fourteenth-century geographer. The data consist of the tax payments of 22 medieval cities to the Marinid treasury under the reign of Abû Sa'îd 'Uthmân II (A.D.1310-1331). As Table 9.1 shows, the taxes paid by Fez and Marrakech are substantially larger than any other city in medieval Morocco. It equals the tax payment of the cities of Sijilmâsa and Dar'a combined and is 2.5 higher than Maknâsa, the city with the next largest tax contribution. Al-'Umarî's tax information clearly shows that Fez and Marrakech were the most dominant cities in medieval Morocco, indicating that a primate settlement distribution most likely prevailed at least until the Marinid period (A.D. 1258-1420).

In order to test the second component of my hypothesis, I correlated al-'Umarî's tax information with settlement

Table 9.1. Tax Payments of Marinid Cities

Settlement name	Tax payment (in thousands of mithqâl[1])
Tijissâs	5
Tît	5
Safrawi	6
al->Arâ`ish	10
Bâdis	10
Azammûr	20
Qasr >Abd al-Karîm	20
Aghmât	25
Asafî	25
Tâzâ	30
Tangier	30
Ghasâsâ, al-Mazamma, Malîla	30
Anfa	40
Salâ	40
Sabta	50
Maknâsa	60
Fez	150
Marrakech	150
Sijilmâsa, Dar>a	150

Note: Data from al-'Umarî (1927:171).
[1] One mithqâl, or dinar, equals 4.25 grams of gold (Devisse 1972a:58, note 69; Miles 1965:297).

size data derived from Godinho's work (1947:134-135).[17] (See Table 9.2.) It should be stressed at the outset that, in the absence of secure settlement size data for medieval Morocco, the results presented below are tentative. Figure 9.8 shows that there is a meaningful correlation between settlement size and the amount of tax payment (Spearman rank-order correlation: -0.843). This graph also shows that the two inland capitals of Fez and Marrakech are substantially larger (Class I) than the other cities within the Marinid settlement system. In a primate settlement pattern, one would expect an absence of second-ranking urban centers (Class II). Although one value is shown in Class II, it represents the population estimate for an entire region (Sijilmâsa-Dar'a) and not for an individual city. Godinho's settlement data that was used to establish this graph do not show any Class II (50,000-100,000 inhabitants) urban centers (see also Boone et al. 1990:Table 1).

Although still preliminary, this study shows that there is a potential for using tax payment information to predict settlement size. These findings may have important implications for studies of settlement systems, particularly those based on documentary sources, since tax information is less elusive than settlement size information.

Duration of Settlement Occupation

Another component of the Boone et al. model that needs to be addressed is the process of urban growth and the long-term survival of a number of urban centers. Figure 9.9 shows the distribution of settlements in northern

Table 9.2. Settlement Size Estimates for Selected Medieval Moroccan Cities, Based on Documentary Data

Number of inhabitants	Settlement name
More than 100,000	Fez and Marrakech
50,000-100,000	No cities
25,000-50,000	Tâza, Sabta (before A.D. 1415), Maknâs[a], Azammûr (heyday), Tît (heyday), and Aghmât-Urîka
10,000-25,000	Malîla, Tangier, Qasr al-Kabîr [Qasr >Abd al-Karîm] (heyday), Salâ-Rabat, Safim [Asfî], Tît (decline), al->Arâ=ish (?) (15th-16th A.D.), and Anfâ
2,000-10,000	Bâdis, Tagaca [Tijissâs], Qasr al-Kabîr [Qasr >Abd al-Karîm] (decline), al->Arâ=ish (12th-13th A.D.), Azammûr (decline beginning of 16th A.D.), Tît (16th A.D.), Safrû (?) [Safrawi], Cacaca (?) [Ghasâsâ], al-Mazamma (?), and Aghmât-Aylân (?)

Note: Data from Godinho (1947:134-135).

[17] Population estimates for the cities of Sijilmâsa and Dar'a were derived from Massignon (1906:148) based on information found in Leo Africanus and Marmol.

Anatomy of a Medieval Town

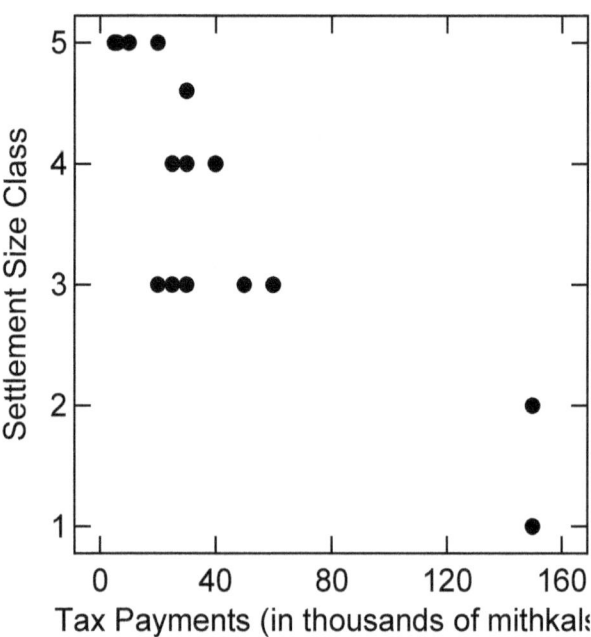

Figure 9.8 Correlation between city tax payments and settlement size classes during the Marinid period. (Based on Godinho 1947:134-135; Massignon 1906:148; al-'Umarî 1927:171)

Morocco according to their length of occupation from the eighth to the fifteenth century. Those with a relatively short occupation period (between two to three centuries) are the most abundant. Interestingly, Idrisid and pre-Almoravid sites dominate this group (29 and 10, respectively). These are mid-sized inland settlements that were abandoned and/or destroyed during the Almoravid invasion of northern Morocco. Only 10 settlements in northern Morocco were occupied for eight centuries or longer.[18] Significantly, half of these settlements functioned as coastal entrepôts.

Of 14 coastal entrepôts analyzed, 11 (80 percent) survived more than seven centuries and were settled before the Almoravid period. The shift in the political economy that occurred during this period apparently triggered a change in the role played by coastal entrepôts. Under the Idrisids, coastal entrepôts were economically and politically tied to provincial capitals (e.g., Buḥayrat Aryagh functioned as the port of al-Basra). After the eleventh century and the rise of inland dynastic capitals, they assumed much greater importance. Dynastic control of long-distance trade offered new economic opportunities to coastal entrepôts. They were involved in a variety of mercantile activities, first under the watchful eye of state officials and later on for their own benefit.

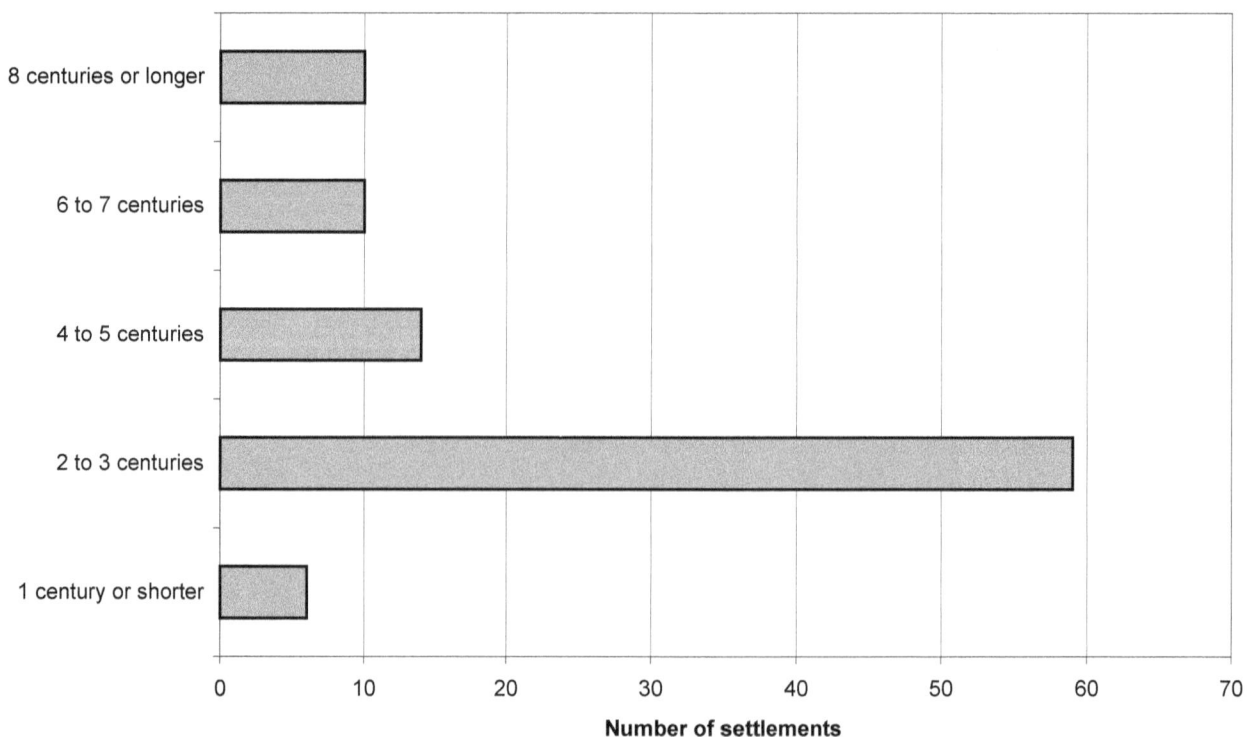

Figure 9.9 Distribution of settlements, by length of occupation. (All periods are combined)

---

[18] The settlements in question are the following Pre-Idrisid and Idrisid sites: al-Jazîra (Gezira), Fez, Ijâjîn, al-Qaṣr al-Kabîr, al-Qaṣr al-Ṣaghîr, Khamîs Matghâra (Camis Metgara), Maghîla, Sabta, Salâ, and Tangier.

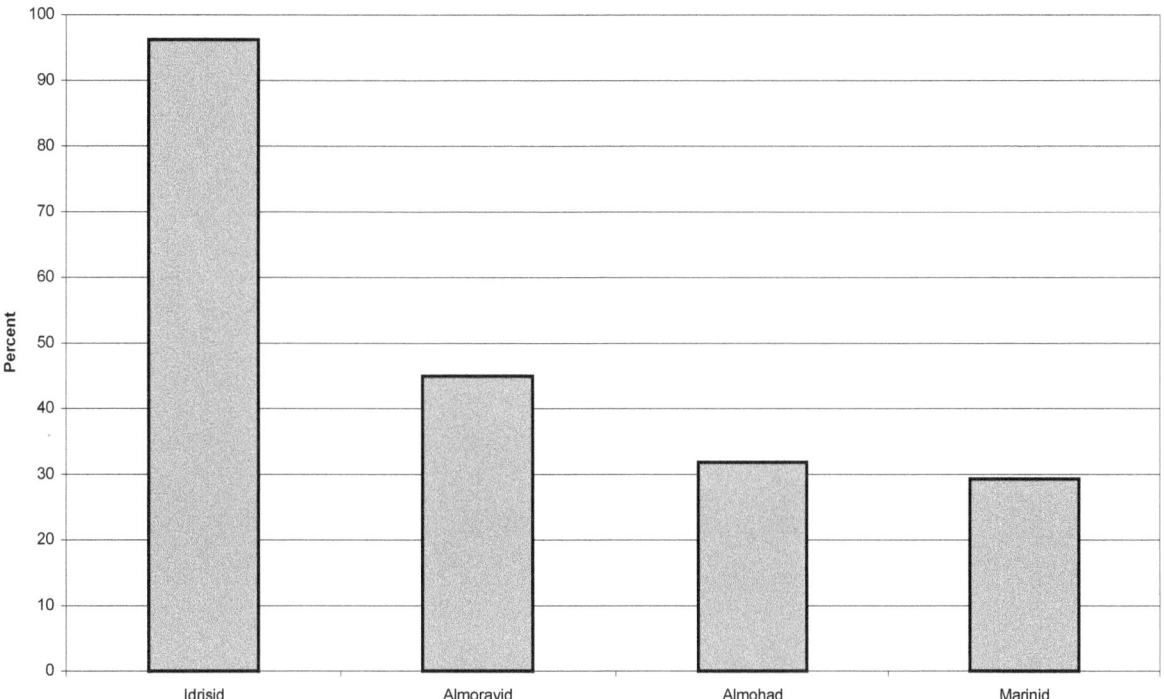

Figure 9.10 Percentage of occupied settlements, by dynastic period.

Discussion and Conclusions

As these analyses indicate, textual evidence strongly supports the main premises of the Boone et al. model (1990). The texts clearly demonstrate that the shift in the medieval Moroccan political economy had major implications for settlement systems. They also support the model's explanations of urban growth. They show that medieval Moroccan urban networks declined continuously and irreversibly after the Idrisid period (Figure 9.10). The Almoravid period marked the threshold at which the number of abandoned or destroyed settlements exceeded that of occupied ones.

Although the texts cite warfare as the major cause of settlement abandonment, other factors, such as famine and epidemics, may have been equally devastating. Ibn Abî Zar' (1843:21) mentioned the "great famine" of A.D. 1222-1240 which, in his terms, caused "the abandonment of the country." A plague in A.D. 1348-1350 may also have caused significant reductions in population size and settled life. In Europe, the plague decimated between one-eighth and two-thirds of the population, and similar estimates could be applied to medieval Morocco (Brignon et al. 1967:153). Episodes of famines and epidemics are often accompanied by the disruption of public order and political stress; these elements could have weakened dynastic control and impeded the course of settled life. By the beginning of the fifteenth century, only about 30 percent of all the original settlements of northern Morocco were still occupied (Figure 9.10).

The promising results discussed in this study show that the information found in medieval Arabic textual sources can be effectively used to address specific anthropological questions. Unfortunately, documentary evidence has often been regarded by archaeologists as merely a source for historical background knowledge on archaeological sites. The field of Islamic archaeology in Morocco will certainly achieve significant growth, both in method and theory, when researchers begin to recognize the full potential of using historical data in evaluating existing anthropological models or formulating new ones.

Acknowledgments

Travel and analytical costs for this research were generously supported by the National Science Foundation (Doctoral Dissertation Improvement Grant: SBR-9808443), the Wenner-Gren Foundation for Anthropological Research (Predoctoral Grant: 6388), the Arizona State University Chapter of Sigma Xi, and the Department of Anthropology at Arizona State University. Travel and fieldwork were also partly funded through a National Science Foundation grant awarded to Nancy Benco (SBR-9618369).

References Cited

Benco, N. L.
  1987 *The Early Medieval Pottery Industry at al-Basra, Morocco*. BAR International Series 341. British Archaeological Reports, Oxford.
  2001 Five Seasons of Archaeological Research at al-Basra, Morocco: 1980, 1981, 1990, 1994, and 1995. *Actes du colloque sur plus d'un siècle de recherches archéologiques au Maroc, 1998*. Sociéte Marocaine d'Archéologie et du Patrimoine, Rabat.
  2002 Archaeological Investigations at al-Basra, Morocco. *Bulletin d'archéologie marocaine* 19:293-340.

Boone, J. L., and N. L. Benco
  1999 Islamic Settlement in North Africa and the Iberian Peninsula. *Annual Review of Anthropology* 28:51-71.

Boone, J. L., E. Myers, and C. L. Redman
  1990 Archaeological and Historical Approaches to Complex Societies: The Islamic States of Medieval Morocco. *American Anthropologist* 92:630-646.

Brignon, J., A. Amine, B. Boutaleb, G. Martinet, and B. Rosenberger
  1967 *Histoire du Maroc*. Hatier, Casablanca.

Cressier, P.
  1992 Le développement urbain des côtes septentrionales du Maroc au moyen age: frontière intérieure et frontière extérieure. In *Castrum IV: frontière et peoplement dans le monde Méditerranéen au moyen âge*, pp.173-187. Casa de Velazquez, Madrid.

Cressier, P., and M. Garcia-Arenal (editors)
  1998 *Genèse de la ville islamique en al-Andalus et au Maghreb occidental*. Casa de Velazquez, Madrid.

D'Altroy, T. N., and T. K. Earle
  1985 Staple Finance, Wealth Finance, and Storage in the Inka Political Economy. *Current Anthropology* 26:187-206.

Devisse, J.
  1972a Routes de commerce et échanges en Afrique occidentale en relation avec la Méditerranée. Un essai sur le commerce Africain médiéval du XIe au XVIe siècle, 1re partie. *Revue d'histoire économique et sociale* 50:42.
  1972b Routes de commerce et échanges en Afrique occidentale en relation avec la Méditerranée. Un essai sur le commerce Africain médiéval du XIe au XVIe siècle, 2e partie. *Revue d'histoire économique et sociale* 50:357.
  1988 Trade and Trade Routes in West Africa. In *UNESCO General History of Africa: Africa from the Seventh to the Eleventh Century*, vol. 3, edited by M. El Fasi, pp. 367-435. University of California Press, Berkeley.

Devisse, J., and I. Hrbek
  1988 The Almoravids. In *UNESCO General History of Africa: Africa from the Seventh to the Eleventh Century*, vol. 3, edited by M. El Fasi, pp. 336-366. University of California Press, Berkeley.

Eustache, D.
  1955 El-Basra, capitale idrissite et son port. *Hespéris* 42:218-238.
  1970a Idrisids. *Encyclopaedia of Islam*, vol. 3. E. J. Brill, Leiden.
  1970b Les ateliers monétaires du Maroc. *Hesperis-Tamuda* 11:95-102.
  1970-71 *Corpus des dirhams idrissites et contemporains: études sur la numismatique et l'histoire monétaire du Maroc I*. Banque du Maroc, Rabat.

Garcia-Arenal, M., and E. Manzano Moreno
  1995 Idrissisme et villes idrissides. *Studia Islamica* 82:5-33.
  1998 Légitimité et villes idrissides. In *Genèse de la ville islamique en al-Andalus et au Maghreb occidental*, edited by P. Cressier and M. Garcia-Arenal, pp. 257-284. Casa de Velazquez, Madrid.

Godinho, V. M.
  1947 *Historia economics e social da expansao Portuguesa*. Marroco I. Terra Editora, Lisbon.

Ibn Abî Zar', al-Fâsî (died A.D. 1315)
  1843 *Annales regum mauritaniae (al-Anîs al-mutrib rawd al-qirtâs)*. Translated by C. J. Tornberg. 2 vols. Litteris Academicis, Upsaliae.
  1860 *Roudh el-Kartas, histoire des souverains du Maghreb et annales de la ville de Fès*. Translated by A. Beaumier. Paris.

Ibn Hawqal (died ca. A.D. 988)
  1967 *Kitâb sûrat al-ard* (Opus Geographicum). *Bibliotheca geographorum Arabicorum*, vol. 2, edited by J. H. Kramers. E.J. Brill, Leiden.

al-Idrîsî, Muhammad ibn Muhammad al-Sharîf (died A.D. 1166)
  1957 *Description de l'Afrique septentrionale et saharienne (Texte arabe extrait du Kitâb nuzhat al-mushtâq fî ikhtirâq al-âfâq)*. La Maison des Livres, Algiers.

Leo Africanus, al-Hasan ibn Muhammad al-Wazzân (died ca. A.D. 1548)
  1956 *Description de l'Afrique (Della descrittione dell'Africa e delle cose notabili che quivi sono)*. Translated by A. Epaulard, T. Monod, H. Lhote, and R. Mauny. 2 vols. Maisonneuve, Paris.

Levtzion, N., and J. F. P. Hopkins (editors)
1981 *Corpus of Early Arabic Sources for West African History*. Cambridge University Press, Cambridge.

Massignon, L.
1906 *Le Maroc dans les premiéres années du XVI siècle ap. J.C.: tableau géographique d'après Léon l'Africain*. Mémoires de la Société Historique Algérienne I, Algiers.

Miles, G. C.
1965 Dînâr. *Encyclopaedia of Islam,* vol. 2. E. J. Brill, Leiden.

Miquel, A.
1967-1968 *Géographie humaine du monde musulman jusqu'au milieu du XIe siècle. Géographie et géographie humaine dans la littérature Arabe (des origines à 1050)*. Ecole Pratique des Hautes Etudes. Civilisations et Societés: 7, 37, 68, and 78. 4 vols. Mouton, Paris-La Haye.

al-Muqaddasî, Muhammad ibn Ahmad (died ca. A.D. 990)
1950 *Description de l'occident musulman au IVe-Xe siècle*. Translated by C. Pellat. Bibliothèque Arabe-Française, Algiers.
1994 *The Best Divisions for Knowledge of the Regions: A Translation of Ahsan al-taqasim fi mar'ifat al-aqalim*. Translated by B. A. Collins, reviewed by M. H. al-Tai. Center for Muslim Contribution to Civilization. Garnet Publishing, Reading, Pennsylvania.

Redman, C. L.
1983 Comparative Urbanism in the Islamic Far West. *World Archaeology* 14:355-377.
1983-1984 Survey and Test Excavation of Six Medieval Islamic Sites in Northern Morocco. *Bulletin d'archéologie marocaine* 15:311-349.
1986 *Qsar es-Seghir: An Archaeological View of Medieval Life*. Academic Press, Orlando.

Rosenberger, B.
1964 Autour d'une grande mine d'argent du moyen age Marocain: le jbel Aouam. *Hesperis-Tamuda* 5.
1967 Note sur Kouz, un ancien port à l'embouchure de l'Oued Tensift. *Hesperis-Tamuda* 8:23-66.
1970a Les vieilles exploitations minières et les centres métallurgiques du Maroc: essai de carte historique. *Revue de géographie du Maroc* 17:71-108.
1970b Les vieilles exploitations minières et les centres métallurgiques du Maroc: essai de carte historique. *Revue de géographie du Maroc* 18:59-102.

Siraj, A.
1995 *L'image de la Tingitane: l'historiographie arabe médiévale et l'antiquité Nord-Africaine*. No. 209. Collection de l'Ecole Française de Rome, Paris.

al-'Umarî, Ibn Fadl Allâh Ahmad ibn Yahya (died A.D.1349)
1927 *Masâlik al-absâr fi mamâlik al-amâr*. Translated by M. Gaudefroy-Demombynes. Bibliothèque des Géographes Arabes, Paris.

Vanacker, C.
1973 Géographie économique de l'Afrique du nord du IX au milieu du XII siècles selon les auteurs arabes. *Annales: economie, sociétés, civilizations* 28 (3):659-680.

al-Ya`qûbî, Ahmad ibn Abî Ya`qûb (died A.D. 897)
1937 *Al-Buldân (Les pays)*. Institut Français d'Archéologie Orientale, Cairo.

Anatomy of a Medieval Town

Scientific Applications

Chapter 10

An Archaeomagnetic Study of Two Kilns at Al-Basra

Abdelkrim Rimi
Donald H. Tarling
Sidi Otman el-Alami

Traditionally, the earliest settlement at the site of al-Basra in northern Morocco has been attributed to the Idrisid Arabs at the end of the eighth or the beginning of the ninth century A.D. (Eustache 1955). Radiocarbon dating, however, has suggested that the site was originally settled earlier, possibly as early as the fifth or sixth century A.D., not long after the end of Roman rule in Morocco (Benco 2002).

In order to examine this age discrepancy, in 1990 our team conducted an archaeomagnetic study of two previously excavated rectangular-shaped updraft kilns within the industrial zone near the western wall of the ancient city. It was hoped that a comparison with published archaeomagnetic studies of kilns at the late Roman site of Volubilis (Kovacheva 1984; Najid 1986), located 80 km away, could help confirm the likely date of the last firings of the two al-Basra kilns. In addition, the study would provide a comparative record that could be used for future archaeomagnetic dating of sites elsewhere in northwestern Africa and southern Spain.

Methodology

The two kilns, located about 50 m apart, have been labeled as F3 and F1. Both kilns are of an updraft type and were apparently used for the production of both roof tiles and pottery vessels (Benco 1987, 2002; Lundquist and Benco, this volume).

For the archaeomagnetic study, a total of 33 oriented samples (labeled F) were obtained from the F3 Kiln (Figure 10.1a) and 28 samples (labeled B) from the F1 Kiln (Figure 10.1b). In both cases, samples were obtained by the disk method (Tarling 1983), in which nonmagnetic disks are attached to potential samples using nonmagnetic epoxy glue. The surfaces of the disks were then oriented using both magnetic and sun compasses prior to the removal of samples with the disks still attached. Although the difference in orientations by the two methods was generally less than 10°, they differed by as much as 37° (B9). This was thought to be caused by the strong magnetic remanence in parts of the site that may have affected the magnetic compass readings. Because of this, only sun compass orientations were used in the study.

All measurements of the magnetic remanence of the samples were undertaken with a large-access Digico spinner magnetometer. The characteristics of the remanent magnetization were established using alternating magnetic field demagnetization in which every sample was subjected to peak fields of 3, 7, 10, 15, 20, 30, 50, and 70 mT (and 90 mT for F1 Kiln samples), with the remanence being re-measured after each incremental demagnetization step.

F3 Kiln

The F3 Kiln (Figure 10.1a) was 3.5 m wide and 4 m long and comprised a firing chamber of 4 large vaulted arches, each ca. 3.5 m long and .55 m thick, that supported a plaster floor with flue holes. The structure itself was oriented approximately northeast/southwest with access on the northeastern side. It was built of fired bricks interspersed with tiles, and the interior walls were coated with mud plaster. The kiln was located stratigraphically in the lowest levels of the site, resting on sterile soil, and was associated with the earliest phase pottery. A wood charcoal sample from the kiln floor has provided a radiocarbon age of 1380 ± 80 B.P. (Beta-39976), which calibrates to A.D. 540-790 at a 95 percent (2 sigma) probability (Benco 2002). Other samples from the lowest levels of the residential quarter of the site have given equally early dates.

All archaeomagnetic samples were taken from the kiln floor (Figure 10.1a), with 16 (F1-F16) from the northwestern edge, 3 (F17-F19) from the near the western corner on the southwestern side, 9 (F21-F28, F32) from the southeastern edge, and 2 (F30-F31) from the northeastern edge. Three samples did not survive transport to the laboratory and are thus not included in this analysis.

The initial intensity of magnetization (Table 10.1) was high, ranging between 220 and 11,757 A/m/kg, with an arithmetic average of 4,589 ± 3,556 A/m/kg. (The log mean intensity was 2,942 A/m/kg.) All sample directions showed very high consistency during alternating magnetic field demagnetization as the Consistency Indices (Table 10.1) were all greater than 20, except for 3 samples (F13, F23, and F24). The arithmetic average Consistency Index was 34 (log mean 28 ± 2). Since a Consistency Index greater than 5 is considered to indicate high consistency, only sample F23 can be regarded as of low consistency. Most of the samples had high coercivities, and their initial

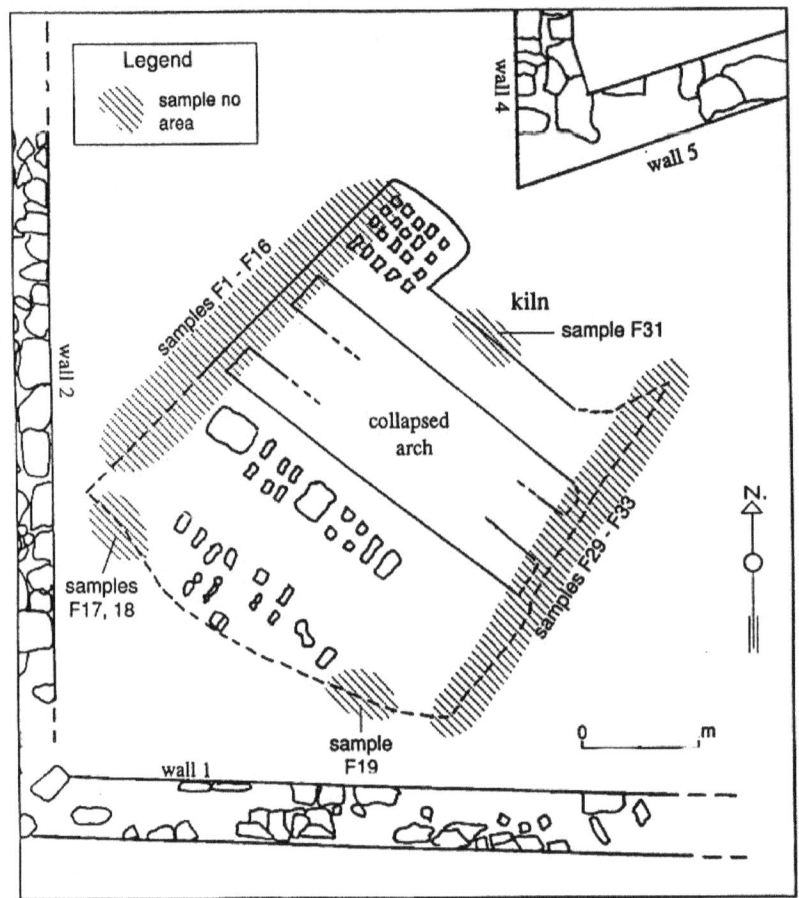
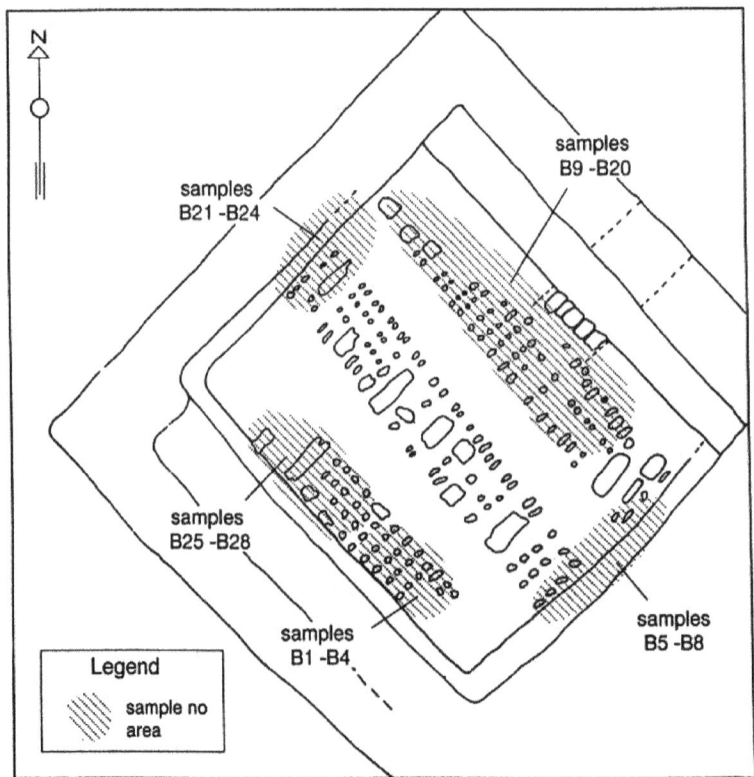

Figure 10.1 Sketch plans of the sampled floor areas: (top) Kiln F3, (bottom) Kiln F1. Shading indicates the areas that were sampled for archaeomagnetic analysis.

intensity of remanence did not decrease to less than 50 percent until, on average, a peak field of 40 mT was applied (Table 10.1). The lowest mean destructive field (MDF) was for samples F23 (7 mT) and F12 (15 mT). Principal component analyses (Kirschvink 1980) showed clear characteristic remanent vectors (Table 10.2) with linearities defined within a diagonal angle (d.a.) of less than 2° in all but 6 samples. This linear vector was defined between 10-15 mT and included both the final demagnetization and theoretical zero in all cases except F23 (end point 20 mT) and F9 (50 mT). No secondary components could be identified that differed significantly in direction from the characteristic components and were defined by a diagonal angle of less than 5°. On this basis,

Table 10.1. F3 Kiln Intensity, Coercivity, and Consistency Characteristics

Sample No.	M_{init}	MDF	CI	N	Min	Max	Decl.	Incl.
Northwestern edge								
F 1	4640	50	22.3	5	15	70	17.7	49.5
F 2	2433	50	41.6	4	15	50	26.8	53.5
F 3	1664	>70	30.6	3	30	70	27.6	45.0
F 4	8638	50	77.4	4	20	70	32.5	53.4
F 5	3826	20	21.5	5	0	15	16.7	51.8
F 6	1505	50	61.3	3	10	20	26.6	58.1
F 7	11757	50	31.3	3	30	70	20.7	46.3
F 8	9984	70	27.3	3	30	70	16.5	51.5
F 9	3642	30	28.1	5	10	50	(216.1	-1.5)
F10	6374	50	21.0	3	20	50	15.5	48.8
F11	2662	>70	24.3	3	20	50	31.5	53.5
F12	2410	15	29.0	3	30	70	20.7	60.4
F13	4210	70	17.6	6	0	20	13.5	53.5
F14	1284	50	39.0	3	10	20	24.7	51.2
F15	2478	50	21.2	7	7	70	18.5	56.7
F16	4886	50	21.7	4	3	20	20.4	53.3
Southwestern edge								
F17	7145	50	34.0	4	7	20	22.6	54.5
F18	9646	50	25.1	5	10	50	23.1	56.8
F19	4241	>70	43.2	3	20	50	21.4	48.1
Southeastern edge								
F21	823	30	28.8	4	7	20	22.5	38.5
F22	3995	30	82.0	3	30	70	24.4	49.5
F23	220	7	1.1	9	0	70	(44.8	51.4)
F24	284	20	10.1	3	30	70	34.3	55.7
F25	642	30	26.4	4	20	70	9.3	58.0
F26	9141	50	42.0	3	7	15	25.9	46.7
F27	9793	30	29.8	6	10	70	21.1	47.8
F28	9312	50	101.7	5	15	70	9.1	65.5
F32	433	30	22.5	7	3	50	16.3	50.0
Northeastern edge								
F30	8736	30	28.3	3	20	50	30.2	41.0
F31	880	30	29.4	3	30	70	34.3	51.4

M_{init} is the initial intensity of natural remanence in A/m/kg; MDF is the value of field applied at which the initial intensity had decreased to at least half of its original value. The directional consistency during demagnetization is defined by the Consistency Index (CI) which is based on the Stability Index of Tarling and Symons (1967) and involves N successive vectors over a demagnetization ranging from Min to Max (in mT peak field). Decl., Incl. are the declination and inclination of the most consistent directions of remanence identified over this range of demagnetization treatment. Excluded data are given in parentheses; see text for discussion.

Table 10.2. F3 Kiln Principal Component Analyses

Sample No.	Most Linear Component					
	Min	Max	N	d.a.	Decl.	Incl.
Northwestern edge						
F 1	20	zero	5	1.2	18.0	49.4
F 2	15	zero	6	0.7	26.6	53.6
F 3	30	zero	4	1.1	27.6	45.0
F 4	30	zero	4	0.4	32.7	53.4
F 5	10	zero	7	1.3	17.1	52.5
F 6	50	zero	3	0.2	25.4	58.0
F 7	30	zero	4	0.7	20.4	46.4
F 8	30	zero	4	0.8	16.6	51.7
F 9	10	50	5	1.6	(215.5	-1.5)
F10	50	zero	3	1.9	14.7	48.4
F11	30	zero	4	1.8	32.5	53.3
F12	15	zero	6	2.1	17.6	59.8
F13	30	zero	4	4.3	17.1	53.0
F14	10	zero	7	1.3	25.2	51.4
F15	30	zero	4	2.1	20.7	56.9
F16	30	zero	4	1.4	24.8	53.6
Southwestern edge						
F17	30	zero	4	1.6	20.5	54.4
F18	10	zero	7	1.2	23.1	56.8
F19	20	zero	5	1.2	21.6	48.0
Southeastern edge						
F21	10	zero	7	2.0	22.5	38.9
F22	30	zero	4	0.3	24.6	49.5
F23	10	20	3	3.7	(308.2	82.6)
F24	15	zero	6	2.4	26.6	54.2
F25	15	zero	6	1.1	9.1	57.4
F26	20	zero	5	1.3	25.9	46.6
F27	30	zero	4	0.3	21.1	47.8
F28	3	zero	9	0.5	8.9	65.8
F32	20	zero	5	1.1	15.6	50.0
Northeastern edge						
F30	7	zero	8	1.7	29.7	41.5
F31	30	zero	4	1.0	34.6	51.2

Note: Min., Max. are the minimum and maximum peak applied fields (mT) over which the linear vector is defined using N successive demagnetization step within which the vector is confined to a linear box with a diagonal angle (d.a.) less than 5°. Decl., Incl., are the declination and inclination of the vector defined over the stated demagnetization range.

it was concluded that no significant secondary components are present in this kiln site and that the directions isolated during demagnetization can be considered to be the characteristic remanent directions.

All sample characteristic directions are well grouped, whether considered in terms of consistency or linearity (Tables 10.1 and 10.2, Figure 10.2a, b), with the notable exception of F9 and possibly F23 and F28. The deviation of the direction for sample F9 is well defined and cannot be explained by an orientation error in the field. Its magnetic characteristics are also similar to those for all other samples. Thus, it seems most probable that this sample had been moved after it had been last fired and, on this basis, it is excluded from further consideration. The remanence of sample F23 has a low coercivity and its direction is poorly defined during demagnetization; as a result, the direction for this sample is also excluded. There are no physical grounds for excluding sample F28, so this direction is included in subsequent analyses, although it is suspected that it might have been subject to a minor tilt prior to collection and subsequent to the original firing.

F3 Kiln Summary

The agreement between both the consistency and linear analyses was within 0.5°. This indicates that the remanence associated with this kiln was acquired when it was last fired and provides a reliable estimate of the direction of the Earth's magnetic field at that time (Table 10.3). The direction of this field is best given as the mean direction of the two analytical techniques, each based on the same 28 samples, with a conservative estimate of the overall precision being given by the average of the precisions determined for each analytical procedure:

F3 Kiln: 22.5°, 52.0°, $k = 164$, $\alpha_{95} = 2.1°$

F1 Kiln

This kiln (Figure 10.1b) was 3.2 m by 2.4 m in size, with its central axis oriented approximately northeast /southwest. Its construction was similar to that of the F3 Kiln, with a plaster floor supported by a series of transverse brick arches. The kiln opening was on the northeastern side. A total of 28 oriented samples was taken from the floor area, and included 8 samples (B1-B4 and B25-B28) from the southwestern edge; 4 samples (B5-B8) from the southeastern edge, 12 samples (B9-B20) from the northeastern edge, and 4 samples (B21-B24) from the northwestern edge. Of the 28, two samples (B15 and B21) did not survive transport to the laboratory and thus are not included in the analysis.

The initial intensity of magnetization (Table 10.4) was high, ranging between 77 and 17,275 A/m/kg, with an arithmetic average of 3,926 ± 4,358 A/m/kg. (The log mean intensity was 1,697 A/m/kg.) All sample directions showed high consistency to alternating magnetic fields as the Consistency Indices (Table 10.4) were all greater than 10, except for 4 samples (B3, B8, B25, and B27). The arithmetic average Consistency Index was 23 (log mean 18 ± 3). Since a Consistency Index greater than 5 indicates high consistency, only samples B3 and B27 are regarded as possibly low reliability. The samples, except for B2, B4, B9, and B28, had high coercivities, with the

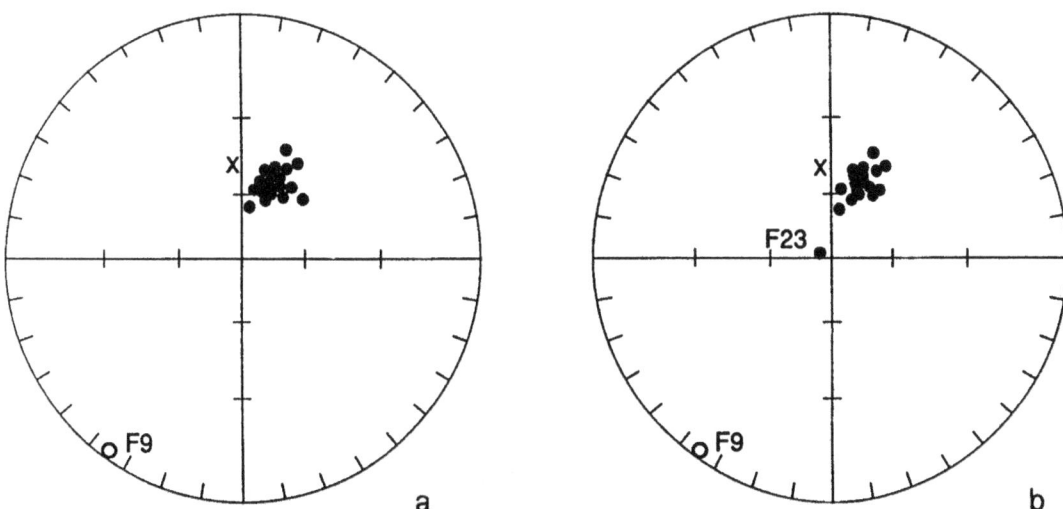

Figure 10.2 Stereographic projections of the sample directions for Kiln F3: (a) most stable directions for each sample, (b) most linear vector directions. The projection is an equal area, lower hemisphere projection in which upward directions are shown as circles. The present geomagnetic field direction is marked by a cross.

Table 10.3. F3 Kiln Mean Sample Directions from Different Edges and the Combined Mean Direction

Edge	Stable Directions					Linear Vectors			
	N	Decl.	Incl.	k	$\alpha_{95}°$	Decl.	Incl.	k	$\alpha_{95}°$
NW[1]	15	22.0	52.6	220	2.6	22.4	52.6	227	2.5
SW	3	22.3	53.1	319	6.9	21.7	53.1	309	7.0
SE	2	32.1	46.2	113	23.7	31.9	46.4	125	22.6
NE[2]	8	21.0	51.7	73	6.6	20.8	51.5	81	6.2
Combined[1,2]	28	22.6	52.0	186	2.0	22.4	51.9	143	2.3

Note: The declination (Decl.) and inclination (Incl.) for N samples define the mean direction. The estimate of precision is k and the radius of a circle of 95% confidence about the mean is α_{95} (Fisher 1953).

[1] Excluding sample F9.
[2] Excluding sample F23.

initial intensity of remanence decreasing to less than 50 percent at 30 mT or higher; the median destructive field averaged 46 mT (Table 10.4). No linear components could be identified in two samples, B3 and B27, but well-defined linear vectors (Table 10.5), defined by a diagonal angle (d.a.) of less than 3°, were isolated in all but 2 samples (B6 and B25). The well-defined linearities were mostly defined at high coercivity levels, usually up to the final demagnetization level (90 mT) and including the theoretical zero. No superimposed secondary vectors could be identified.

It is evident, however, that while there is general agreement in the individual sample directions isolated by either consistency or linearity criteria, all of the directions isolated from samples from the northeastern edge of this kiln differed markedly from those taken from the other three edges (Tables 10.4 and 10.5; Figures 10.3 and 10.4). The directions from each edge are, therefore, considered separately.

Table 10.4. F1 Kiln Intensity, Coercivity, and Consistency Characteristics

Sample No.	Minit	MDF	CI	N	Min	Max	Decl.	Incl.
Southwestern edge								
B 1	574	30	20.8	3	7	15	14.6	52.2
B 2	1125	20	32.1	6	7	70	19.9	47.5
B 3	276	70	1.0	3	7	15	(37.8	66.3)
B 4	950	20	22.7	4	20	70	17.0	56.8
B25	111	50	6.2	3	20	50	6.5	55.0
B26	97	30	44.2	3	20	50	12.8	70.0
B27	77	70	1.1	10	0	90	(336.8	-2.8)
B28	686	20	18.1	8	7	90	11.8	67.9
Southeastern edge								
B 5	225	30	21.5	9	3	90	337.6	45.2
B 6	3955	50	37.7	3	30	70	(292.2	8.6)
B 7	2807	70	27.2	4	10	70	191.1	-16.4
B 8	593	30	8.2	7	0	90	22.3	53.5
Northeastern edge								
B 9	780	20	21.7	3	50	90	(223.4	-20.4)
B10	17275	30	23.6	4	30	90	(310.2	2.2)
B11	3118	30	14.6	10	0	90	80.6	-28.7
B12	6991	30	19.1	9	3	90	43.0	-28.7
B13	3949	70	24.5	4	30	90	44.6	-31.2
B14	6000	30	31.9	3	0	7	30.0	-47.8
B16	3511	30	21.0	5	20	90	17.3	-36.2
B17	1717	90	52.0	3	20	50	19.5	-22.5
B18	8445	50	26.2	3	30	70	18.7	-29.4
B19	3767	50	30.0	5	10	50	20.0	-29.0
B20	6120	70	15.4	5	10	50	15.4	-47.5
Northwestern edge								
B22	13456	70	29.2	4	20	70	16.1	51.7
B23	8089	50	25.2	3	20	50	24.4	47.5
B24	7382	50	26.6	4	20	70	17.0	47.5

Note: Minit is the initial intensity of natural remanence in A/m/kg; MDF is the value of field applied at which the initial intensity had decreased to at least half of its original value. The Consistency to demagnetization is defined by the Consistency Index (CI), based on Tarling and Symons (1967), involving N successive vectors over a demagnetization ranging from Min to Max (in mT peak field). Decl., Incl. are the declination and inclination of the most consistent component of remanence identified over this range of demagnetization treatment. Poorly defined directions (CI less than 1.5) are given in parentheses.

Southwestern Edge

Two samples (B3 and B27) have both a low directional consistency with no linear vector identifiable and, on this basis, are excluded as being inadequately defined. The remaining 6 samples have similar directions, whether defined on consistency or linearity, although the directions of samples B26 and B28 are steeper than the others. However, there were no physical grounds for excluding these samples and all 6 samples directions are used to calculate the mean direction for this edge (Table 10.6).

Southeastern Edge

The sample directions from this edge are highly scattered, although all show good consistency in direction during demagnetization and the linearities are well defined, except for sample B6. This sample has low linearity and its most consistent directions are only defined at low coercivities and may not be representative of the original remanence acquired as it cooled. This sample is, therefore, excluded. There are no objective grounds for excluding the remaining 3 samples, but they are so scattered that they have no significant mean direction (Table 10.6).

Northeastern Edge

All samples have highly consistent directions during demagnetization and all have well-defined linearities. The directions isolated, using either analysis, are also very

Table 10.5. F1 Kiln Principal Component Analyses

Sample No.	Min	Max	N	d.a.	Characteristic Vector Decl.	Incl.
Southwestern edge						
B 1	70	zero	3	1.8	13.3	52.5
B 2	20	zero	5	0.7	19.0	47.5
B 3	None					
B 4	20	zero	6	0.9	17.0	56.4
B25	30	90	4	3.8	22.2	56.8
B26	20	zero	6	1.2	12.7	70.1
B27	None					
B28	7	zero	9	2.0	12.0	67.6
Southeastern edge						
B 5	20	70	4	2.2	337.9	41.7
B 6	0	7	3	6.2	(109.2	-8.3)
B 7	20	zero	4	0.4	191.5	-15.6
B 8	10	50	4	2.6	28.4	51.9
Northeastern edge	(All excluded in final average)					
B 9	50	zero	4	1.4	(223.5	-20.4)
B10	20	zero	6	1.9	(309.3	3.1)
B11	20	zero	6	2.8	79.1	-28.4
B12	30	zero	5	2.5	43.9	-27.8
B13	30	zero	5	1.0	44.2	-31.3
B14	20	70	4	1.9	32.7	-46.1
B16	10	zero	8	2.2	15.4	-35.5
B17	20	zero	6	1.0	19.6	-22.3
B18	30	zero	5	1.8	18.2	-29.2
B19	10	zero	8	1.4	20.2	-29.0
B20	20	70	4	2.2	7.0	-48.8
Northwestern edge						
B22	30	70	3	2.1	16.4	50.1
B23	20	zero	6	2.0	24.5	47.7
B24	20	zero	6	1.3	17.3	47.2

Note: Min., Max. are the minimum and maximum peak applied fields (mT) over which the linear vector is defined using N successive demagnetization step within which the vector is confined to a linear box with a diagonal angle (d.a.) less than 5°. Decl., Incl., are the declination and inclination of the vector defined over the stated demagnetization range. Excluded directions are given in parentheses.

Anatomy of a Medieval Town

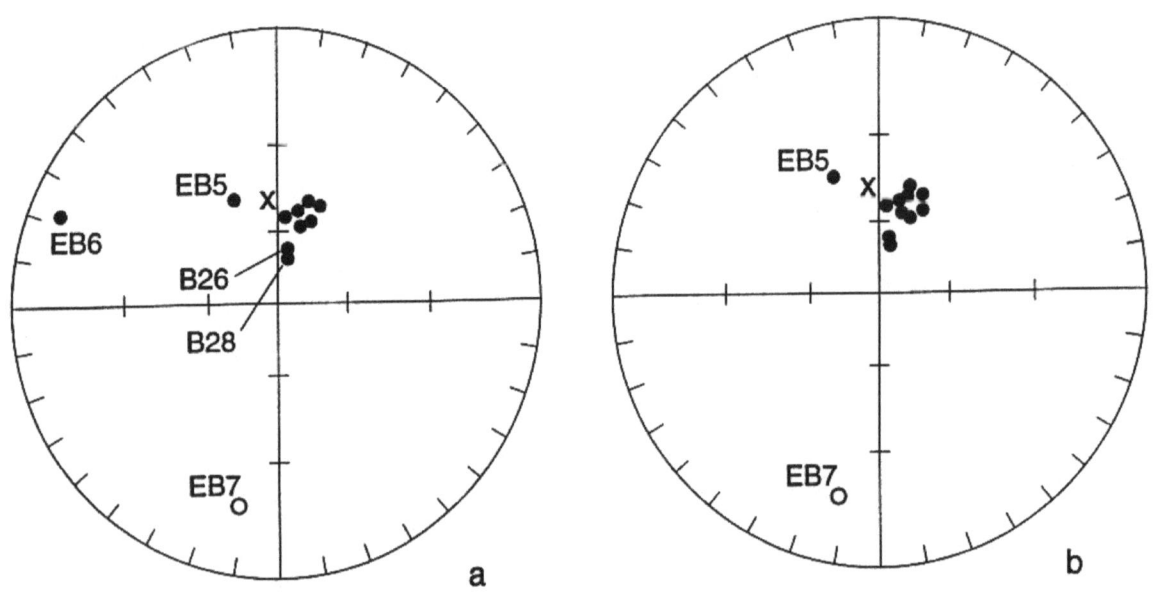

Figure 10.3 Stereographic projections of the sample directions for the northwestern, southwestern, and southeastern edges of Kiln F1: (a) most stable directions for each sample, (b) most linear vector directions. The projection is an equal area, lower hemisphere projection in which upward directions are shown as circles.
The present geomagnetic field direction is marked by a cross.

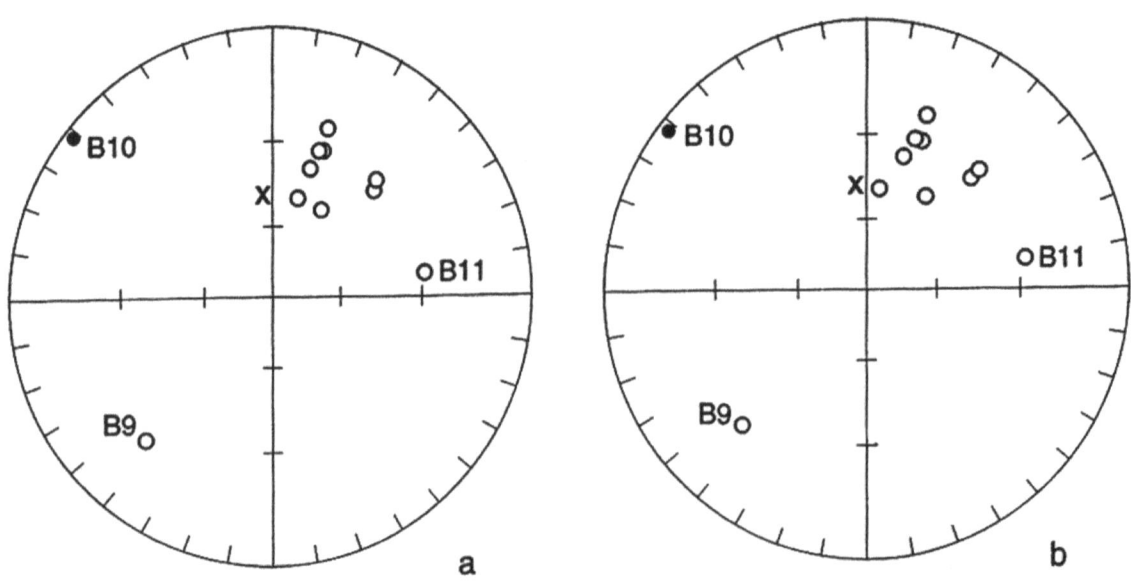

Figure 10.4 Stereographic projections of the sample directions for the northeastern edge of Kiln F1: (a) most stable directions for each sample, (b) most linear vector directions. The projection is an equal area, lower hemisphere projection in which upward directions are shown as circles.
The present geomagnetic field direction is marked by a cross.

Table 10.6. Mean Directions for F3 Kiln Southwestern, Northeastern, and Northwestern Edges

		Mean Consistency				Mean Linearity			
	N	Decl.	Incl.	K	$\alpha_{95}°$	Decl.	Incl.	k	$\alpha_{95}°$
Southwestern edge	6	13.7	58.3	78	7.6	16.5	58.5	82	7.5
Southeastern edge	1	22.3	53.5	-	-	28.4	51.9	-	-
Northwestern edge	3	19.3	49.0	449	5.9	19.5	48.4	590	5.1
Combined SW, SE, and NW edges	10	16.5	55.1	90	5.1	18.8	54.8	87	5.2
Northeastern edge	9	32.0	-35.1	17	12.8	31.3	-34.9	16	13.2

Note: The mean direction is defined by the declination (Decl.) and inclination (Incl.) for N samples. The estimate of precision is k and the radius of a circle of 95% confidence about the mean is α_{95} (Fisher 1953).

similar. Thus, there are no physical reasons for not considering these sample directions as representative of the characteristic directions of remanence acquired as they originally cooled following the last firing of this part of the kiln. However, the directions of samples B9 and B10 are strongly deviant from those of the other samples and are, therefore, considered to have been moved, relative to the other samples, sometime after the final cooling. Thus, these samples are excluded from the determination of the mean direction for this edge (Table 10.6).

Northwestern Edge

All three samples from this edge show good consistencies and well-defined linearities, and their characteristic directions are similar. The mean directions are given in Table 10.6.

F1 Kiln Summary

Three of the four edges (SW, SE, and NW) show similar mean directions, the mean of which is:

F1 Kiln (SW, SE, and NW):
17.7°, 55.0°, $k = 93$, $\alpha_{95} = 3.4°$

This is considered to represent the direction of the Earth's magnetic field at the time that this kiln last cooled.

The mean direction for the northeastern wall samples (Table 10.6) is quite different from the other edges, particularly in having a negative inclination. All other magnetic parameters (intensity of magnetization, consistency, and linearity characteristics) are similar for all samples from this kiln. Within the northeastern edge, there is also very close agreement between the directions isolated using consistency and linearity criteria, and the mean declination is broadly similar to that of the other three edges. However, the mean inclination is not only inconsistent with that of the other three edges but also with any likely Earth magnetic field direction during the last 720,000 years, i.e., since the Earth's magnetic field last changed polarity.

The consistency of the sample directions indicates that these samples are still in the same relative positions to each other as they were when they last cooled. They do not have the mean direction of randomly oriented samples. There is also a potentially significant geometric relationship between the mean inclination value, - 34.5°, with that of the other three edges, +55.0°, i.e., it corresponds to 55.0° - 90° = 35.0°. Such a relationship suggests that if the samples from this edge originally had an identical direction to that of the other edges, then they must have moved systematically (as a whole or individually) since then, i.e., they rotated by some 90°C around an east-west axis.

Comparison between F3 Kiln and F1 Kiln

The mean directions of both al-Basra kilns are statistically similar. The solid angular difference between their two mean magnetic directions is 4.1° while the individual 95 percentage probability errors on each direction are 2.1° (F3) and 3.4° (F1). The angular difference is, therefore, within the 95 percent range of the combined errors. This suggests that while both kilns could have been last fired at the same time, it is more likely that there is an age difference during which the direction of the Earth's magnetic field changed. Unfortunately, the rate of change in the direction of the Earth's magnetic field in Morocco has not yet been defined, but it is unlikely to have been radically different from that of Western Europe during the last 2,000 years (0.2° per year). Based on this rate, the kilns appear to have been fired within some 50 to 60 years of each other.

Comparison with Other Moroccan Kilns

As the geomagnetic field varies both spatially as well as temporally, it is generally necessary to correct the observed values to some central location prior to discussing the differences (Tarling 1983:116). In this case, however, the site of al-Basra (34.8°N, 5.9°W) is only some 80 km from Volubilis (34.0°N, 5.5°W), where most of the late Roman archaeomagnetic Moroccan observations have been made (Table 10.7). The only other relevant Roman archaeomagnetic data currently available are from Spain (Oyamburu et al.1996), but these need correction for the spatial variation of the geomagnetic field (Tarling 1983). The Spanish data, although somewhat distant, are consistent with the similarly aged data from Volubilis (Figure 10.5).

Although the F3 Kiln has a mean inclination identical to that of the youngest determination in Volubilis, attributed to the third and fourth centuries A.D. (Najid 1986), both F3 and F1 kilns have declination values that are quite distinct from all other Roman age determinations. It can, therefore, be concluded that the final firing of the al-Basra kilns must have occurred some time after the late Roman period that was sampled in Volubilis.

Table 10.7. Relevant Archaeomagnetic Observations from Morocco (300 B.C.-A.D. 500) and Spain

Site Name	Archaeological Age Max.	Min.	N	Decl.	Incl.	α_{95}
Early Moroccan sites						
Dchar Jdid Citadel (30.5° N, 6.0° W)	300 BC	100 BC (Kovacheva 1984)	10	1.8	53.0	1.8
Al Kouass Chkakra (35.5° N, 6.0° W)	100 BC	0 AD (Kovacheva 1984)	5	353.9	54.3	3.3
Volubilis, Morocco						
Volubilis Furnace (34.0° N, 5.5° W)	200	0 AD (Kovacheva 1984)	4	349.0	49.9	-
Volubilis Big Furnace (34.0° N, 5.5° W)	200	300 AD (Kovacheva 1984)	10	352.2	50.3	3.6
Volubilis N.E. Kiln (34.0° N, 5.5° W)	200	390 AD (Najid 1986)	3	0.1	44.7	1.8
Volubilis Oven (P.Justice) (34.0° N, 5.5° W)	200	390 AD (Najid 1986)	4	351.6	47.2	8.5
Volubilis Thermal Bath (34.0° N, 5.5° W)	250	390 AD (Najid 1986)	9	358.2	47.5	3.1
Volubilis S. Furnace (34.0° N, 5.5° W)	400	500 AD (Kovacheva 1984)	5	353.3	51.7	2.5
Al-Basra, Morocco (34.8° N, 5.9° W)		(This paper)				
F3 Kiln			29	22.5	52.0	2.1
F1 Kiln			10	17.7	55.0	5.1
Madrid, Spain (40.3° N, 3.4° W)		(Oyamburu et al. 1996)				
Villa Panuelo 1[1]	100	250 AD	31	357.1	45.5	2.2
Villa Panuelo 2[1]	100	250 AD	25	354.7	51.8	2.6

Note: The max. and min. ages are those assigned on archaeological criteria. Decl., Incl. are the mean declinations and inclinations reported for N samples from each site. α_{95} is the estimate of the radius of the cone of 95 percent confidence about the mean direction (Fisher 1953).

[1] The Madrid data are corrected to al-Basra using the inclined dipole geomagnetic model (Tarling 1983).

Declination

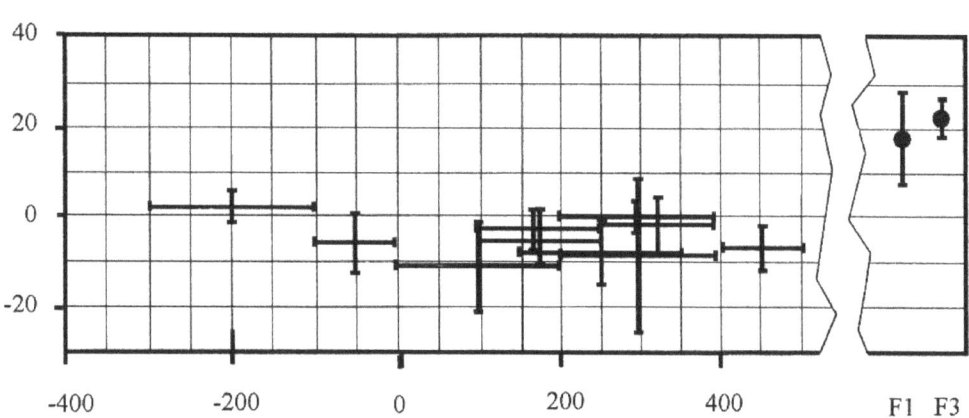

Inclination

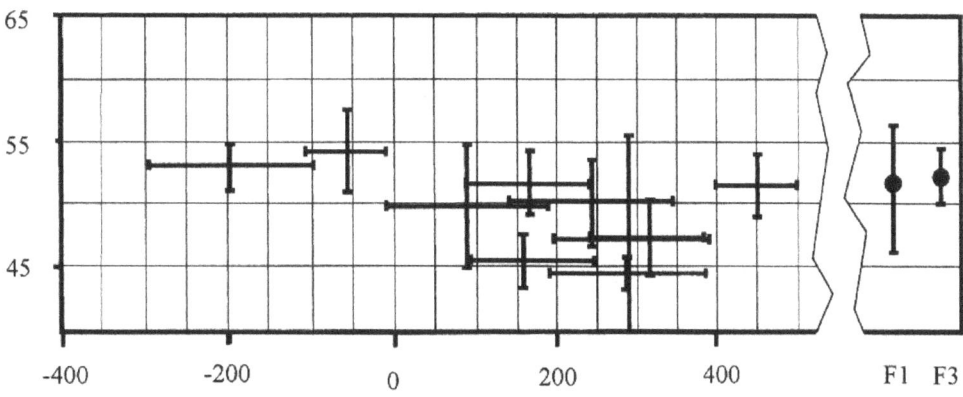

Figure 10.5 Mean declination and inclination values for relevant sites (200 B.C. to A.D. 600). The mean values are shown with the standard deviation of the age estimate. The errors on inclination are α_{95} and twice α_{95} for declination (to approximate the solid angle error).

Unfortunately, the direction for later centuries has not yet been established, but the al-Basra kilns have directions that could well be consistent with that expected for the latter part of the fifth- to sixth-century age indicated by the radiocarbon determinations obtained for the site. However, there are no actual archaeomagnetic controls yet available for the post-Roman direction of the Earth's magnetic field in Morocco. Clearly, archaeomagnetic data from well-dated younger sites in Morocco, Algeria, or southern Spain would provide a more reliable archaeological age assessment for these two kilns.

Acknowledgment

We thank Nancy L. Benco for her suggestion to sample this site and for her advice on the archaeological background.

References Cited

Benco, N. L.
    1987 *The Early Medieval Pottery Industry at al-Basra, Morocco.* BAR International Series 341. British Archaeological Reports, Oxford.
    2002 1990 Archaeological Investigations at al-Basra, Morocco. *Bulletin d'archéologie marocaine* 19:293-340.

Eustache, D.
    1955 El-Basra, capitale idrissite et son port. *Hespéris* 42:218-238.

Fisher, R. A.
    1953 Dispersion on a Sphere. *Proceedings of the Royal Society.* A217:295-305.

Kirschvink, J. L.
  1980 The Least-Squares Line and Plane and the Analysis of Palaeomagnetic Data. *Geophysical Journal of the Royal Astronomical Society* 62:699-718.

Kovacheva, M.
  1984 Some Archaeomagnetic Conclusions from Three Archaeological Localities in North-West Africa. *Comptes rendus academia Bulgaria sciences* 37:171-174.

Najid, D.
  1986 Palaeomagnetic Studies of Morocco. Ph.D. thesis, University of Newcastle, Newcastle.

Oyamburu, I., J. J. Villalain, M. Osete, M. Zarzalejos, and C. Blasco
  1996 Estudio paleomagnetico del yacimento de Villa del Panuelo (Villamanta, Madrid). *Geogaceta* 20:1044-1046.

Tarling, D. H.
  1983 Palaeomagnetism: Principles and Applications in Geology, Geophysics and Archaeology. Chapman and Hall, London.

Tarling, D. H., and D. T. A. Symons
  1967 A Stability Index of Remanence in Palaeomagnetism. *Geophysical Journal of the Royal Astronomical Society* 12:443-448.

www.ingramcontent.com/pod-product-compliance
Lightning Source LLC
Chambersburg PA
CBHW041707290426
44108CB00027B/2879